The Art of Writing Fiction

For Lynne

The Art of Writing Fiction

ANDREW COWAN

Longman
is an imprint of

Harlow, England • London • New York • Boston • San Francisco • Toronto
Sydney • Tokyo • Singapore • Hong Kong • Seoul • Taipei • New Delhi
Cape Town • Madrid • Mexico City • Amsterdam • Munich • Paris • Milan

PEARSON EDUCATION LIMITED

Edinburgh Gate
Harlow CM20 2JE
United Kingdom
Tel: +44 (0)1279 623623
Fax: +44 (0)1279 431059
Website: www.pearsoned.co.uk

First edition published in Great Britain in 2011

© Pearson Education Limited 2011

The right of Andrew Cowan to be identified as author of this work
has been asserted by him in accordance with the Copyright,
Designs and Patents Act 1988.

Pearson Education is not responsible for the content of third party internet sites.

ISBN: 978-1-4082-4834-8

British Library Cataloguing in Publication Data
A CIP catalogue record for this book can be obtained from the British Library

Library of Congress Cataloging in Publication Data
Cowan, Andrew.
    The art of writing fiction / Andrew Cowan.
        p. cm.
    Includes bibliographical references and index.
    ISBN 978-1-4082-4834-8 (pbk.)
 1. Fiction–Authorship.   2. Creative writing.   I. Title.
    PN3355.C69 2011
    808.3–dc22
                                    2010049764

10   9   8   7   6   5   4   3   2   1
15   14   13   12   11

Set by 35 in 11/13pt Bulmer MT
Printed and bound in Malaysia, CTP-VVP

Contents

and exercises

Publisher's acknowledgements		viii
Introduction		1
1	**Writers' routines**	5
	1. When where what . . .	8
	2. Timewasting	9
	3. Friends and foes	14
	4. What where when . . .	16
2	**Write about what you know: observational journals**	17
	5. Keeping an observational journal	21
	6. Keeping a scrapbook	23
	7. Weather report	24
	8. Street life	25
	9. Workplace	26
	10. Home life	28
3	**Write about what you don't know you know: automatic writing**	34
	11. First thoughts	36
	12. First things	40
	13. First thoughts, second thoughts	43
	14. First drafts	47
4	**Don't tell me . . .**	49
	15. Telling it slant	52
	16. Don't mention it	54

17.	How does this feel?	55
18.	Sightless	60
19.	Hyacinths	61
20.	Summary and scene	65

5   Write about what you used to know: remembering and place   66

21.	Lost things	69
22.	Lost lands	70
23.	Lost selves	70
24.	Lost loves	71
25.	'Lost'	71
26.	Departures	73
27.	Typical	74
28.	Untypical	75
29.	A place	76
30.	A person	79

6   Write about who you know: character   80

31.	A Portrait of Yourself as You Are Now	83
32.	Twenty questions	85
33.	Q&A gimmick	89
34.	Notes towards a character	90
35.	Envelopes	91
36.	Still life	96
37.	Two characters	99

7   Voices   101

38.	Oral history	104
39.	Conversation	106
40.	Formatting dialogue	107
41.	Dramatic twist	111
42.	Cross purposes	113
43.	Vernacular voices	116
44.	In summary	118

8   Viewpoints   121

45.	Something is happening out there	123
46.	Something else is happening	128
47.	Captors and captives	130

48.	Eye witness	132
49.	You	134
50.	You, too	136
51.	Third, and finally	142

9	**Middles, ends, beginnings: structure**	**143**
52.	Story vs plot	143
53.	Diagnostics	146
54.	Beginning middle end	150
55.	Middle beginning end	152
56.	End middle beginning	153
57.	Sub-plotting	154
58.	Shuffling	155
59.	Rearranging	159

10	**Making strange: defamiliarisation**	**160**
60.	Literally	161
61.	Figuratively	161
62.	Given words	167
63.	Given moods	168
64.	Exercises in style	171
65.	Mathews's Algorithm (almost)	172
66.	Horizontal	174
67.	Vertical	176

11	**Making clear: revision, grammar and punctuation**	**178**
68.	More first thoughts	178
69.	Checklist	181
70.	Next thoughts	182
71.	Simple	190
72.	Compound	192
73.	Complex	196
74.	Compound-complex	199

| **12** | **Workshopping** | **200** |

| *Bibliography* | | 218 |
| *Index* | | 222 |

Publisher's acknowledgements

We are grateful to the following for permission to reproduce copyright material:

Text
Extracts on pages 30–1, page 126, pages 121–2 adapted from *A Common Ground*, Penguin (Cowan, A 1997); Extracts on pages 53–4, page 55, page 197 from *On Becoming a Novelist*, W.W. Norton (Gardner, J 1999); Extracts on pages 81–2 from *Maxims*, Penguin (La Rochefoucauld, trans. L.W. Tancock 1959), Reproduced by permission of Penguin Books Ltd.; Extracts on page 94, page 140 from *Mrs Dalloway*, Penguin (Woolf, V 2000), © The Society of Authors, Literary Representative of the Estate of Virginia Woolf; Extract on page 170 from *Exercises in Style*, Calder (Queneau, R. trans. Barbara Wright 2009), Exerpts from Exercises in Style by Raymond Queneau (published by Oneworld Classics, 2009), translation by Barbara Wright, 2009, reprinted with permission; Extract on page 202 and page 217 from *The Wrench*, Abacus (Levi, P. trans. William Weaver 1988).

In some instances we have been unable to trace the owners of copyright material, and we would appreciate any information that would enable us to do so.

Introduction

Introductions are the first thing a reader will read, but often the last thing a writer will write. This introduction is no different. The book you are about to read has, as I type these words, already been written. I've done all the work, and now I can account for my intentions and the ways in which I may have deviated from them, and perhaps offer some guidance on how to approach the exercises, and explain certain usages and conventions. I might attempt to reassure you about my competence to write a book about writing. Certainly I ought to be clear about my anticipated audience; I should be clear about 'you'.

As originally conceived, then, this book was designed to appeal as a university-level coursebook, and that remains the case. The twelve chapters correspond to the twelve weeks of a university semester, and are structured in line with my undergraduate syllabus at the University of East Anglia, where I've taught since 2002. The chapters resemble my lessons. They come in much the same order, and contain much the same material, and the exercises appear pretty much where they would appear in those lessons.

However, with so much more space on the page than I'm ever allowed in the classroom, the discussion has become longer, the examples more detailed, the exercises more numerous. In places, my book has begun to resemble a memoir, and while I shouldn't be surprised by this, the pleasure I took in writing it may reflect something of my relief at finding I wasn't after all compiling a textbook.

I hope it's less generic, more personal than that, not least because I came to teaching through the residential courses offered by the Arvon Foundation, and my approach in the university classroom – anecdotal, practical, relatively informal – derives from that more 'recreational' experience. Arvon courses happen throughout the year, in remote rural locations, and typically involve sixteen students and two tutors who eat, sleep and drink writing for five days more or less without distraction. Several of the exercises in this book were devised for such courses; several others were filched from my co-tutors while teaching them. This book is therefore intended to appeal to that kind of non-academic audience, too.

That said, a good deal of the more extended commentary between the exercises derives from conversations I've had with my Masters students at UEA – both in workshops and in individual tutorials – and is informed by an awareness of literary theory and of the literary canon, while certain other passages have their origin in conversations with fellow novelists, and so I hope this book might be of interest to them, too. Certainly it is intended for other teachers of writing; it is intended for the likes of me.

But if this is beginning to sound like my anticipated audience is 'everyone' – or that 'you' are pretty much 'anyone' – I ought to offer at least one qualification: I don't believe you can be a writer unless you are also a reader. If writing is the out-breath, the exhalation, then reading should be the in-breath, the inspiration. And if you aren't already an enthusiastic and habitual reader of short stories and novels, I doubt you'll have much use for this book.

Of course, your writing will derive from personal experience (what you know), as well as from research and what you are able to invent or imagine (what you don't know, yet). But it will also spring from your awareness of language, and especially of literary language. This is your medium – the stuff from which you will fashion your fictions – and the more you are aware of the fictions that have preceded you and which surround you, the more conscious you'll become of the possibilities of the form and what you might do with it.

For many of us, that awareness will be acquired by a kind of osmosis, almost unconsciously, since we read in the main for entertainment, for delight. Our lifelong immersion in the fictions of others will help us acquire a degree of technical understanding that may come to feel instinctive or commonsensical. But as writers we will often also want to read analytically and for instruction – to learn about method and style – and this 'reading as a writer' will tend to be deliberate, a fully conscious activity involving marks in the margin, memos to self, scribblings in notebooks.

This is a practice I would encourage. For as long as seems useful at least, I would suggest you keep a record of your reading, making notes on the mechanics – as you observe them – of constructing successful short stories and novels. Chapters 4 to 9 in this book should provide a guide to what to look for, the kinds of questions you might be asking of the writing of others. But this needn't be arduous; it shouldn't be a chore. If your inclination is simply to jot down arresting images, neat turns of phrase, unusual details, then that should be enough. My own notebook, for instance, has come to resemble a swag-bag, a collection of thievings from other writers – all their shiniest sentences – including this line from one of Samuel Beckett's later short fictions, *Worstward Ho*, which has become for me a kind of mantra, a consolation whenever my achievements on the page fall short of my ambitions:

No matter. Try again. Fail again. Fail better.

It is an underlying premise of this book that writing is an on-going process, perfection impossible, completion elusive, and while this line from *Worstward Ho* encapsulates that thought, I know I'm not the first to have discovered it. It appears to have become something of a slogan in the teaching of Creative Writing, in fact. And just as mine is not the first guidebook to quote it, nor will I be the last to draw on the words of Dorothea Brande, Flannery O'Connor or John Gardner, whom I mention in several of the chapters that follow. There is one good reason for this: they are among the wisest of writers on writing. But I have sought to compensate for their ubiquity by incorporating into my commentary several other, less orthodox names: for example, the seventeenth-century French courtier and soldier the Duc de La Rochefoucauld, or the Russian Formalist critics Viktor Shklovsky and Boris Tomashevsky (both of whom are central figures in the history of literary theory, but maybe less central to the teaching of Creative Writing).

Certain of my literary exemplars are likewise already well known. Ernest Hemingway's 'Hills Like White Elephants', for instance, must be the most frequently quoted of all short stories in the Creative Writing classroom. Tim O'Brien's 'The Things They Carried' can't be far behind. But many of my other choices will reflect the idiosyncrasies of my own reading. And of course, despite my best intentions, I frequently use my own novels to illustrate or support my argument, though not necessarily because I believe them to be particularly fine examples of how to write well. Every example is in some way provisional – merely an example – and often the easiest way to explain myself is to point to a passage from my own work. Besides which, as I know from the classroom, the process of learning to write is an intensely personal process that may best be encouraged through the example of personal experience.

This mix of the familiar and less familiar may be found in the exercises, too, many of which are my own invention, some of which are not. A few were devised in good faith – as if they were my own – only to surprise me in similar guise elsewhere, evidently not my idea at all. But the provenance of Creative Writing exercises is notoriously difficult to establish, and while those that appear in a guidebook may take on the authority of being the official or original version, often they are adaptations of exercises that are already in general circulation, and with this in mind I have taken care to acknowledge my sources where I am aware of them, while of course offering my own (or rather, those I believe to be my own) to the Creative Writing commons.

Finally, three other, minor points of explanation. If this book was always intended to appeal as a university-level coursebook, it was also, initially, designed to look like one, with all the apparatus of an academic textbook, including footnoted citations. However, these quickly became so much clutter on the page, and so I've limited myself to a bibliography at the end of the book, listing all the works I mention without giving page numbers for each and every quotation. The footnotes that remain are there to allow me to contradict or further explain myself.

English pronouns are always problematical and while it's rightly no longer acceptable to say 'he' when we mean 'he or she', or 'his' when we also mean 'hers', none of the alternatives strikes me as particularly elegant: 'he or she' is unwieldy; 's/he' is ugly; and the use of the plural form 'they' when we mean the singular 'he' or 'she' is not only ungrammatical, but inelegant and unwieldy. My solution – for the most part – is to use 'she' on some occasions and 'he' on others, more or less randomly (which may or may not be equally inelegant).

Meanwhile, you may notice that the phrase 'Creative Writing' is capitalised throughout, while the word 'writing' is not. This may be splitting hairs, but I wish to preserve the sense that writing is what writers do – and is an art – whereas Creative Writing is a subject of study – a regulated set of educational activities that occurs in an institution and results, usually, in a qualification. This isn't to suggest that the two can't coincide, or that Creative Writing is not an enjoyable, instructive, or personally improving set of activities. But it is to suggest that writing need not occur in an institution, or in response to a syllabus. The hope of the Creative Writing tutor, always, is that the student will surpass the syllabus. And that, ultimately, is the hope of this Creative Writing guidebook, that it will enable you to surpass the instructions, and your own expectations, and become a book about the art (and the craft, and the graft) of writing.

1.   Writers' routines

I imagine most decorators will be interested in the brushes and solvents that other decorators use, and where they get them, and on what terms, and I expect they'll be just as interested in each other's methods and how they get the best use out of those solvents and brushes. They may even be curious about each other's lives, how they organise their weekends, and if they pay into a pension plan, and whether they know a good osteopath. And no doubt the same will go for plumbers, photographers, ceramicists, chefs . . .

I'm always interested in how other writers write, when and where they do it, and what implements they use. I'm especially interested in how they organise their lives. And being a writer, if I come across some information I will squirrel it away – I'll jot it down – though being a fiction writer I won't always remember it accurately. I might well embellish it, or believe what I want to believe, and so the list I've compiled of writers' working routines might not be quite accurate, however much it suits me to think it is.

Here is my list:

The novelist and biographer Peter Ackroyd ('as prolific a writer as he is a drinker', according to the *Guardian*[1]) writes from seven in the morning till nine in the evening, often lying down in a semi-slumber. After which he drinks, prolifically.

Douglas Adams was either Apple Macintosh's number one fan or was sponsored by Apple Macintosh to use their computers. Either way, he wrote directly onto his Mac, which coincidentally often appeared just over his shoulder in photographs.

---

[1] If there's a libel here, it's the *Guardian*'s (11 August 2003).

Martin Amis used to rent a flat as an office and work there in the morning, then play tennis, then read all afternoon. Now he works in a 'garden studio'.

Jeffrey Archer likes to line up a row of freshly sharpened pencils and a team of editors.

Paul Auster writes with a fountain pen into notebooks of squared paper, and endlessly revises. If he manages a page in a day he's happy. After which he types up his 'scratchings' so he can read them properly, and makes further corrections in pencil.

The playwright Edward Bond writes in a shed – which might also be known as a 'studio' – at the end of his garden, as does Philip Pullman, as did Roald Dahl and Arthur Miller.

Paul Bowles, author of *The Sheltering Sky* and husband of the novelist Jane Bowles, wrote longhand and claimed that 95 per cent of his writing was done in bed. Jane, he said, took a week to write a page and the effort 'cost her blood'.

Barbara Cartland dictated her novels from a *chaise longue* to a secretary.

Just as Martin Amis once did, Margaret Drabble rents a room without a telephone and writes from 9.45 a.m. until lunchtime. She types directly onto her computer, and doesn't revise much. She doesn't play tennis.

The novelist and biographer Margaret Forster also works until lunchtime, in a room without a telephone, though she doesn't own a typewriter, let alone a computer. She writes with a fountain pen.

Ernest Hemingway wrote standing at a lectern, and often wrote naked. He used a pencil, and only sat down to type when writing dialogue.

In common with Barbara Cartland, Henry James dictated his later novels to a secretary.

James Joyce sometimes lounged on a sofa with his feet up and wrote surrounded by domestic chaos.

Philip Larkin wrote, if he wrote at all, for two hours in the evening, but only after he'd eaten and washed the dishes. He wrote with a fountain pen onto lined paper.

Vladimir Nabokov wrote from very early in the morning, initially in pencil onto filing cards, which he would then revise and rearrange to produce his novels. He insisted on pencils tipped with erasers.

Joyce Carol Oates writes mainly in the morning, and mainly before breakfast. If the work is going well she'll delay her breakfast until two or three in the afternoon.

Edna O'Brien writes with a fountain pen into exercise books from first thing in the morning until early afternoon, 'in a kind of trance' as she describes it.

George Orwell wrote much of *1984* sitting up in bed with TB, a pad in his lap.

Anthony Powell wrote mainly in the morning, on a typewriter. He sometimes used the afternoon for corrections.

The poet and novelist Michèle Roberts writes novels directly onto her computer, but sits in bed to write poems, in longhand, with her earlier drafts spread around her.

Philip Roth (like Hemingway) writes standing at a lectern. His lectern is in a twelfth-storey apartment with a view of Manhattan, and his only other item of furniture is a small bed, for catnapping.

Muriel Spark, who lived most of her writing life in Tuscany, would only write in a particular brand of exercise book, which she had sent to her from the Edinburgh stationers, James Thin.

Historical novelist Nigel Tranter sometimes composed directly onto a notepad as he strode through the Scottish countryside. In this way he was able to produce 133 books in his lifetime.

Barbara Trapido wakes at dawn and writes into exercise books until breakfast, correcting her pages until they are almost illegible. She used twenty-five exercise books for *Frankie and Stankie*. She is gregarious the rest of the day.

John Updike wrote every weekday morning, alternating between poetry and prose.

Edith Warton wrote in bed, tossing the pages to the floor for her secretary to collect and type up.

Eudora Welty woke early and typed. Her structural revisions were made using scissors and pins.

P.G. Wodehouse began his working day at seven in the morning and wrote until seven in the evening and aimed to complete a novel in three to six months.

Virginia Woolf (like Hemingway and Roth) sometimes wrote standing at a lectern. More often (like Roald Dahl) she wrote in an armchair with a board on her lap.

Here is a ten-minute exercise:

---

1. When where what . . .

Consider your own writing routines and describe them under these headings:

Where do you write?
When do you start?
Which days of the week?
How long do you write for?
What implements do you use?
What rules do you set yourself?
What excuses do you make?

If there's no discernible pattern, that's fine, for now. We'll come back to this later.

Of course there are exceptions – there will *always* be exceptions – but what strikes me about my list is the number of writers for whom writing happens best in the morning, often very early in the morning (and sometimes without their even getting out of bed). Only a few continue writing into the afternoon, and fewer still into the evening. And then there are those, quite a few of them, for whom writing begins when they are closest to the condition of sleep, or half-sleep: those who write in a semi-slumber, or a semi-trance (or just while reclining).

They seem to be suggesting that the ideal state for a writer – the dream state, so to speak – is somewhere close to the state of dreaming. And this is a theme that emerges in most of the books on Creative Writing that I'm aware of, beginning with one of the classics of the genre, Dorothea Brande's *Becoming a Writer*, first published in 1934. Inevitably it will crop up in this book too, in Chapter 3, when I consider the role of the unconscious in relation to the technique of automatic writing.

But besides the purely psychological argument for writing as soon as you wake, it may be that there's a sound practical reason for starting early. The sooner you get going, the less likely you are to be distracted by *stuff*, the intrusions and interruptions that other people cause: the knocks on the door, the emails, the phonecalls, the demands on your time and attention (and possibly your conscience) that steadily accumulate throughout the day and can so fracture your concentration and calm, and so drain you of energy, that there can be no chance of writing later on.

Though perhaps it isn't the intrusions and interruptions that other people cause that are the issue. Possibly it's your own tendency to niggle away at yourself, forever remembering other things you ought to be doing (and very often doing them). It could be that you are your own worst enemy.

Many writers are.

One of the books on Creative Writing that I turn to most often is called *Taking Reality by Surprise*, edited by Susan Sellers and published by the Women's Press, and one of the exercises I most often use in my teaching is adapted from this book. The original was devised by Nicky Edwards and is called 'A Ten-Minute Exercise on Time-Wasting' and is designed to 'speed the writer from bed to computer, eliminating all forms of procrastination'. Over the years my own version has evolved so that the wording is now very different from hers, though the concept and structure remain the same. (And this perhaps is an example of how we develop as writers, and teachers: first imitating, even copying, then adapting, and eventually – hopefully – originating.)

You will need a pen and paper. Here is my version of Nicky Edwards's exercise:

---

2. Timewasting

Imagine you are sitting at your desk and are ready to write. Let's *assume* there are no family or work demands, no other distractions. Now list all the things you do to avoid starting. Tally up your marks in the style of a *Cosmo* questionnaire.

Fiddling: 1 point each
Stacking and squaring your papers. Cleaning the gunk from your keyboard keys. Cleaning the gunk from your fingernails. Adjusting the height of your chair. Adjusting the tilt of your chair . . .

Almost work-related distractions: 2 points each
Cutting and pasting scraps into a scrapbook. Reading a page or two of a book or a magazine to 'get in the mood'. Rearranging the order of the notes in a ring-binder. Counting the words you've written so far. Tidying, deleting and renaming the files and folders on your computer . . .

Stalling: 3 points each
Tidying your work-room. Re-reading your emails. Making lists of things to do later. Making more coffee . . .

Dreaming: 3 points each
More than ten minutes staring at a window or a wall. More than five minutes with your eyes closed or your head on the desk . . .

Skiving: 5 points each
Writing emails. Making phone calls. Doing the housework. Tackling minor repairs around the house. Walking the dog to the postbox. Doing questionnaires like this one . . .

Absconding: 10 points each
Gardening. Decorating. Shopping. Sleeping. Visiting . . .

Score
0–10 points: Completely abnormal. Try to relax.
11–20 points: A necessary amount of nest-circling. But beware of lapsing once the writing has begun.
21–30: Perhaps you sat down too soon? Surely you're doing things now which were best done earlier?
31+: Completely abnormal. Start worrying.

Initially and for some years I presented this exercise by way of introduction to some stern, admonitory words on the dangers of procrastination and the importance of self-discipline. The fact that the majority of my students owned up to being in the '31+: Completely abnormal' category seemed only to confirm the need for the exercise. The fact that I was also in the '31+: Completely abnormal' category, and that every single one of these displacement activities applied equally to me, seemed only to confirm the need for us all to be more vigilant, less dreamy, more focused, less dilatory.

I've since begun to suspect that procrastination is not only *not* 'completely abnormal' but is an essential part of the process of writing. I've begun to believe that we might benefit as much by gazing at nothing as by staring at the screen, and that we need to distract ourselves from our writing every bit as much as we need to knuckle down to it.

John Keats famously characterised the writer (he actually said 'Man of Achievement especially in literature') as someone who is 'capable of being in uncertainties, Mysteries, doubts without any irritable reaching after fact & reason', and while it may be stretching it somewhat, here perhaps is another realm of uncertainty in which a writer must dwell: whether or not to trust the impulse to delay or to interrupt ourselves, whether to allow ourselves the licence to waste time.

There are limits of course – I once put my first novel *Pig* aside for a couple of days and failed to return to it for nine months, and I still allow whole days to disappear in a frenzy of file rearranging and paper stacking (and emailing; especially emailing) – but often I think we need certain periods of not-writing, or slow writing, so that things can percolate up from the back of our minds and surprise us. Sometimes I think we may even need to defer and delay for so long that we reach such a pitch of anxiety that all our excuses metabolise into nervous energy and eventually, finally, we have the impetus we need to press on.

And energy is important. If you have a fit of the fidgets, or a sudden urge to paint a ceiling or plant some seedlings, that may be because you need to get some distance on the work, so that you can see it more clearly – or it may simply be that you need the exercise. Writing, unlike the other arts, involves little physical activity. Often it requires tremendous physical restraint. Dancers, actors, painters, potters, printmakers, photographers, sculptors and musicians all get to move about a bit – and sometimes to suspend conscious thought, relying instead on the body's intelligence – but with writing the energy is contained, held in; very often the body is clenched. Which is tiring. Writing can be exhausting precisely because it requires so much sitting still. And tired writers produce tired writing. Or none at all.

Tired *people* produce tired writing, or none at all, and one obvious reason why so many of the writers in my list do their writing in the morning is because they have nothing better to do, being writers (by which I mean successful, famous writers), whereas most other people (including most other writers, including me) have to organise their writing time around the need to earn a living, or bring up a family, or complete a college course, or even all three.

Clearly there are some writers who prefer to write in the evening. For them, as for Philip Larkin perhaps, the best defence against the distracting demands of real life and other people is to attend to those demands first, to do the dishes (or the full day at work, or whatever else it may be) and *then* start the writing. Possibly the option of rising at dawn in order to write before work or family life begins is just too heroic or too daunting a prospect: it's the evening (however little remains of it) or nothing.

Curiously, though, too much time may be even more of a problem than too little.

This is especially true for beginning writers (of whatever age), who won't have the pressure of contractual deadlines, or the lure of a readership curious to read what they've written (let alone the fear of that readership browsing in a bookshop and choosing the latest title by a rival writer instead). With certain familiar (and exaggerated) exceptions – the Beats for instance; William

Burroughs and Jack Kerouac, let's say [2] – the lives of writers are generally quite dull, often exceedingly dull. The writing requires it; that's how the writing gets done. And this can be a problem for the beginning writer with too many options: almost anything can seem more interesting and more enticing than writing.

Conversely, sometimes nothing can seem quite so *important* as writing, to the extent that the actual, practical sitting down and doing it becomes fraught with anxiety. Unless the circumstances appear in some way auspicious, or we feel in some way *inspired* – and the writing in some way guaranteed to succeed – then we dare not begin.

A little of both of these attitudes afflicted me in the writing of *Pig*. I know from an old diary that the first twelve pages took me seven months to complete, and that it then took me four years to get as far as page 124, just past half-way. I was a young man drifting along, periodically unemployed, only ever in low-paid, part-time, often menial work, and with no particular ambitions. I had little self-discipline, and next-to-no belief in myself as a writer or in my book as a publishable novel. Despite this, I was also profoundly attached to the idea of writing and of 'being' a writer and of the importance of writing well. The tension between these contradictory attitudes meant that I continually delayed and deferred sitting down with my book until my stars were aligned, my yin–yang in harmony, my in-tray empty, the dishes all done.

The second half of *Pig* was written in just over a year, and two things helped me to accelerate. The first was accepting that I did in fact have a plausibly publishable book, or at least half of one, which encouraged me to believe I could write the other half. The second was acquiring both a proper, full-time job (my first, ever) and a baby daughter (ditto). My working days began and ended with a two-hour commute across Glasgow by bus, tube and overground train; my weekends were organised around Rose. Suddenly I seemed to have no time whatsoever to write, and this, contrarily, made the urge and determination to write all the more pressing.

Somewhat belatedly I realised I needed to designate a time – however limited, or hemmed about with other concerns – that was my writing time, and that this needed to be consistent and protected (not least from my own tendency towards self-sabotage). And so I began to write most evenings between half-nine and midnight, after Rose was asleep and – interestingly (to me at

[2] Burroughs and Kerouac remain very popular with my undergraduate students in particular, heroes of the 'writing while wasted' idea. But Burroughs himself dismissed the usefulness of stimulants, sedatives and, ultimately, hallucinogens to his writing. They were, he said in an interview with *The Paris Review*, 'absolutely contraindicated for creative work'. The example of burnt-out, alcoholic Kerouac perhaps proves his point. Burroughs's own output perhaps doesn't.

least) – after I'd had a short sleep myself, which had an effect similar to that of a wiper on a rain-spattered windscreen: my catnap cleared away the clutter of the day, erased the accumulated aggravations, and allowed me to begin a little closer, perhaps, to the state of dreaming.

It helped for me that my partner was (and is) also a writer. As far as we could, we shared the chores and childcare equally, and took turns on our only computer, and worked as each other's editor and principal reader.[3] But not everyone is so fortunate; in fact, quite often the opposite. Those nearest to us can be the biggest obstacle to our writing, since our writing requires so much of our attention, our energy and time, and this will frequently provoke hostility or jealousy, whether openly expressed, or disguised in the form of indifference or a consistent lack of encouragement.

Alternatively, those nearest to us might be our parents, who can cherish quite different ambitions for us than our own, seeing in writing a particularly hazardous, insecure and uncertain career choice, perhaps even viewing it as a prolongation of adolescence, a wilful or dreamy refusal to accept adult responsibility (both of which views may be quite accurate).

Or the obstacle can be our children. Cyril Connolly famously wrote in *Enemies of Promise* that 'there is no more sombre enemy of good art than the pram in the hall', and while some will find in the birth of a child a spur to their writing (as I did), and some will claim (or cheerfully complain) that each of their children represents a book that will never be written, others may struggle even to get going, since the pram is already there, the soft toys strewn about the floor, the nappies dripping in the kitchen.[4]

All of us are hindered in some way, but what seems a hindrance to one writer may well be a help to another. I know of one novelist, for instance, who claims to work best in the evenings and only after her second glass of wine; yet for most of us even one glass may be too many. On one Arvon Foundation course I taught there was a student who could only write to music and had brought along a pair of plate-sized earphones to plug into his iPod. His roommate, meanwhile, had packed a pair of industrial ear-muffs, since even birdsong would derange him.

---

[3] Lynne might give a differently slanted account of this time, emphasising post-natal exhaustion and the burden of breastfeeding. As I became more productive, she became less so.

[4] J.G. Ballard, a brilliant and prolific writer, brought up three children after the early death of his wife, and wrote this in his autobiography *Miracles of Life*: 'I kept up a steady output of novels and short story collections, largely because I spent most of my time at home. A short story, or a chapter of a novel, would be written in the time between ironing a school tie, serving up the sausage and mash, and watching *Blue Peter*. I am certain that my fiction is all the better for that. My greatest ally was the pram in the hall.'

Whatever they may be, it can be useful to itemise those things we find a hindrance to our writing, as well as those we find helpful. The following exercise is called 'Friends and foes' and is my version of an exercise I first encountered on that same Arvon course. It appears in what might be its original form in Louise Doughty's cheerful guidebook *A Novel in a Year* (where it's called 'Allies and enemies') and in David Morley's *The Cambridge Introduction to Creative Writing* (where it's called 'Enemies and allies'):

---

3. Friends and foes

Take two sheets of paper and give one the heading 'Friends' and the other 'Foes'.

Under 'Friends' make a list of all those things that help you in your writing. Some of these may be people (a supportive partner, perhaps) or the memory of people (a grandparent who always made you feel valued, let's say) or maybe even an animal (the cat in your lap). Some might be objects (a particular pen, the ergonomic chair that means you no longer get backache) or surroundings (this view of your garden, the calm you find in the back bedroom). Other 'friends' might include the coffee you drink in the morning, or the wine you drink in the evening, or your twenty roll-ups a day, or your gunk-cleaning routine, or the hour you spend at the gym, or the cut-and-paste facility on your PC, or the favourite novels you turn to for guidance. And then there are the thoughts about yourself and your writing that console or inspire or encourage you, which may well be your best friends of all.

Under 'Foes' make a list of all those things that hinder you in your writing. Some of these may be people (an unsupportive partner, perhaps) or the memory of people (the parent who is always so critical, let's say) or maybe even an animal (the cat that keeps pestering to sit in your lap). Some can be objects (the keyboard that gives you RSI, the uncomfortable chair that causes your backache) or surroundings (this dismal view of your garden, the constant noise from upstairs). Other foes might be the wine you drink in the evening, or the hangover you wake to each morning, or your constant trips to the kitchen, or your email addiction, or your migraine affliction, or the prizewinning novels you keep comparing your own to. And of course there are the thoughts about yourself and your writing that defeat or depress or discourage you, which can be absolutely your worst foes of all.

The point here is not to cancel out each of your friends with a foe, or to challenge each foe with a friend, but to try to be clear about what enables or inhibits you, and to think about ways in which you might foster the thoughts and circumstances that assist you, while addressing or simply acknowledging the conditions that hinder you, whether they be practical, personal or psychological.

Some things can't be changed. Others can't be changed easily. But recognition may be a necessary first step towards finding the writing routine that best suits you.

It could be, for instance, that starting early is a bargain you need to strike with yourself: if you can get the writing done by mid-afternoon, or by lunchtime, or by breakfast, the day will still be long, so no other chore need be left undone, niggling away at the back of your mind.

Or it may be that all your other chores and obligations must be dealt with first: if you can finish your essay, or get the children to bed, or complete your shift at work, then whatever time remains need not be overshadowed or interrupted by those other concerns. And while it would not be a good idea to trust the urge to daydream, fidget or paint ceilings to such an extent that no writing gets done at all, it may be useful to accommodate these distractions as a necessary precursor to writing, so that they are acknowledged as a part of the process and serve to create the mental space in which the writing can happen.

And ultimately it is a mental space you need to create, some inner place you can retreat to as a way of announcing to yourself 'I am a writer', or if that seems too grandiose or presumptuous, 'I am writing'. You need to create this space, and you need to devise a schedule, a regular and consistent routine, that will take you there. This is partly so that you don't come to depend upon the gift of inspiration, which may strike when you are least ready, or may never strike, or may in fact require you to be fully immersed in the process of writing and rewriting before it can find you. But mainly it is because the unpredictability of writing – the sense of never knowing for sure what will come out today – depends on all other distractions being eliminated.

As I'll explore in Chapters 4 and 10, the measure of successful writing is very often the extent to which it is able to surprise us – as writers and readers – by reawakening perceptions made dull by habit and familiarity. And this ability to 'make strange' or 'defamiliarise' very often depends, paradoxically, on our writing lives being premised on habit, on the dullness of familiar routines.

Now attempt again our first exercise, but this time describe the routine you intend to work to *from now on*:

4. *What where when* . . .

Think about your ideal writing routine. Then modify it so it becomes
more realistic. Now describe it under these headings:

Where will you write?
When will you start?
Which days of the week?
How long will you write for?
What implements will you use?
What rules will you set yourself?
What excuses are you most determined not to make?

Whatever routine you set for yourself, it is inevitable that you will at times
struggle. You should anticipate that you will occasionally fail. Such is the
nature of writing. But you can reduce the chances of failure by being realistic
about the many other demands on your time and your energies, and if it seems
that you may only have a short period each day for writing – thirty minutes
before breakfast, let's say; perhaps an hour before bedtime – then that time is
fine. It is better to know what you have, and to adapt to it, than to condemn
yourself to the frustration of not being able to meet any more challenging
targets. And even thirty minutes may be enough, if you are clear about what
can be achieved. Several of the exercises in the next two chapters are designed
for generating material in short bursts of activity. Often this will be material
that can be developed later into longer works. But the exercises themselves can
become an essential, on-going discipline in the practice of writing, which
is after all what it means to 'be' a writer. Writers write – regularly, habitually,
routinely.

2. Write about what you know: observational journals

Despite the necessity of sitting still for long periods (or of standing, in the case of Ernest Hemingway and Philip Roth), writing has one definite advantage over other, physically more expressive art forms: it requires the barest minimum of tools and materials, and can be accommodated to the smallest of working environments. A pen and paper and something to lean on will do.

Of course, whatever the art form, a good deal of imagination is also required, and the application of that imagination to some raw material, whether it be the dancer's body, the ceramicist's clay, the painter's acrylics, or the conceptualist's dead shark and formaldehyde. In the case of the writer, the raw material is language, which is to say *words*, and the writer's first problem is always to find enough words – or, to put that another way, to choose from among the all-too-many possible words that are out there. Too much choice can be just as disabling as none. Finding the *exact* words can be a torturous business.

In this respect a dictionary will be one helpful addition to the writer's minimal toolkit, while a thesaurus may not be.

Like the Bible to the believer, a dictionary is a constant source of comfort and security, a dependable guide and confirmation in which every word has an origin and a history as well as a stable identity – a consistent spelling and function and a reliable meaning or range of alternative meanings.[1] A dictionary defines and delimits, which makes precision possible, and as a writer you will be as committed to precision – to exactness and clarity – as you are interested

---

[1] Up to a point anyway: unlike the Bible, a dictionary will need to be updated once in a while since the stability of the language is only ever relative – some words become fossils, some simply archaic, others take on new meanings, or shed old ones.

in the nature of the words you use: where they come from, what they can do, where you can take them.

However, as a writer you will also be acutely aware of how words can fail you. The more you engage with the language the more you will come to suspect that its true nature is to be inconsistent and unreliable: meaning often depends on context; ambiguity creeps in; words won't say what you want them to say; they clang when you want them to chime; sometimes they slip away from you.[2]

We've all had the experience of the word on the tip of our tongue for instance, and if we are writing (as opposed to talking) we'll often reach then for a thesaurus, just as I did in the Introduction to this book when I wanted to use the word 'provenance'. Unfortunately, just as usually happens, I went through my thesaurus from possibility to possibility – via many impossibilities – and failed to find the exact word I wanted. In the end I asked my wife.

In this respect a thesaurus is the epitome of what language is like – so many words, each defined by what it is not, the exact definition never quite certain, the exact word forever elusive. . . . Having had one since I was at school, I haven't yet summoned the courage to discard my own thesaurus, though I use it less and less. I'm not sure I would recommend you acquire one.[3]

I would however recommend you acquire a notebook, or several.

Neither the dictionary nor the thesaurus quite qualifies as *source* of raw material for the writer of fiction (though either could be employed as a prompt to the kind of automatic writing exercises I describe in Chapter 3). Your source, very often, will be your own experience and your awareness of the world around you – at least initially – and one way in which you can begin to generate your own raw material is to keep a notebook, or a series of notebooks.

Here you can record your observations – your eavesdroppings and noticings – and so accumulate a bank of words and phrases, descriptive paragraphs and character sketches, snatches of dialogue and (perhaps) quotations from

---

[2] The unreliability of language is something you may want to explore, of course; eventually you may wish to exploit the possibilities of imprecision, the suggestiveness of ambiguity. But how to be imprecise without being obscure, how to be ambiguous without becoming confusing? Perhaps even vagueness requires exactness. I'll come back to this in Chapter 11.

[3] Then again, Jonathan Safran Foer's novel *Everything is Illuminated* makes good comic use of the possibilities of the thesaurus. One of its narrators, Alex Perchov, is a Ukrainian translator whose voice is composed of a stream of bad thesaurus choices: he doesn't spend money but 'disseminates currency'; his hair isn't centre-parted but 'split in the middle'; he doesn't sit but 'roosts', doesn't explain but 'illuminates', doesn't sign his letters sincerely but 'guilelessly', etc.

other writers that will act as a kind of deposit account of language from which you can later make withdrawals to adapt or incorporate into your work-in-progress, or to form the basis from which you can begin to build a new work.

This writerly discipline of observing and notetaking is a crucial means to fixing experience in words (particular words, in a particular order) and therefore of fixing those words in your mind. And when you are feeling especially impoverished – lacking ideas, struggling for words – your bank of phrases and paragraphs can be what sustains you. The potential danger in this is that you may come to depend too much on your notebooks and so become overly shy of invention, of 'simply' making it up. This possible pitfall, and the benefits of notetaking, are nicely described by W. Somerset Maugham in *A Writer's Notebook*:

> I forget who it was who said that every author should keep a notebook, but should take care never to refer to it. If you understand this properly, I think there is truth in it. By making a note of something that strikes you, you separate it from the incessant stream of impressions that crowd across the mental eye, and perhaps fix it in your memory. All of us have had good ideas or vivid sensations that we thought would one day come in useful, but which, because we were too lazy to write them down, have entirely escaped us. When you know you are going to make a note of something, you look at it more attentively than you otherwise would, and in the process of doing so the words are borne in upon you that will give it its private place in reality. The danger of using notes is that you may find yourself inclined to rely on them, and so lose the even and natural flow of your writing which comes from allowing the unconscious that full activity which is somewhat pompously known as inspiration.

Having kept notebooks for many years, and having drawn on them heavily for at least one novel – *Common Ground* – and somewhat less heavily for my other books, I'm inclined to disagree with the idea that you should take care never to refer to your notebooks. In fact, just the opposite: I trawl through mine regularly, though I am often acutely aware of how the pre-prepared phrase might work against the 'even and natural flow' of what I've already written. It's encouraging therefore to find a contemporary novelist as significant as Richard Ford – a writer of richly detailed, absorbing depictions of what he calls 'the normal applauseless life of us all' – admitting in an interview to generating new work in just the way I am advocating here:

> I'm a noticer and a prolific taker of notes. If I see something, I try to write it down because I know I'll forget it otherwise. So when I start a story, while I

may not have the story itself, I do have a collation of raw materials – details written in words, sentences that I've heard over time and thought were interesting, descriptions of people, memories of my own. That's the raw material for what will become a story.[4]

A more extreme form of this approach is presented in a short story by the Canadian writer Norman Levine. 'Tricks' describes a residential writing course very similar to those run by the Arvon Foundation, and the speaker here is one of the tutors:

'Take things from life,' Adolphe said. 'Bad experience is better than no experience. Invent as little as possible. You are inventing the piece the way you use words and the way you are telling it. Wherever you go you will notice things.'

Adolphe is a faded poet, and despite his name – 'like Hitler but with an e' – he isn't as dictatorial as this may make him sound; his dogmatism in fact disguises a deep ambivalence about his authority as a teacher and about the nature of literary fame (as well as a profound sadness about life). However, even if he were a mini-Hitler, I suspect I would still find myself agreeing with him here, both with the somewhat contentious suggestion that you should invent as little as possible (though only initially, and only up to a point) and with the more straightforward notion that wherever you go you will notice things.

This latter idea does require one small qualification, though: wherever you go you will notice things, but only if you have trained yourself in the habit of noticing.

A useful analogy might be the small fortune my daughter and I have accrued in lost coins over the years. When Rose was much younger there was a fashion among the boys who hung around our local shops to throw away their small change, what they called their 'shrapnel'. One day we decided we would gather up this discarded money, and gradually, as the weeks went by, we began to notice coins outside other shops too, and along kerbsides, on buses, wherever we happened to go. We collected them all, and by the end of the year we'd

---

[4] This is from a collection of interviews called *Writers on Writing*, which is based on an Australian TV series. The interviewers' questions have been edited out, so that the writers' answers take the form of critical (and sometimes quite uncritical) self-commentaries. I sometimes worry about the academic practice of requiring students to write critical reflections on their own work, but if the practice does have an equivalent in the world beyond the academy, this may be it: the author interview.

amassed £27.55, which seemed so large a windfall we decided to continue for another year, then another, and another, and now we can't stop.

The boys may no longer discard their shrapnel, but people are always losing money, and each year our total has steadily risen: £32.35, £34.49, £40.56, £47.49, £63.13, £70.04 and, last year, £86.84. Mostly we find coppers and silver, but there are pound coins too, and sometimes notes. And what has happened, I believe, is that we have become uncommonly attuned to something most people would overlook: because we've schooled ourselves in the habit of looking, we now notice lost money wherever we go; we can't help it.

Similarly, once you get into the habit of keeping notebooks, you will begin to notice noteworthy things; you will become uncommonly attuned to all manner of things you might not normally see, and this noticing will become ingrained, almost a reflex.

In an essay called 'The Art of Fiction', published in 1884, Henry James imagined saying to a novice writer, 'Write from experience, and experience only', to which he then added, 'Try to be one of the people on whom nothing is lost!'

This has since become something of a slogan in Creative Writing teaching – echoed by Adolphe with an e – but it is nonetheless the best of advice, as useful now as it was then, and the first step to becoming a person on whom nothing is lost is to acquire the habit of collecting (that is, noticing, recording, and saving in your notebook) the particulars of everyday experience.

There are two ways of going about this. The first is to keep a general, all-encompassing observational journal. The second, which has been my own habit, is to keep specific journals for specific periods of time on specific themes. But the first approach first:

---

5. Keeping an observational journal

You will need a notebook compact enough to take with you wherever you go. This shouldn't be something too precious (leather-bound with premium-grade paper, let's say) as that might make you overly precious about what you put in it (you may feel that every sentence has to be leather-bound and premium-grade too). The purpose of the notebook is to gather up raw material. Rawness is fine. Any old notepad will do.

Once you have your notebook, go and sit somewhere public. If I were teaching a university class, at this point I would open the door and send the students away for a while – to the campus coffee bar, the steps overlooking the plaza, the pub, the library, or simply to wander the walkways and corridors. I would ask them to be extra-attentive to their surroundings, and to jot down whatever strikes them as interesting. At the appointed time, everyone should return to the seminar room prepared to read out some of their findings to the rest of the group.

What might those findings be? What might you record in your notebook as you sit in your chosen place? Remember that this is an observational journal, an objective record of things seen and heard, rather than a place to express your hopes and fears, to explore your emotions, or even to set down your memories. In this notebook you might:

- record an overheard conversation, perhaps only a snatch, perhaps a mere phrase, possibly the entire exchange;
- record your own conversation with someone, not necessarily a friend, and not necessarily very long;
- describe an unusual or puzzling scene, something glimpsed through a window perhaps, something whose meaning isn't necessarily obvious;
- describe in detail an incident whose meaning may seem obvious, but which you might not normally observe so closely;
- make a note of interesting, intriguing or amusing shop names, graffiti, public notices, newspaper headlines, etc.;
- describe the weather, the way the light falls, the way the rain falls;
- jot down the details of something you might not normally notice, or might not normally need to find the words for: the design of things, the decay of things;
- make a sketch in words of someone observed on a bus, in a café or a bar, walking down the street, sitting in the park, etc., and perhaps speculate on their character, their story.

And having begun, having made your first entry, you should keep going. Make this a practice you continue indefinitely, replacing one notebook with another, and then another, and another.

For the purposes of an exercise that comes later in this book, you should be especially observant of strangers in public places while keeping this journal. In addition, it might be useful if you gathered other, 'found' material in the form of magazine photographs and newspaper clippings. These will not only be useful for later exercises, but the clippings in particular can be an excellent starting point for generating stories.

6. Keeping a scrapbook

You will require a scrapbook, some scissors, a glue stick.

Collect photographs from magazines of people who strike you as interesting, but avoid celebrities: you don't want anyone whose face is instantly recognisable or whose 'character' may already be known to you. Newspaper supplements tend to be better for this, as they usually depict their subjects in natural poses, as themselves. Fashion glossies are all about the image, which makes the personality less easy to access.

Collect pictures of interesting locations, too – both interior and exterior. Empty locations are particularly useful, full of potential, a sense of 'something might happen'. Crowd scenes can have a similar effect, the more crowded the better.

Look out for human interest stories in newspapers, whether tragic or comic, distressing or funny. The local evening paper is often best for this: ordinary people surprised by something slightly out of the ordinary.

We'll return to this material in later chapters.

In one obvious sense there's an artificiality to the way I've described the observational journal exercise. In reality it would be impractical to banish personal, subjective material to another notebook, or to carry around different notebooks for different purposes. Very often the writer's notebook is a scrappy, all-inclusive compendium of observations, reflections, quotations, other people's book recommendations, memos-to-self, names and addresses, shopping lists, to-do lists, et cetera.

The crucial point here, however, is to emphasise the importance of looking outwards rather than inwards, and to stress that writing from experience is very often as much a matter of observation as it is of introspection.

My own notebooks tend towards the observational end of the spectrum, recording even the most personal experience dispassionately, hardly ever becoming introspective. They are also particularly scrappy, and the material in them particularly raw, but for me there is always a second stage to the process: once a notebook is full I'll transfer the most usable bits to my computer, and as I type them up I'll begin to refine the phrasing; I'll begin to shape the material. (The filleted notebook I'll then throw away.)

In part this practice is conditioned by the fact that I began keeping journals soon after I acquired my first computer, which happened to coincide with a period when almost all my experiences were new experiences. I'd just begun my first proper job, after years of odd-jobbing and drifting. I'd also recently moved from low-rise, leafy Norwich to high-rise, post-industrial Glasgow, three hundred miles to the north. The weather, apart from anything else, was very different. And my not-yet-wife was pregnant.

The computer, with its organisation of files within folders, and folders within bigger folders, seemed to offer a way of managing this welter of new experience by compartmentalising it under separate headings, and so I began one journal about my job, another about my new neighbourhood, another about the grey Glaswegian weather, another about Lynne's pregnancy. There were several more besides, and while some ran concurrently, most didn't. As one drew to a close, I would begin the next, and in each case I would set myself three rules or parameters: what the journal should be about; how long it should run for; and how frequently I should make an entry.

This approach encouraged a certain self-discipline and gave focus to my noticing, and eventually these particular journals came to furnish the material for *Common Ground*. The following exercises should demonstrate the process.

---

7. *Weather report*

Here are two entries from my journal 'Weather':

14th February
Snow is predicted but hasn't yet fallen. The wind is bitterly cold and forces you along the street from behind. Getting onto a warm bus a skim of icy cold remains on the face. There's a bed of wind-blown leaves and litter at the top of the Underground escalators. And yet, this being Glasgow, young men pass me in shirt-sleeves, a girl in a strapless dress, bare legs.

31st March
The winds are sometimes fierce, gale force. A beer can pursues me up the street, rattling along the centre of the road as if kicked. Plastic bags are caught high in the trees.

Whatever the weather now, go and stand outside for ten or fifteen minutes, or go for a short walk. When you come back indoors, write a short paragraph in which you attempt to capture something of your impressions. Draw on all your senses. And keep it economical.

The rules: this should be the first entry in a journal you will keep for exactly one year, at the end of which you will have a record of the seasons. The entries should be occasional: each time you notice a change in the weather, set it down in words.

The idea is that whenever you then need to describe the weather in a story – particularly if you're writing in the middle of winter about summer, or in the middle of summer about winter – you can refer to your notebook. The phrases should have retained the clarity and specificity of the recently seen, the freshly experienced.

It may or may not be obvious that my 'Weather' entries are quite 'worked'. At the time I wrote them I was still learning the discipline of journal keeping, and although I would jot down my notes on any old scrap of paper, I would then over-compensate for this scrappiness at the typing-up stage. In one sense, I thought of my journals as an end in themselves; I laboured over the phrasing until each sentence, and each paragraph, seemed 'finished'. I now realise that these journals are only ever a step on the way, and while I will begin to revise the phrasing at the typing-up stage, I will only *begin*. The completion of the entries comes later, in the context of a novel or story.

8. Street life

Here are two entries from my journal 'Glasgow' (I've chosen a couple that again mention the weather, and again they're quite 'worked'):

Wednesday 26th August
The weather has been wet for weeks, but now the winds have started. They sough through the sycamores, rattle the windows at night. There's a chill in the air, a draught in the bedroom. Coming home from work under grey skies this evening I see only one other person out of doors, a small boy wearing giant flapping elephant ears, a plastic trunk attached to his forehead.

Thursday 3rd September
There are gusting winds all night and a wheelie bin is blown the length of the street, colliding with cars and setting off their alarms. In

the morning the litter is everywhere, stuck to the sides of buildings, strewn across lawns, still blowing in the sky. I see whirlwinds of rubbish on street corners. There's a smell of perfumed washing powder at the top of our road, the stench of the sewage works when I get to the shops. In the back courts the lines are flapping with clothes, the trees are rustling, and on the side of a tenement block there's the whipping shadow of a telephone line.

You may like to go for another short walk, or simply stand at your front or back window. Your aim is to notice things in your immediate neighbourhood, and this might take one of two forms: you could either describe something you see every day, setting it down for the first time; or you could look to describe something brand new (this needn't be anything extraordinary, but should be something you may not see again).

The rules are these: beginnning today, this should be a journal you keep for exactly three months, and you should aim to add one entry a day.

Occasionally in keeping this kind of observational journal you may notice an incident that gives rise to a story, or a series of events that seem to connect in the way of a story, but for the most part the material you gather will be detail, the stuff of backdrop or setting. Selectively incorporated into your fiction, this material can lend texture, the grain of the real. The next two exercises are more concerned with recording your active participation in the world around you. As a consequence they are more likely to generate the stuff of narrative, of stories.

9. Workplace

I was appointed as librarian to a large Glaswegian high school and kept a journal for the duration of one term. Here are three entries:

Tuesday 10th September
At three in the morning I turn off my alarm. 'I'm going to have to take a sicky,' I tell Lynne, 'I can't sleep.' 'What's your excuse?' she asks. 'Migraine, double-vision and nausea.' She shakes her head, goes back to sleep. It took me an hour to decide my symptoms, visualising the headmaster as he read them on my sick note, imagining his thoughts. It had to be something stress-related, so he'd understand that I'm working too hard.

Thursday 12th September
After I've wound up my study skills lesson an English teacher says to
me, 'You're sounding very hoarse, Mr C.' 'It's the sixth time I've given
this *spiel* this week. My throat's sore.' 'Occupational hazard,' she says
cheerfully. 'I've had a permanent sore throat since the day I started
teaching. Never goes away.'

Monday 9th December
A new teacher joined us in September. She wears soft clothes which
sag where she sags. Her hair is black and white, her complexion grey,
and she speaks in a voice which is never stable, sometimes high
pitched, sometimes throaty, always with a slight tremor. She constantly talks to herself, giggles at her own private jokes. But what distinguishes her most is her shortness of breath, bronchial wheezing,
constant sniffling and sneezing. I thought at first she had a slight cold,
but it has never left her. She keeps a box of tissues in her handbag, a
hanky tucked under both sleeves, usually another crumpled in her
fist. This evening I was leaving on foot by the car park exit when she
passed me in her car. It fits her as her clothes fit her, an old model, too
small and seeming to bulge to accommodate her. Its engine works as
poorly as her lungs, coughing and spluttering, bellowing exhaust as it
goes, leaving a cloud for the kids to walk through, a trail of grey from
the school to the next junction.

You needn't be in employment to keep this kind of journal. School
or college are equally good, or any other social environment that you
regularly go to: church, club, pub, community centre, wherever . . .
Your rules are these: decide on the social context you wish to record,
then set your own time limit, depending on how often you go there (if it's
five days a week, three months might be enough; if it's once a fortnight,
a full year would be better); then each time you attend, bring back an
incident, a conversation or a character sketch to record in your journal.

Graham Greene famously remarked[5] that there needs to be a sliver of ice in
the heart of every writer, and while my sketch of the bronchial teacher may be
unkind, it is a reasonably truthful depiction not only of her but of my reaction
to her. The paradox of short stories and novels is that they are *untrue* – in that

[5] So famous is this remark that a Google search will throw up dozens of references to it,
and many variations upon it, but will fail to give the precise source of the phrase. It's in his
memoirs, I believe, somewhere.

they are made up – yet their success so often depends upon how *truthful* they seem to us. This can be expressed as 'true to life' or 'true about life'.[6]

In either case the truthfulness will be registered emotionally and will spring from the writer's willingness to be honest – and even unsparing – in recording his or her experiences (however radically those experiences are transformed in the transition from notebook to fiction).

---

10. Home life

I kept a journal of Lynne's pregnancy, which concluded with a lengthy description of Rose's birth. I tried to keep this as descriptive as possible, though my hopes and fears inevitably crept into it (I tried to be objective about those too). Here are three entries:

22nd October
At midnight Lynne was still awake, unable to breathe or get comfortable, and becoming very angry. She turned over, dragging her extra pillow with her, and almost immediately went back the other way. Her sighs were as much to catch her breath as to vent her frustration, but I lay stiffly beside her, afraid to move in case I disturbed her, convinced she was angry with me, becoming angry myself. Once she'd found a comfortable position she went straight to sleep, and started to snore. The snoring became louder, stopping briefly when I nudged her, but continuing for almost twenty minutes. I went for some aspirin. Then I said, 'Lynne, you're snoring.'
'I'm not, I'm awake, how can I be snoring!'
'You've been snoring for the last twenty minutes!'
'Well I can't help it, it's not my fault is it!'
So she lay awake, trying not to snore, unable to breathe or get comfortable and becoming even more angry.

27th October
Coming home on the bus from our ante-natal class we were attacked by a gang of kids at Partick Cross. They threw stones at the windows,

---

[6] This isn't to argue for literary realism, especially. Even the least realistic writing will carry an emotional charge. In fact, the less conventionally realistic – the more exaggerated, distorted or fragmented, let's say – the more true to life's complexity a novel may seem, the closer to life's underlying realities, or to life's apparent absurdity and lack of any underlying stability.

and shattered two behind us. When the driver noticed he stopped the bus and refused to go on. We had to get off. I was furious. I wanted to hit the driver. I wanted to go back and start a fight with the boys. Instead we hurried to catch the last tube train to Govan, then waited for the last bus from Govan Cross, and arrived home an hour and a half after we left the class, cold, miserable, exhausted.

2nd November

As I sat writing Lynne got into bed and held her face in her hands. I thought she was crying, but she was yawning. 'You okay?' I said.

She looked at me crossly. 'No,' she said, and picked up the pregnancy book. She read out her symptoms as they were listed:

She has shooting pains down her thighs and pelvis, caused by the baby's head pinching a nerve in her pubic bone.

She has tingling fingers (carpal tunnel syndrome) caused by fluid retention in her wrists.

She has frequent peeing, caused by the baby's head pressing down on her bladder.

She has indigestion and heartburn.

She has breathlessness, caused by her uterus pressing against her diaphragm and compressing her lungs.

She has practice contractions, known as Braxton Hicks contractions. And she has amnesia. (She read from the book: 'Some women find that their memory comes back after the birth. Others feel that it is never quite the same again.')

The only thing she hasn't got is piles.

Today marks the 28th week since conception. The chapter commencing the 28th week is called 'THE STRANDED WHALE'. And it seems from now on it can only get worse.

For the next few minutes you should close your eyes and think of those people to whom you are closest and whom you see most frequently: parents, partner, siblings, children, etc. Some very recent event or exchange should come to you, happy or sad, humdrum or unusual. Set this down, being as detached as possible. Observe yourself as objectively as you view the other person.

These are your rules: record one incident a day (whether large or small, trivial or significant); continue for the next six weeks; confine your entries to this one person only.

There is a reason why I've chosen to illustrate these last four exercises with these particular journal extracts. I might have selected other entries from other journals. But what the extracts have in common is that they all feed into the following passage from my novel *Common Ground* and demonstrate, firstly, I hope, the way in which writing may sometimes be a process of stitching together disparate bits of other writing, and secondly, how journals can act as a source of material for fiction.

(A brief contextualising note: the novel is written partly as a series of italicised letters from an expectant father, Ashley, to his brother Douglas, who is backpacking around the world. The letters alternate with a third-person narrative that is also from the expectant father's point of view. Jay is the expectant mother.)

Beaches, we know all about beaches. Jay officially became a BEACHED WHALE whilst you were resting up on the sands of Kovalam, Douglas. This is the title of chapter six in her guidebook and describes the period from twenty-eight weeks to childbirth. There are no palm trees or pineapples unfortunately, but thankfully no sweating eyeballs either. Our weather continues to run the precipitational gamut, and if India really does boil your brains to slurry, then I'm glad. Jay hasn't an opinion either way, meteorologically speaking, as she has too much else on her plate, including all of the following:

> *CRIPPLING PAINS IN THE PELVIS (baby's big head squashing a nerve on her pubic bone)*
> *CONSTANT PEEING (baby's big head squashing her bladder)*
> *CONSTIPATION (baby's big head squashing her bowels)*
> *BREATHLESSNESS (baby's big bum squashing her diaphragm)*
> *BACKACHE (baby's big everything)*
> *BRAXTON HICKS CONTRACTIONS (caused by Braxton Hicks)*
> *CARPAL TUNNEL SYNDROME (or 'tingly fingers', caused by fluid retention)*
> *SWOLLEN ANKLES (caused by a gloomy outlook, the result of all of the above)*
> *And AMNESIA ('Some women find their memory is never quite the same again')*
> *But not PILES ('Yet')*
> *Or SUNBURN (Ha!)*

Apparently it can only get worse. But, as the book also says, 'Pregnancy is not an illness but a natural life transition with important holistic and spiritual dimensions.' Rather like South East Asia, I suppose.

....

Jay lay on her side, facing away from him. It was dark outside but not yet late. Cars passed at intervals beneath their window; a black cab thrummed to a halt, doors slammed and a man began shouting. Ashley extended a hand to Jay's hip. The wind soughed through the sycamores. A wheelie-bin was blown the length of the street, colliding with parked cars and setting off their alarms. Jay sighed and pushed his hand away. As the alarms began to expire she turned laboriously towards him, dragging her pillow with her, but almost immediately went back again. Ashley lay close to his edge of the bed, afraid to move in case he disturbed her. She tugged the bedclothes and left him uncovered.

He stared at the twitching curtains, felt the cold of the draught from the window. His fists were clenched. He splayed his fingers until he felt the stretch in the tendons, then laid his hands flat to his stomach. A bus moved off in the distance and his mind returned to his journey from school that evening, some boys at a shopping parade hurling stones at the traffic. They had shattered the window immediately behind him, another in front, and the driver had accelerated beyond the next stop to the nearest depot, from where he'd refused to continue. The following bus was twenty minutes behind. Too weary to argue, Ashley had walked half a mile to a windowless shelter beside a dual-carriageway, hoping to catch a bus on a different route. But nothing had appeared for nearly an hour. A skim of icy cold had remained on his face until he arrived home; his throat was too raw to speak and he had barely listened as Jay described the events of her own day. She later accused him of being this sullen every evening, whatever his reason, and then they had bickered till bedtime. He swallowed painfully now, and realised his hands were clenched as tightly now as before.

He closed his eyes and rolled on to his side, pulled the bedspread across him. Jay was starting to snore. For several minutes he tried to ignore her, then reached to the floor for his alarm clock. He held the dial close to his face. It was a quarter past ten. He turned on to his front and wondered if he could afford another day's sick leave, and what symptoms he might use. On his previous sick-line he'd claimed migraine, double-vision and nausea, all stress-related, and all invented, as his head of department surely knew. In their monthly meeting she had queried his performance in class, his attendance and timekeeping, even his standard of dress. He wasn't delivering the curriculum, wasn't managing his workload or controlling his pupils. He pictured her now as she had appeared at her desk, her soft pink jersey sagging where she sagged, a hanky tucked into each sleeve, another crumpled into her fist. Her complexion was grey and there were pouches under her eyes. She had a bronchial wheeze, and coughed and sniffed constantly, but she worked late every evening and he had never known her to be absent. Sore throats, she had told him on another occasion, were an occupational hazard.

And so it goes on . . .

Although the deck of details has been shuffled to some extent, this excerpt from *Common Ground* reveals an especially close correspondence between my journals and my fiction, and would appear to illustrate Adolphe's injunction to 'invent as little as possible' and Henry James's advice to 'write from experience, and experience only'. In fact, the connection between my notebooks and my novels is only ever occasionally *this* close. Usually the gap is much wider, and the degree of disguise and displacement much greater.

The relationship between the autobiographical and the fictional is similar, perhaps, to that between a tree and its roots. If the tree is the novel, the roots will be that novel's origins in experience, in the facts of your life. But the tree is never a mirror image of the roots. It takes on a very different shape, a much fuller form, expanding upwards and outwards, growing leaves and blossom and fruit, perhaps becoming host to a whole ecology of new connections. The stability of the tree, the very possibility of there being a tree, depends upon its being anchored and nurtured by its roots, but the roots remain in darkness, out of sight, underground. Which is where they belong, of course.

This is to offer a particular slant on the familiar adage that you should 'write about what you know'. My own understanding of this is that you should use 'what you know' to write about 'what you don't know', whether you are writing historical romances, police procedurals, wizarding fantasies, or English provincial realist novels like mine. We all know what it is to be human – in all its complexity and contradictoriness – and this knowledge is what will give substance to our characters, however different they might be from us, and however distant their world might be from our own.

We all have a sense of what it is to be a small child, for instance, with that knee-high perspective on things, just as we've all experienced the intensities of adolescence, those extremes of boredom and absorption, estrangement and excitement. We know what it means to fall in love, to think of someone first thing in the morning, last thing at night, and to yearn for them every moment that they're absent. We know too what it means to lust after someone, to feel the restlessness of desire, that physical reflex, just as we know what it is to loathe, fear or despise someone, to be bullied perhaps, or to behave like the bully ourselves. We've all been vindictive and cruel, and will know the satisfaction that comes with that, as well as the shame. We've all suffered remorse and regret; we've all enjoyed moments of calm and contentment, and sometimes euphoria.

There are these common experiences and the emotions they give rise to, and of course there are many others besides – the list would be limitless – but in every instance the particulars will be different, unique to ourselves. And then there will be the uncommon experiences that we have lived through, and the places we've been to – geographical, social, emotional – that others won't necessarily know. In either case it is the discipline of observing and notetaking, of being a person on whom nothing is lost, that will allow us to capture these particularities of our experience in words so that those words may later be used to furnish our fictions. And the more precise our observations, the more vivid the imaginary worlds we will be able to create; the more we record of our own life, the more we will be able to donate to our characters, and the more they will be able to take on a life of their own.

3. Write about what you don't know you know: automatic writing

If the previous chapter was premised on the idea that you should write about what you know, this chapter is concerned with the possibility that you may know more than you think you know.

The discipline of keeping journals is a discipline in being observant and in recording what you have observed, and in both these respects it's a discipline in being wide awake, in being consciously aware. The practice of 'automatic writing', on the other hand, is a technique by which you might reveal to yourself what is going on in the back of your mind, the stuff you aren't consciously aware of, the stuff of your unconscious – the stuff, in a sense, that you don't know you know.

In Chapter 1, I suggested that procrastination might be as essential to the process of writing as actually sitting down and doing it, that allowing yourself to dally or daydream might be just as important as schooling yourself in self-discipline. The danger in this is that the procrastination may become so prolonged it settles into a kind of inertia. At its most benign, little or no anxiety will attach to this inertia – the stillness and silence may even become permanent and the idea of becoming a writer will simply fade away. If so, you may want to rejoice, for at its most malign the procrastination can assume the agonising form of writer's block – a deep psychological inability or refusal to commit words to the page, or an equally soul-destroying sense that there are no words *to* commit, alongside a deep psychological inability or refusal to give up on the idea of being a writer.[1]

---

[1] What makes this so agonising is that you can only 'be' a writer by writing. Which is to say, writing is an activity not an identity (or is only an identity when it coincides with the activity). Even a shelf of published works won't make you a writer if you are not still

A great deal of anxiety will attach to this.

Besides having other or better things to do, there are perhaps two main reasons why someone might not be able to put any words on the page: the first is that they're waiting for inspiration to strike, and the second is that they're paralysed by perfectionism. Sometimes these two come together.

The former assumes a 'genius' view of the writer, owing much to the Romantic fantasy of the divinely gifted poet, uniquely touched by the hand of the muse, though sometimes 'touched' in the other, more colloquial sense of being slightly mad – or worse: possessed by the muse and made temporarily (or even terminally) insane. Not surprisingly, this tends either to inhibit or excuse the merely mortal from making the effort.

The latter, 'perfectionist' view of the writer is more inclined to accept the need for some perspiration in addition to the inspiration, and assumes that craft and technique can improve a piece of work – draft by laborious draft – but is undermined by the writer's fear of being insufficiently skilful, of being hamfisted and getting it wrong. Which is a fear ultimately of being judged and found wanting (in relation, perhaps, to a Romantic 'genius' idea of what is 'right').

These two views of writing and the writer find a more-or-less correspondence in the two main types of Creative Writing handbook: the 'inspirational' guides, such as Natalie Goldberg's *Writing Down the Bones* and Julia Cameron's *The Artist's Way*, and the more practical (or 'perspirational') guides, such as *Taking Reality by Surprise* and, indeed, this one. In either case, some variation on the technique of automatic writing is almost bound to appear. Ironically, the version you're most likely to find in the 'inspirational' guides will usually be offered as a remedy for the underlying psychological causes of perfectionism, while the version in the practical guides will usually be offered as a means of accessing the muse (reconceived in our post-Freudian age as the unconscious).

I'll come back to this, but in the meantime here's a variation I very often use in the classroom:

---

writing; they make you a former writer. Authorship is another thing entirely. You *can* be an author even if you're not writing. Authorship is the public or social aspect of writing. It's what happens when, to paraphrase Philip Larkin, you go about pretending to be yourself, i.e. the name on the spine of the book (which is why Larkin refused to do public readings; he couldn't bear the public role of being 'Philip Larkin', particularly when the real Philip had stopped writing).

---

11. First thoughts

Think of the person you are closest to in the world, the person whose life you know the most intimately. You are going to write for fifteen minutes, describing in detail what you imagine that person to be doing (and thinking and feeling) at this very moment. Write in the present tense, and address it to 'you' – e.g. *You are humming to yourself. Standing on tip-toe, you are scanning the top shelf of the cupboard for the pistachio nuts I hid there last night . . .*
  The rules are these:

- You are free to write illegibly and ungrammatically.
- You are free to be clumsy and clichéd.
- You are free to repeat or contradict yourself.
- You are free to write rubbish.
- You are free to write anything.
- You are free to go completely off the point.
- But you must write without a moment's pause for exactly fifteen minutes.

No one is going to read what you write – not your teacher or your classmates, and especially not the person you're describing.

The rules for this exercise aren't exactly mine. They're adapted from an exercise in *Writing Down the Bones* that Natalie Goldberg describes as the 'basic unit of writing practice' and upon which most of her creative method is predicated. Its purpose is to outwit the internal critic or censor, to sidestep conventional or habitual modes of thinking, and to release a spontaneous, energetic flow of writing that reveals, in Goldberg's words, 'the truth of the way things are'.

Goldberg doesn't give this exercise a name – other than 'the timed exercise' – though the chapter in which it appears is called 'First Thoughts'. This connects her interestingly (and possibly intentionally) with the Beat writers of the fifties and sixties, and particularly with Allen Ginsberg and Gregory Corso – the latter of whom once said:

At the time of writing I don't rewrite. First thought best thought. We were always into that. You know, first words that are down, best words that are down. The first thought is the purest thought. The pure stuff is spontaneous.[2]

Corso was speaking here as a guest lecturer at Allen Ginsberg's Creative Writing class at New York University, where earlier in the semester Ginsberg had distributed a sheet of what he called 'Mind Writing Slogans'. These were sub-headed by the dictum 'First thought is best in Art, Second in other matters', which Ginsberg attributed to the archetypal Romantic poet and painter William Blake, though his friend and fellow Beat poet Lawrence Ferlinghetti identified it more as 'a Buddhist concept' (and indeed the first 'mind writing slogan' on Ginsberg's list is 'First Thought, Best Thought', attributed to his Buddhist teacher, Chogyam Trungpa).

While hardly as significant a writer as Allen Ginsberg, Natalie Goldberg is likewise a Buddhist, and *Writing Down the Bones* is perhaps as much about spiritual enlightenment and a version of inspiration she calls 'breathing in God' as it is about creative writing. Throughout the book she quotes the sagacities of Katagiri Roshi, her Zen guru, and she describes the practice of 'timed writing' as 'a way to help you penetrate your life and become sane'. For Goldberg, in other words, automatic writing appears as both an end in itself – a form of meditation – and a means to self-discovery or self-understanding, possibly even self-healing.

This emphasis on personal growth is especially pronounced in Julia Cameron's *The Artist's Way*, where the practice of automatic writing is called 'the morning pages' and consists in filling three sheets of paper with random outpourings immediately on waking in order to 'forge a creative alliance, artist-to-artist, with the Great Creator' and so achieve, among other things, 'forgiveness and self-forgiveness' and 'a sense of safety and hope'.

There is little suggestion in *The Artist's Way* that this daily routine of spooling words onto the page has much in common with *writing* as most practising poets, playwrights and novelists would understand it. The 'morning pages', she says, 'are a meditation, a practice that bring you to your creativity and your creator God'. And given that everyday life is presented throughout *The Artist's Way* as an illness or addiction from which we are all in recovery, the morning pages are also a form of medication. But they are not designed to generate

---

[2] This is in Elissa Schappell's account of attending Ginsberg's ramshackle class, 'A Semester with Allen Ginsberg', which is in *The Paris Review Interviews: Beat Writers at Work*. Ginsberg's Mind Writing Slogans, which he passed around in class, can easily be found online.

the kind of raw material that might later be worked up into more finished or structured pieces of writing. Indeed, to revise, edit or improve this material would be to exercise judgement, and the morning pages are not to be judged, even aesthetically.

'Remember, your artist is a child', Cameron says. It is 'afraid of the dark, the bogeyman, and any adventure that isn't safely scary. As your artist's parent and guardian, its big brother, warrior and companion, it falls to you to convince your artist it is safe to come out and (work) play.'

And as its parent, big brother, warrior, and so on, it apparently follows that the exercise of judgement must be a form of child cruelty or 'artist abuse'.

Both *The Artist's Way* and *Writing Down the Bones* have become international bestsellers, and while Cameron *has* written two novels and Goldberg one, their principal output as writers is in the form of autobiographical spin-offs and sequels to these two guidebooks, with Cameron so far publishing no less than twenty-two related titles, including *The Writing Diet: Write Yourself Right-Size*. Both authors have struggled with demons, as their memoirs are keen to reveal, and presumably as life gurus they do have something to offer their readership, but I doubt whether either would be worth a moment's consideration in the Creative Writing classroom were it not that the technique of automatic writing as practised in particular by Goldberg is a genuinely useful and productive *writerly* discipline, and that Julia Cameron in particular has some pertinent things to say about perfectionism. Besides which, a quasi-religious conception of inspiration is one with a long and continuing literary history – as expressed by contemporary writers of the stature, for instance, of Margaret Atwood, who writes in *Negotiating with the Dead*:

> An art of any kind is a discipline; not only a craft – that too – but a discipline in the religious sense, in which the vigil of waiting, the creation of a receptive spiritual emptiness, and the denial of self all play their part.

This ideal of ego-less receptivity recalls not only the Buddhist precepts of Ginsberg and Goldberg, but their literary antecedents among the Romantics for whom inspiration was achieved – or so they sometimes claimed – in a state of semi-wakefulness or *reverie*, which the novelist Patricia Duncker (writing about the genesis of Mary Shelley's *Frankenstein*) describes as 'that state of wise passiveness in which the ego relinquishes control to the unconscious, the state that allows ideas to surface and be remembered without censorship or restraint'.

The suggestion that the ego might act as an internal censor, or even that there are such entitites as the ego and the unconscious, derives of course from Freud, as does the suggestion (as I expressed it in Chapter 1) that the dream state for a writer might be somewhere close to the state of dreaming. This emphasis on the fruitfulness of semi-wakefulness also underlies much of Dorothea Brande's *Becoming a Writer*, a hybrid inspirational-practical guide written, as Malcolm Bradbury's foreword points out, 'in Freudian times' (the America of the 1930s).

Here is Dorothea Brande, being very Freudian:

> . . . if you are to have the full benefit of the richness of the unconscious you must learn to write easily and smoothly when the unconscious is in the ascendant.
>
> *The best way to do this is to rise half an hour, or a full hour, earlier than you customarily rise. Just as soon as you can – and without talking, without reading the morning's paper, without picking up the book you laid aside the night before – begin to write.* Write anything that comes into your head: last night's dream, if you are able to remember it; the activities of the day before; a conversation, real or imaginary; an examination of conscience. Write any sort of early morning reverie, rapidly and uncritically.

There is an obvious resemblance between this version of automatic writing and 'the morning pages' described by Julia Cameron some sixty years later, the principal difference being the absence in Brande of any suggestion that our dreams come from a divine source or that the practice of recording them will connect us to that divinity. What is also absent, however, is much in the way of solid guidance on *what* to write about, and while this can be a liberation – another freedom from constraint, another means by which you might surprise yourself – should you be experiencing any reluctance to commit words to the page, perhaps connected to a sense of having nothing to say that's worth saying, it may be helpful to be given some themes or headings to write to. (Conversely, you may be experiencing no reluctance at all, but would welcome some means of shaping or directing your output.)

In the previous chapter I suggested that your writing might begin with what you know. In Chapter 5, I'll pursue this theme by considering how you might begin to mine your memories for workable material. In anticipation of that, here is an automatic writing exercise that draws upon the earliest of your memories:

12. First things

As Dorothea Brande suggests, you should attempt to rise half an hour or an hour earlier than you would normally rise. Then, without delay, begin to write – though not, in this case, whatever comes to mind.

On the first morning you should aim to produce a list of your earliest memories – merely a list. For this part of the task you can pause and ponder and take your time, though you needn't go into any detail. All you require is a series of headings. For instance, if it were me:

- *Mimi next door and her towering black beehive, black eyeliner, arched eyebrows*
- *our sky-blue kitchen: curtains, formica, cupboards and drawers, two vinyl-covered stools, two vinyl-backed chairs*
- *Dad changing for his nightshift, his cigarette burning a black groove on my dressing table*
- *the night-time roar of the blast furnace; the clanking of the trains*
- *the earwigs beneath the metal dustbin; the ladybirds on the leaves*

As a minimum, try to come up with a list of fourteen headings. Then, for the next two weeks, work your way down the list, writing for exactly half an hour each morning in response to just one heading each day.

Apart from the timing, the rules are the same as before: you are free to write illegibly and ungrammatically, to be clumsy and clichéd, to repeat or contradict yourself . . . but you must write for exactly thirty minutes without pause.

The heading is your prompt, and you should attempt to supply as much related incident and detail as you can think of. In all likelihood you will find yourself remembering things you thought you had forgotten, or wandering far from the original prompt, which is fine – go wherever your pen takes you.

At the end of the process you will have a mass of material – some good, some useless – in which you may discern recurrent themes, or the germ of a story, or a clear chronology of related events. The material may suggest fictions, or demand to be written as a true account of your earliest years.

You may want to continue, producing another series of headings, and then another. But the end of this process is only the beginning. The real work of writing is still to come . . .

It was a scientist, Thomas Edison, who first defined genius as one per cent inspiration and ninety-nine per cent perspiration, and almost everywhere you look you are likely to find this confirmed in the statements of other creative thinkers, whether scientists or artists – including writers – few of whom will deny the possibility of inspiration, but most of whom will insist on the necessity of hard graft and a more earth-bound, workaday notion of genius than is associated with the Romantics – something more in line with Thomas Carlyle's suggestion that 'genius is an infinite capacity for taking pains'.[3] In other words, it is only by adopting regular routines and doggedly persisting with difficult problems that the possibility of self-surprise (the inspired idea) can arise.

This is a view typified by John Braine – one of the 'angry young men' generation of British writers – in his book *How to Write a Novel*:

> . . . for the majority of novelists, the difficult way is the only way. A novelist's vocation is like any other; discipline and technique are infinitely more important than inspiration . . . You must never wait for inspiration before you write. It isn't that inspiration doesn't exist, but it comes only with writing. I've never met any writer who waited for inspiration.[4]

Braine's insistence (contrary perhaps to Atwood's 'vigil of waiting') that you shouldn't be passive, shouldn't allow yourself simply to wait, but should roll up your metaphorical sleeves and get busy, is echoed by Stephen King in his book *On Writing: A Memoir of the Craft*, which offers this corrective to the conventional idea of the muse as some sort of heavenly spirit or wand-waving sprite (usually female):

> There is a muse, but he's not going to come fluttering down into your writing room and scatter creative fairy-dust all over your typewriter or computer station. He lives in the ground. He's a basement guy. You have to

---

[3] Like Graham Greene's sliver of ice in the heart, Carlyle's is an often quoted, but rarely referenced remark (it may have been said in an after-dinner speech) and takes a variety of forms, the most common misquotation being 'genius is the capacity for taking infinite pains', and the most wincingly wrong: 'genius is the capacity for causing infinite pain'.

[4] Odd to consider that Braine's generation of no-nonsense English provincial realists coincided with Ginsberg's generation of mind-expanding Beats, that Braine's *Room at the Top* was published the same year as Jack Kerouac's *On the Road*, and that both literary currents were considered equally culturally radical.

descend to his level, and once you get down there you have to furnish an apartment for him to live in. You have to do all the grunt labor, in other words, while the muse sits and smokes cigars and admires his bowling trophies and pretends to ignore you . . .

On the face of it, King's cigar-smoking 'basement guy' bears little or no relation to Julia Cameron's artist-child with its terror of 'the dark, the bogey-man, and any adventure that isn't safely scary'. (The basement guy would probably make a very good bogeyman, in fact.) But what King and Cameron do share is a conception of the writer as comprised of two people, one of whom must be indulged and protected by her more hard-working and responsible companion.

This is a popular notion. Dorothea Brande similarly conceives of the writer as a dual personality, and in common with Cameron she uses the metaphor of the adult and child, although unlike Cameron she welcomes the application of grown-up judgement and accords the internal critic – the critical faculty, in other words – an equal value in the production of any creative work that's worthwhile.

In Brande's Freudian scheme, the child-artist is associated with the spontaneity and surprise of unconscious processes, while the adult-critic represents the careful discriminations of conscious thought. Often the adult is equated with the 'craftsman', the 'artisan' or the 'workman', whereas the child is always the 'artist' and somewhat unruly. These two sides of the writer require each other. And the healthy, fully-functioning writer is the one who is able to hold them in balance:

The unconscious must flow freely and richly, bringing at demand all the treasures of memory, all the emotions, incidents, scenes, intimations of character and relationship which it has stored away in its depths; the conscious mind must control, combine, and discriminate between these materials without hampering the unconscious flow.

The following exercise – like the previous one – is intended to help you access some of those 'treasures of memory' by using the technique of automatic writing, though in this case there is a second stage that requires the conscious participation of the artisan – the craftsman or craftswoman. The first part of this exercise is loosely adapted from one I came across in a neat little book of routines and suggestions (it resembles a volume of poems) called – perhaps tellingly – *Writing Without the Muse*, by Beth Joselow:

13. First thoughts, second thoughts

This exercise is organised into two stages, morning and evening. As before, you will be writing in response to a list of fourteen headings. Here are the headings:

early morning
early hours
car window
a gap in the curtains
something there
falling
first kiss
the seashore
undressing
dressing up
winning
losing
the garden in summer
gone forever

Beginning as soon after waking as possible, write for twenty minutes in response to each of these headings, one heading per day.

As before, you are free to write illegibly and ungrammatically, to be clumsy and clichéd, to repeat or contradict yourself, but this time you should try to recall in particular the emotions that attach to each word or phrase.

When your twenty minutes are up, put the writing aside and don't look at it again until the afternoon or evening. In the second session of the day you are going to require an hour to re-read what you have written and then to re-write it.

The punctuation, spelling, grammar and phrasing will probably need some finessing. The order may be wrong. There may be lines you'll want to remove, and lines you'll want to improve. There will be gaps to fill; other associations may occur to you.

It isn't necessary to turn your rough writing into a story, or even the start of one. Simply use this as an exercise in second thoughts – in refining, rephrasing, redrafting. And when your sixty minutes are up: stop.

(I've suggested sixty minutes, which may be too long. Half of that may suffice, but whatever time-limit you settle on, stick to it, and keep it consistent for each of your fourteen evenings.)

Given that Dorothea Brande herself recommends rising early in order 'to have the full benefit of the richness of the unconscious', it would seem to follow – as I've arranged it in this exercise – that automatic writing is the work of the morning while editing is the work of the afternoon (or alternatively, automatic writing could be the work of this month, editing the work of next month). And indeed it's hard to see how the critical operations of 'weighing, balancing, trimming, expanding', as Brande describes them, could occur without there being some raw material for the craftsman or critic to work upon. But Brande's proposition is perhaps more subtle than this, in that it recognises the need for an on-going to-and-fro, a reciprocal exchange between the two sides of the personality, with the successful writer being someone who is able to 'suppress one or the other at discretion'.

The key point is that neither should dominate, for if either is allowed the upper hand for too long the result will be 'bad work, or no work at all'.

By 'bad work' Brande presumably means the formless outpourings of the unfettered unconscious, mere splurge, a kind of linguistic diarrhoea (otherwise known as logorrhoea), while 'no work at all' is what occurs when the critic or internal censor is so much in the ascendancy that a form of linguistic constipation sets in (otherwise known as writer's block).

Such a blockage, suggests Brande, is frequently the result of 'such ideals of perfection as can hardly bear the light of day', though sometimes it can be due to 'a kind of touchy vanity . . . which will not risk any rebuff and so will not allow anything to be undertaken which is not assured in advance of acceptance'. Unsurprisingly Julia Cameron picks up on this theme of perfectionism and its relation to the need for approval (conceiving again of the critic as some kind of domestic bully, an internalised Bad Dad):

> The critic reigns supreme in the perfectionist's creative household. A brilliant descriptive prose passage is critiqued with a white-glove approach: '*Mmm*. What about this comma? Is this how you spell . . . ?'
>
> For the perfectionist, there are no first drafts, rough sketches, warm-up exercises. Every draft is meant to be final, perfect, set in stone . . .
>
> The perfectionist is never satisfied. The perfectionist never says, 'This is pretty good. I think I'll just keep going.'
>
> To the perfectionist, there is always room for improvement. The perfectionist calls this humility. In reality, it is egotism. It is pride that makes us want to write a perfect script . . .
>
> Perfectionism is not a quest for the best. It is a pursuit of the worst in ourselves, the part that tells us that nothing we do will ever be good enough – that we should try again.

It might be objected that no genuine artist could produce anything of value without reference to some personal aesthetic, and that any aesthetic must imply an ideal, some notion of the perfect form, however unattainable.[5] Achievement in almost any creative endeavour will inevitably fall short of the ambition – but, to recall Samuel Beckett: 'No matter. Try again. Fail again. Fail better.' In other words, without an ideal of perfection, there can be nothing to aim for, and no progression. But while Cameron is doubtless wrong to object to the idea of 'room for improvement' or the necessity of 'trying again', she is clearly right to insist that perfectionism is not a quest for the best, since a 'quest' implies a journey, and perfectionism is, as she says, 'a refusal to let yourself move ahead. It is a loop – an obsessive, debilitating closed system that causes you to get stuck in the details of what you are writing or painting or making and to lose sight of the whole.'

Here then is Joseph Conrad, describing in a letter to Edward Garnett in 1898 what it is like to be stuck in that loop:

I sit down religiously every morning, I sit down for eight hours every day – and the sitting down is all. In the course of that working day of 8 hours I write 3 sentences which I erase before leaving the table in despair. There's not a single word to send you. Not one! . . . I assure you – speaking soberly and on my word of honour – that sometimes it takes all my resolution and power of self-control to refrain from butting my head against the wall. I want to howl and foam at the mouth but I daren't do it for fear of waking the baby and alarming my wife.

This, unfortunately, has all too often been me. I am a perfectionist, and therefore a particularly slow writer, inclined to much suppressed foaming at the mouth and a great many days when 'the sitting down is all'. And I am like this despite being fully conscious of the debilitating effects of perfectionism, and despite being fully aware that perfectionism and perfection are two quite distinct things – the first almost guaranteeing the impossibility of achieving the second. And I am like this despite consistently counselling my students against any habits that will lead them into the same obsessive closed system – the 'loop' that is also, creatively, a noose.

---

[5] Which is not to rule out an aesthetic based on rawness, randomness, or the primacy of 'first thoughts'. To hold to such an aesthetic, and to discern what 'works' and what doesn't within it, may be even more challenging than to operate within the parameters of an established or conventional genre.

Or at least, I am like this sometimes – which is to say, I am like this less than I was, since latterly, belatedly, I have begun to combine a degree of anti-perfectionism with my perfectionism, and begun to achieve something of the balance between the craftsman-critic and the artist – or between conscious intention and unconscious expression – that is advocated by Dorothea Brande. And the key, for me, to effecting this change was reading *Becoming a Writer*[6] just as I was approaching something close to paralysis in the writing of my third novel *Crustaceans*.

Ever since school, and whatever the form – whether poem, short story or essay – my habitual method has been to begin with minimal preparation (rough notes seeming altogether too rough, too messy) and to proceed strictly from the beginning, painstakingly building one slow sentence upon another, until finally, eventually, I arrive at the last sentence and can declare my job done, no further revision required, no overhaul possible.

The assumption underlying this approach is 'first thought, worst thought', and the consequence is that I will feel compelled to rewrite each line I put down, and to continue rewriting that line until I feel certain – in Cameron's words – that it is 'final, perfect, set in stone'. Only then will I be able to move on to my next line. Except that the rhythm or sense of the next line will inevitably require me to go back and re-revise the previous line, and the one before that. And though I will, eventually, achieve a paragraph in this manner, every subsequent paragraph will require me to comb back through the previous paragraphs, just as every additional page will require me to refine every previous page. More agonising still, just as this method requires me to make judgements based on the rhythm and sense of everything that has preceded the current sentence, it also requires me to anticipate the sense and rhythm of everything that is still to come, which I would rather hold in my head than commit to the page, however sketchily, however provisionally.

Clearly this is to describe a form of madness – or at the least an obsessive compulsive disorder – and the symptoms became particularly acute when I was writing *Crustaceans*. In part this was because the novel is about a child who dies, and I became convinced that the writing must therefore stand as a kind of memorial to him – 'perfect, set in stone' – even though he was entirely

---

[6] My gratitude to this book should explain my reluctance to admit (anywhere but in this sheepish footnote) that Brande is no more of a *writer* than Goldberg and Cameron, and every bit as much an entrepreneurial guru. Principally a journalist and editor, her creative output was negligible and she followed up her bestselling *Becoming a Writer* with the even more lucrative *Wake Up and Live: A Formula for Success that Works*, which was – bizarrely – made into a musical by Twentieth Century Fox in 1937. She was also married to a prominent American fascist.

imaginary. Partly, too, it was because I felt obliged to reward my reader for engaging with such emotionally taxing material by attempting to make the novel aesthetically irreproachable, every sentence just so, every chapter just so. Which was to place far too much pressure on the writing: it collapsed; it couldn't go on.

Having read *Becoming a Writer*, I didn't immediately begin rising half an hour earlier than I customarily would: my days were hardly cluttered; they were as blank as my next page. Instead, one afternoon, I decided on some headings: one for each of my characters, one for each of the main themes, one for each of the settings, one for each of the events still to be written. Then I filled my days, and my pages, with automatic writing in response to these headings, until I had enough raw material to finish my book. And the great surprise that emerged from this process was that I found I knew more than I thought I knew: things emerged on the page that I hadn't anticipated, some of them major – solutions to compositional problems – and some minor – small details of character, nice turns of phrase.

Perhaps inevitably the process of refining and revising this raw material returned me to my perfectionism – or, perhaps, to my infinite capacity for taking pains – but at least now I had something to work with and to work against. The book was soon finished. And this has remained my method. Whatever I am writing, I will spool material for a week, or a month, or just in the mornings, and then I will revise and refine for a week, or a month, or just in the afternoons – and whenever I find I am stuck, I will turn off my computer and take up some scrap paper, set the alarm, and splurge. It usually works.

Earlier I mentioned Allen Ginsberg's 'Mind Writing Slogans'. Eclectic as they are, gnomic and playful as they are, they would have been no use to me then, but here finally are a few of my own, conceived since reading Dorothea Brande, and all concerned with lifting the pressure on a mind beset by perfectionism:

---

14. First drafts

Whenever you begin a new piece of writing, bear the following in mind:

1. Writing is a form of thinking. But don't expect to think perfect thoughts which you will then transcribe to the page. Expect much muddle to begin with. Allow for the muddle.
2. Most writing is re-writing. Always expect to have to revise. It doesn't have to be perfect now.

3. Give yourself permission to splurge. Get the stuff down. The real work of writing comes later – in the shaping, revising, refining, redrafting, combining.

4. You won't know what to leave out until you have first got it down, just as you won't be able to see what is missing.

5. Write in drafts, and use your first draft as a way of clarifying to yourself what it is you think you think, what it is you think you are writing about.

6. Ernest Hemingway said, 'The first draft of anything is shit.' Refinement is for later drafts.

7. In a first draft you can be inconsistent and contradictory. But with the words on the page you will then be more able to *see* the contradictions and inconsistencies.

8. You don't need to begin at the beginning. You don't have to proceed in strict sequence to the end. You can proceed as randomly as need be.

9. Begin in the middle if it helps. The true shape and sequence of a piece of writing will only emerge over time.

10. Right now, you are providing yourself with the raw ingredients; you can cook them later.

4.   Don't tell me . . .

The previous chapter was particularly heavy on commentary and relatively light on practical examples. There was a lot of discussion but not too many exercises. Another way of expressing this is to say there was more telling than showing. In factual or expository writing – essays, articles, reviews and the like[1] – this is generally a good thing. In imaginative or creative writing it often isn't.

The American poet Emily Dickinson once wrote, 'Tell all the Truth but tell it slant', which is a very flexible (and widely adopted) axiom for Creative Writing, not least because it suggests the importance of 'defamiliarisation' (or 'making strange'). The art of 'showing' often depends on the technique of defamiliarisation, which is a concept I will explore more fully in Chapter 10, though the gist of it goes something like this: the more familiar we are with something the less we will notice it since our perceptions will have become habitual, dulled by routine and convention. That 'something' could be anything, whether small – the texture of train-carriage upholstery; the smell of greenhouse tomatoes – or medium-sized – the view from our living-room window; the layout of our workplace – or really quite large – the layout of London; the distribution of wealth in society. And the older we get – which is to say, the further we drift from what Coleridge called 'the child's sense of wonder and novelty' – the less vivid and immediate our perceptions will become, and the less inclined we might feel to question our day-to-day world.

It might then be said that the moral and aesthetic purpose of art is to reveal the world from unusual or unexpected perspectives, to 'defamiliarise the

---

[1] Including, of course, chapters in how-to-write books . . .

familiar' in order to revivify or refresh our perceptions and so deepen our understanding of the world and our place in it. And one of the ways in which literature does this is through the avoidance of bald, factual statements that merely deliver information or name the already named ('telling'). Instead, literature proceeds by indirection, by suggestion and implication, which often means through the depiction of concrete particulars whose significance is left unstated ('showing').

This technique of leaving certain things unsaid invites the reader to imagine the rest, to fill in the gaps, and in this way – sentence by sentence – the reader becomes a partner in the construction of a story's meaning. In effect, the author's intentions and reader's imagination meet somewhere half-way – in the spectral white space around the words, perhaps – and the more involved the reader becomes in this process, the more compelling and memorable is the experience of reading the story. And it *is* an experience; that seems to be crucial.

I might for instance decide to begin a short story with the sentence: 'Ruby arrived home exhausted with the groceries.' This has the virtue of succinctness, and it tells you several things: that Ruby is called Ruby; that she has just arrived home; that she's exhausted; that she's carrying groceries. But it doesn't reveal much more than that, and it doesn't invite you to participate in the experience of being Ruby. It doesn't show you what Ruby is like in appearance or manner, or what her home is like, or how she expresses her exhaustion. It doesn't give you much sense of the particular texture and atmosphere of her world.

This then is the beginning of Flannery O'Connor's short story 'A Stroke of Good Fortune':

> Ruby came in the front door of the apartment building and lowered the paper sack with the four cans of number three beans in it onto the hall table. She was too tired to take her arms from around it or to straighten up and she hung there collapsed from the hips, her head balanced like a big florid vegetable at the top of the sack. She gazed with stony unrecognition at the face that confronted her in the dark yellow-spotted mirror over the table. Against her right cheek was a gritty collard leaf that had been stuck there half the way home. She gave it a vicious swipe with her arm and straightened up, muttering, 'Collards, collards,' in a voice of sultry subdued wrath.

Here we have a lot of information, more than we might immediately realise. The implication that she has had to walk some distance with heavy groceries suggests a great deal about her circumstances. The fact that she lives in an apartment building with a shared hall suggests more, as does the fact that the hall mirror is yellow-spotted and dark. And as we read on we will doubtless accumulate more detail, more hints, and acquire a much fuller sense of the down-at-heel drabness of her situation. But what I principally take from these few sentences is an almost palpable sense of the experience of being Ruby as she dumps that paper sack – she is not only worn-out, but cross about it too, and probably, given her big florid head, unfit and overweight (perhaps as a consequence of eating so many number three beans).

To offer another, less sultry example, I might want to begin a short story with the sentence: 'It was cold.' But while this also has the virtue of succinctness, and conveys a necessary piece of information, I doubt that you as a reader would feel much sense of that coldness. You wouldn't begin to share in the experience; you would simply know 'it was cold' because I had told you so.

A better beginning might then be: 'The temperature gauge showed minus eighteen.' This at least presents you with a visual detail, which will appeal to the mind's eye, as well as suggesting a character's point of view – the character who is looking at the gauge – which you can share and so find a way into the world of the story. Crucially, it requires you to supply the information that 'it was cold'. On which principle, a more effective beginning might then be: 'The inspector's breath plumed white as he scratched the glaze of ice from the temperature gauge. The panel showed minus eighteen. Shivering beneath his many layers, he turned to examine the beef carcasses.'

This isn't great – it hasn't any of Flannery O'Connor's richness or peculiarity, and 'breath plumed white' is a bit of a cliché, and I'd prefer something less vague than 'his many layers' – but it is both more particular and less direct than the statement 'it was cold'. And what characterises 'showing' over 'telling' is often just these two things: particularity and indirectness.

Anton Chekhov's much-quoted injunction – 'Don't tell me the moon is shining; show me the glint of light on broken glass'[2] – exemplifies this nicely.

---

[2] Like Greene's sliver of ice in the heart, and Carlyle's infinite capacity for taking pains, this phrase is everywhere quoted and nowhere sourced. Maybe Chekhov did say it, but the nearest I can find is this from a letter to his brother in 1886, quoted in Miriam Allott's *Novelists on the Novel*: '. . . you will get a moonlight night if you write that on the dam of the mill a fragment of broken bottle flashed like a small bright star, and there rolled by, like a ball, the black shadow of a dog, or a wolf – and so on.'

15. Telling it slant

Following Chekhov, here is a sentence:

The moon was shining.

And here are three possible ways of showing without saying this:

1. Quietly they strolled along the shoreline that evening and gazed at the light glinting on the ocean's vast stillness.
2. As he crossed the dark field he glimpsed something, an animal, the sudden bright flash of its eyes, gone in an instant.

Or, to take Chekhov's own example:

3. On the dam of the mill a fragment of broken bottle flashed like a small bright star, and there rolled by, like a ball, the black shadow of a dog, or a wolf.

The moon isn't mentioned in any of these three examples. Instead the moon is implied. We are given an effect of the moon; the moon is shown to us slant.

Here are ten more sentences. Try to come up with three alternative ways of expressing these. Place the emphasis on precise sensory detail. Tell it slant:

It was cold.
It was hot.
The rain was heavy.
The car was loud.
She was clumsy.
He was fat.
The room smelled unpleasant.
The chair was uncomfortable.
Her drink was sour.
His meal was delicious.

This exercise can be done in groups of three by discussion: what works? what doesn't?

In the introduction to this book I emphasised the importance of reading as a writer, and noted how this might not coincide with reading for delight. When I 'read as a writer' I am uncommonly self-aware, more than usually conscious of the act of reading a book, which I understand to be both a physical object in my hands (which I periodically disfigure with pencil marks) and a linguistic construct, the outcome of an author's applied expertise in the craft of arranging words for moral, emotional and aesthetic effect. When I read for delight, however, I am more inclined to lose my self-awareness, becoming uncommonly elsewhere, lost in my imagination in the lives of made-up people in made-up places (albeit that some of my delight will be linguistic, a response to the writer's 'music', the rhythms of her prose).

The best novels and stories, the ones we call our favourites and remember the longest, exist in the memory almost as experiences we once had, though the experience ought properly to be called a quasi-experience, since it was vicarious, entirely imaginary, and was likely to have required – again in Coleridge's words – a 'willing suspension of disbelief', which is to say a willing suspension of the usual laws or logic by which our lives are lived. In a sense we submit to the logic of a novel or story as we might submit to the logic of a dream. Both are 'events' that couldn't exist outside of the imagination. Both will mean far more than is evident on the surface. And for the fictional dream to bewitch us – to become as compelling as an actual dream – it will need to be unusually striking to our perceptions and uninterrupted by reminders that we are 'only' reading a novel or story: it will need to be, in other words, vivid and continuous.

This notion of the 'vivid and continuous fictional dream' belongs to the American novelist and teacher John Gardner and was first introduced in his book on Creative Writing – another classic of the genre – called *On Becoming a Novelist* which, like its much longer, seemingly more cobbled-together sequel *The Art of Fiction: Notes on Craft for Young Writers*, was published posthumously. (He died in a motorcycle accident in 1982 at the age of 49.) This is how he describes the vivid and continuous dream in *On Becoming a Novelist*:

> We read five words on the first page of a really good novel and we begin to forget that we are reading printed words on a page; we begin to see images . . . We slip into a dream, forgetting the room we are sitting in . . . We recreate, with minor and for the most part unimportant changes, the vivid and continuous dream the writer worked out in his mind (revising and revising until he got it right) and captured in language so that other human beings, whenever they feel like it, may open his book and dream that dream again. If the dream is to be *vivid*, the writer's 'language signals' – his words, rhythms, metaphors, and so on – must be sharp and sufficient; if they're vague, careless, blurry, or if there aren't enough of them to let us see clearly

what is being presented, then the dream as we dream it will be cloudy, confusing, ultimately annoying and boring. And if the dream is to be *continuous*, we must not be roughly jerked from the dream back to the words on the page by language that's distracting.[3]

Gardner elaborated on this notion in *The Art of Fiction*, where he emphasised the importance of showing over telling and further glossed the term 'continuous' by explaining that 'a repeatedly interrupted flow of action must necessarily have less force than an action directly carried through from its beginning to its conclusion' – the 'interruption' coming, presumably, in the form of narrative commentary on the unfolding events. As a lesson in the avoidance of such intrusive telling, Gardner proposed this now-famous exercise in descriptive writing: 'Describe a barn as seen by a man whose son has just been killed in a war. Do not mention the son, or war, or death. Do not mention the man who does the seeing.'

---

16. Don't mention it

Following Gardner, attempt two of these five exercises in descriptive writing. In each instance aim to write a continuous scene of between 250 and 300 words, and again place the emphasis on precise sensory detail:

1. Describe a party from the point of view of a soldier on leave from a war-zone. Don't mention the war or the fact that he is a soldier.
2. Describe the same party from the point of view of a child. Don't mention the child.
3. Describe a suburban street from the point of view of someone who has just been involved in a car accident. Don't mention the accident.
4. Describe a room from the point of view of a woman whose husband has just left her. Don't mention the husband, or the fact that her marriage is over.
5. A man and a woman meet a year after their marriage has ended. Describe their encounter. Don't mention the fact that they used to be married.

---

[3] This is right at the beginning, page 5, and is Gardner's key concept. On the face of it, all the great works of modernism and postmodernism would then fail Gardner's test of what makes good or satisfying fiction since it is often a ploy on the part of the author of such works to draw attention to the language or to the fictionality of the fiction – in other words, to be linguistically 'distracting'. But then it could be argued that these more challenging fictions create their own logic, and the reading of them becomes a different kind of dream, a different kind of experience. It might also be argued that vivid and compelling scene building can coexist with intrusive narrators and attention-grabbing language, that one need not rule out the other.

What is most noticeable about John Gardner's barn exercise is that it so determinedly steers the writer away from any direct expression of the man's grief. The implication of this is twofold: firstly, that a character's emotional state will inevitably colour the description by determining which details are noticed; and secondly, that those details will get closer to the truth of the man's grief than any direct statement of it. This is made explicit later in *On Becoming a Novelist*, where Gardner states:

> The writer with the truly accurate eye (or ear, nose, sense of touch, etc) has an advantage over the writer who does not in that, among other things, he can tell his story in concrete terms, not just feeble abstractions. Instead of writing, 'She felt terrible,' he can show – by the precise gesture or look or by capturing the character's exact turn of phrase – subtle nuances of the character's feeling . . . One can feel sad or happy or bored or cross in a thousand ways: the abstract adjective says almost nothing.

Gardner then goes on to insist that pretty much anything may be 'told' in fiction except the main characters' feelings, which will only become real for a reader if they are 'shown' in the form of action, gesture, speech, 'or physical reaction to setting'. In which spirit:

---

17. How does this feel?

Again following Gardner, here is a sentence:

He was afraid.

And here are three possible[4] ways of showing without saying this:

1. The door was before him, implacable. He breathed deeply, and swallowed. He wiped his palms on his trousers. At last he reached for the handle.

---

[4] It might not show but I laboured for ages over these examples, which still strike me as overly reliant on cliché, and the reason I think I found my own exercise so difficult is that the details we use in a story are so often determined by the larger context, by the rhythm of the sentences leading up to this point, by the tone or atmosphere we've already established, by the metaphorical threads we've already stitched in. Everything connects. But in writing these sentences I'm trying to imagine the story to which they *might* connect, but of course that story doesn't exist, and so I find myself resorting to conventional scenarios, to clichés.

2. The minutes dragged on and I smiled at him, observing the starkness of his complexion, the fixity of his gaze. Beads of sweat broke on his forehead. When I offered him my handkerchief he flinched.
3. Keeping his back to the wall he edged into the alleyway, alert to every shadow, every noise. 'Hello?' he called out, and heard his own voice echoing back, as small as a boy's.

Here are ten more sentences, each expressing a character's feelings as a 'feeble abstraction':

The girl was overjoyed.
The boy was despondent.
I am so tired.
You are in love with him.
They were uncomfortable.
They were relaxed.
He is infatuated.
She is filled with disgust.
The woman was furious.
The man was satisfied.

Now try to come up with three alternative ways of showing each of these emotions or feelings in 'concrete terms'. Avoid naming the feeling. Concentrate on the particularities of speech, gesture and physical detail.

In a classroom, your descriptions can be tested on the group: you read aloud some of your lines; the group identifies the feelings they express (and comments constructively on possibilities for further improvement).

I quoted earlier from a short story by Flannery O'Connor, and although the choice of that passage was fairly random, the choice of O'Connor was not. In common with John Gardner, she was a graduate of the Iowa Writers' Workshop, which was established in 1936 as the first Master's programme of its kind in the world (and the model for most that have followed), and she has since become recognised, again like Gardner, as something of a posthumous authority on the teaching of Creative Writing. Usually described as belonging to 'the American Southern Gothic tradition' (meaning, broadly, that she depicted grotesque or freakish characters in order to illuminate social or moral themes such as racism or 'Christ-haunted' fanaticism), O'Connor died of lupus at the age of 39 in 1964, having produced two novels, thirty-one brilliantly strange and resonant short stories, and a body of miscellaneous speeches and articles that were collected after her death as *Mystery and Manners* and have become, almost incidentally, one of the key texts on the craft of writing fiction. Her essay 'Writing Short Stories' is particularly influential, and it is here that she says:

> Fiction operates through the senses, and I think one reason that people find it so difficult to write stories is that they forget how much time and patience is required to convince through the senses. No reader who doesn't actually experience, who isn't made to feel, the story is going to believe anything the fiction writer merely tells him. The first and most obvious characteristic of fiction is that it deals with reality through what can be seen, heard, smelt, tasted, and touched.

By way of illustration we might return to 'A Stroke of Good Fortune' and follow Ruby as she makes the arduous journey up four flights of stairs to her apartment, during which climb she encounters certain of her freakish neighbours, suffers a great deal of dizziness, and comes to fear that the pain and fatigue she is experiencing might be explained by the possibility that she is pregnant, a prospect that terrifies her almost as much as the idea that she might also have cancer. To my list of 'feeble abstractions' in the last exercise I could have added: 'She was filled with despair.' But here is how O'Connor conveys the reality of Ruby's despair in 'concrete terms', mainly through what can be seen, felt and heard:

> On the sixth [step], she sat down suddenly, her hand slipping weakly down the bannister spoke onto the floor.
> 'Noooo,' she said, and leaned her round red face between the two nearest poles. She looked down into the stairwell and gave a long hollow wail that widened and echoed as it went down. The stair cavern was dark green and mole-colored and the wail sounded at the very bottom like a voice answering her. She gasped and shut her eyes. No. No. It couldn't be any baby.

O'Connor's insistence on the importance of appealing to the senses finds one obvious endorsement in John Gardner's acknowledgement that a writer's 'eye' might also mean a writer's 'ear, nose, sense of touch, etc'. Another comes in Gardner's further explanation in *The Art of Fiction* of the concept of the vivid and continuous dream:

According to this notion, the writer sets up a dramatised action in which we are given the signals that make us 'see' the setting, characters and events; that is, he does not tell us about them in abstract terms, like an essayist, but gives us images that appeal to our senses – preferably all of them, not just the visual sense – so that we seem to move among the characters, lean with them against the fictional walls, taste the fictional gazpacho, smell the fictional hyacinths.

It should be clear by now that Gardner was principally interested in the techniques and rewards of realist fiction, where language is deployed to create an illusion of transparency, almost as if we were looking through the language to the experience it describes (or if 'looking' is too visually biased a word, then 'stepping'), and presumably he would have approved of the craft of a writer such as Ian McEwan, who is especially adept at rendering precise sensory detail in prose of exceptional, almost 'filmic' clarity, and who – in his early fiction at least – achieved a kind of English equivalent to Flannery O'Connor's Southern Gothic, though one that was more 'Freud-haunted' than 'Christ-haunted', and far more concerned with sex than with race.

I suggested earlier that our favourite novels and stories tend to linger in the memory almost as experiences we once had, and while my own list of favourites is ever-lengthening, McEwan's debut collection of short stories, *First Love, Last Rites*, is one of those that has lingered the longest for me, and partly accounts for my supposing I might want to be a writer too. In McEwan's early stories I found for the first time a world that smelled and sounded and looked like my own.

I should say that my background is not at all bookish. Not only did I not come across anyone in my childhood who wrote books, I knew hardly anyone who bought or borrowed or read books either. And although I did well in the English classroom, and often lost myself in the novels I was required to study, it was rare that I recognised much in those books that chimed with my own experience, or encouraged me to believe that the world I knew might be depicted in a book, much less a book that people like me might be required to study (much less a book that I might myself write). I did become a somewhat restless reader, my imagination forever elsewhere, but it's possible I might have dropped out of formal education, and even ceased to be a reader, except that I wandered into a stationery shop one afternoon when I was eighteen and noticed *First Love, Last Rites* on a carousel of Picador paperbacks. Its cover image of a naked girl lying on a bed in the soft light of dawn immediately appealed to the habitually lovelorn late-adolescent I then was.[5] I bought a copy (it cost £1.25), the first 'grown-up' book I'd ever owned that wasn't on a school syllabus, and seemed to discover something of myself inside it: here was a book that appeared to chime with what I knew of the world. Only in retrospect did it occur to me that most of the stories concerned incest, masturbation and the killing of children. But what principally captured me, I'm sure, wasn't so much the depravity as McEwan's ability to 'operate through the senses': all of them. In the sometimes sordid world of *First Love, Last Rites* – which also appeared to be my world – I could lean against the fictional walls and smell the fictional hyacinths. Or rather, as in these opening sentences of 'Last Day of Summer', I could lie on the fictional lawn and smell the fictional soil:

> I am twelve and lying near-naked on my belly out on the back lawn in the sun when for the first time I hear her laugh. I don't know, I don't move, I just close my eyes. It's a girl's laugh, a young woman's, short and nervous like laughing at nothing funny. I got half my face in the grass I cut an hour before and I can smell the cold soil beneath it. There's a faint breeze coming off the river, the late afternoon stinging my back and that laugh jabbing at me like it's all one thing, one taste in my head. The laughing stops and all I can hear is the breeze flapping the pages of my comic, Alice crying somewhere upstairs and a kind of summer heaviness all over the garden. Then I hear them walking across the lawn towards me and I sit up so quickly it makes me dizzy, and the colours have gone out of everything.

What is interesting to me here (now that I've come to read this story for instruction rather than delight) is not just the extent to which the boy's experience is registered in terms of sensory detail, but the extent to which McEwan combines the senses in unfamiliar or 'defamiliarising' ways. This is synaesthesiac prose. The young woman's laugh is not registered in terms of sound but

---

[5] I say *First Love, Last Rites* is *one* of those books that has lingered the longest for me, and that it partly accounts for my first supposing I might want to be a writer. Before *First Love, Last Rites* there was James Joyce's *A Portrait of the Artist as a Young Man*, which I read for English A level and which seemed to resonate most with the mysterious intensities of my inner world at that time, for all its remoteness from a British industrial new town in the late 1970s. 'He wanted to meet in the real world the unsubstantial image which his soul so constantly beheld', writes Joyce of his younger self. 'And me!' I thought, identifying with Stephen Dedalus's earnestness and yearning, but missing Joyce's gentle self-satire. McEwan seemed to describe my situation more plainly, and in a way I sometimes thought I might be able to emulate.

of touch: it *jabs* at him. The smell of the cold soil, the faint breeze off the river, the sun stinging his back, as well as the jabbing laugh: all of these come together as a *taste* in his head. There are other sounds, too – the flapping pages, Alice crying – as well as the 'heaviness' of the atmosphere, but the only appeal to our *visual* sense is a negative one: the colours going out of everything when the boy becomes dizzy (which in itself appeals to another sense, that of balance or 'equilibrioception').

McEwan is of course capable of equally arresting visual details – a few sentences later he has the boy describe the young woman as 'so fat her arms can't hang right from her shoulders. She's got rubber tyres round her neck' – but much of his ability to create a 'vivid and continuous dream' derives from this ability to register experience in terms of all the senses, and in this respect, if no other, his early fiction offers a useful model to follow. In our attempts to show what we know, it can be surprising how much we rely mainly on what we can see.

---

18. Sightless

In the previous chapter I gave you fourteen headings for an automatic writing exercise (Exercise 13, 'First thoughts, second thoughts'). Choose any one of the pieces you wrote in response to those headings. It doesn't matter whether you choose the first thoughts splurge, or the second thoughts rewrite.

Now go through and underline each instance of the use of a sensory detail. Then tally up how many times you've appealed to:

sight
sound
smell
touch
taste

It's highly likely that you will have used visual details the most, with one or two instances of sounds, and probably no instances of taste.

Write now for twenty minutes on one of the following topics. This time you are strictly forbidden from registering any detail in terms of the sense of sight; you can use all the other senses, but not the visual.

in the woods
stormy weather
sports day
clothes shop
fight

Such is the primacy we tend to accord our visual sense we often use the metaphor of sight for cognition or understanding more generally – 'I can see that'; 'do you see what I mean?' – and can experience some descriptive inadequacy when it comes to registering the world in terms of the other senses, so here in passing is an enjoyable exercise in smelling some actual hyacinths, leaning on some actual walls, even tasting some actual gazpacho (it assumes that the flowers are in bloom, and the weather is fine, and – perhaps crucially – that we happen to be on a residential writing course, and that everyone is willing).

---

19. *Hyacinths*

The class divides into pairs.

One in each pair is blindfolded. The other acts as the guide, gently leading the blindfolded one towards interesting smells, sounds, tastes and textures, both indoors and out.

Neither talks. After ten to fifteen minutes, they swap.

The tutor calls the students back into the classroom. Without further ado, the students write out the sensations they've experienced. They must write quickly, without pausing, for twenty minutes.

And of course, if you happen not to be on a residential writing course, you can always ask a friend or family member to act as your guide.

One obvious observation to make about each of the examples and exercises in this chapter is that 'showing' invariably takes longer than 'telling'. More words are required to show that Ruby arrived home exhausted with the groceries than to state that she did. And the obvious danger in this is that too much description might impede the progress of the story: Ruby might never begin to climb the stairs, might never turn away from her reflection in the mirror, or let go of her groceries, and the reader might just decide to leave her to it.

Clearly no narrative could be written entirely in the mode of showing, however precise the sensory detail. Or rather, it *could*, but it would take forever to write and to read. It would be infinitely slower than real time because in real time we appear to apprehend a scene or situation in its totality, using all of our senses simultaneously.[6] In an instant we take in the dimensions of the space, the arrangement of the furniture, the quality of the light and the atmosphere, the presence of noises and smells, the colours, and if there are people we will be alert at once to the particularities of their appearance, to their posture and shape and what they are wearing and, above all, to their facial expressions. We will also be aware of our own reaction to them and to the situation more generally, however subtly nuanced or fluctuating our emotions might be.

All of this will come to us in a moment, which will be succeeded by another moment, and another, then another, and while the medium of film may appear to get close to this instantaneous, on-going awareness of the whole, any attempt to render an equivalent amount of detail in prose fiction is likely to bore and alienate the reader.

It will be boring because the reader will be impatient for development in the story, for something intriguing to happen. And it will be alienating because the reader will have no room for manoeuvre, no scope for imaginative engagement, no role in the construction of the story's meaning.

The novelist Paul Auster addresses this issue in his reflections on writing in *The Red Notebook*:

> There's a way in which a writer can do too much, overwhelming the reader with so many details that he no longer has any air to breathe. Think of a typical passage in a novel. A character walks into a room. As a writer, how much of that room do you want to talk about? The possibilities are infinite. You can give the colour of the curtains, the wallpaper pattern, the objects on the coffee table, the reflection of the light in the mirror. But how much of this is really necessary? Is the novelist's job simply to reproduce physical sensations for their own sake? When I write, the story is always uppermost in my mind, and I feel that everything must be sacrificed to it. All the elegant passages, all the curious details, all the so-called beautiful writing – if they are not truly relevant to what I am trying to say, then they have to go.

---

[6] When I say we *appear* to apprehend everything it's because in fact the brain is busily selecting, filtering out certain details, focusing on others, organising the welter of information so that the world makes manageable sense to us.

Something of this view is echoed by Flannery O'Connor, again in her essay 'Writing Short Stories':

> . . . to say that fiction proceeds by the use of detail does not mean the simple, mechanical piling-up of detail. Detail has to be controlled by some overall purpose, and every detail has to be put to work for you. Art is selective.

In truth, what often happens in effective writing is that the showing is accompanied by some measure of telling, and both are deployed with equal selectivity. For instance, McEwan's 'Last Day of Summer' begins with the words, 'I am twelve', which is a clear instance of telling. But in the description that follows – in the scene that's then shown to us, and especially in the narrative voice with which it is shown – McEwan allows us a much fuller recognition of the boy's twelve-year-old-ness.

A less striking example might be the entry from the journal 'Weather' that I included in Chapter 2. To say that, 'The winds are sometimes fierce, gale force', is to tell you something, while to add that, 'A beercan pursues me up the street, rattling along the centre of the road as if kicked. Plastic bags are caught high in the trees', is to amplify or illustrate what I've just told you with some specific detail. And what is equally as important as the specificity of the detail is its significance. It *means* something that a beercan is rattling up the street, and that a plastic bag is snagged in a tree: both images suggest something about the shabbiness of the neighbourhood I was living in (and possibly hint at the prevalence of drunkenness).

Selectivity of detail would then appear to have three dimensions: the detail should be concrete and appeal to the senses; it should advance or enhance the storytelling; and it should signify or resonate at a thematic level.

Again McEwan's 'Last Day of Summer' offers an instructive example. When the boy gets up to greet the fat girl (whose name is Jenny), we are told that, 'she makes a kind of yelping noise like a polite horse'. This is her laugh, and over the next few pages it becomes her signature, an indicator of her nervousness and estrangement from the rest of the household. The boy lives in a failing hippy commune with his older brother, their parents having died two years previously, and among the other residents is a beautiful but haughty young woman called Kate, who is described throughout the story in terms of her quietness and seeming abhorrence of noise. Alice, the child we heard crying in the first paragraph, is Kate's daughter, but while 'Kate is always so quiet and sad with her', the new girl Jenny plays with her and sings to her. And gradually, as the story progresses, Jenny becomes a surrogate mother not only to

Alice and the boy, but to the entire household, and her signature sound changes: no longer the yelping laugh, but the songs she sings to Alice and a very different laugh, which is 'easy and kind of rhythmic'. In other words, her development as a character in relation to the other characters is registered in terms of a sensory detail whose significance is never spelled out.

All of this (and a lot more) happens not on the 'last day of summer' (the climax to the story comes then) but over the course of many weeks, which are described to us in less than twenty pages, and this brings me to the final point I want to make in relation to showing and telling, that it operates not only at the level of the sentence but at the larger structural level, too, where it might be reformulated as the difference between 'scene' and 'summary', the former giving us a great deal of detail about an event of relatively short duration, and the latter covering a much longer period in substantially less detail.

One problem of the insufficiently 'shown' story is that it may come to resemble a synopsis, and synopses are invariably dull to read because they are only ever a summary of the experience, never the experience itself. A poor short story often reads like the synopsis of the good short story it is yet to become. Lacking descriptive particularity, it fails to engage us, and seems to get through the events far too quickly. The opposite of this is the story that is overly descriptive, that is so cluttered with detail the mind's eye can't decide what to focus upon, with the paradoxical effect that the more information the picture contains, the less clear it becomes. So as writers we do two things: we select what to include, and we summarise so that we can move on. And this is how all narratives are constructed, as a constant oscillation between showing and telling, between dramatising and summarising, and while a story is principally constructed as a series of scenes, the necessary stitching that binds these scenes together is summary. In effective storytelling, both are required.

Up to now the exercises I have set you have been concerned with generating material, or with gathering the elements that might later be incorporated into a complete work of fiction. To conclude this chapter I want to set an exercise that requires you to write an entire short story, though one based upon a model of your own choosing.

20. Summary and scene

Select a short story you particularly admire. Re-read it carefully, itemising what happens in the form of a series of notes. The notes should be brief, no more than a page or so.

Use these notes to write a summary or synopsis of the story. You are aiming to 'tell' the story as succinctly as you can by identifying what happens in what order. The summary should be no longer than a page.

You are now going to attempt to rewrite the story from scratch. The summary provides you with the structure, the basic outline of events. Use this as your guide.

You are not attempting to recreate the original but to reimagine it. The basic story will be the same, but the way you tell it will be different – different details, dialogue, phrasing; different names and locations.

Build your story as a series of scenes. And attempt to write from what you know: draw on the journals you've been keeping. Incorporate material you have produced in your automatic writing sessions.

This exercise should demonstrate the difference between scene and summary, as well as revealing something of the difference between 'story' – a mere sequence of events – and 'storytelling' – the way in which those events are conveyed to the reader. As likely as not, however closely your story follows the structure of the original, its meaning and effect will be subtly different because the rhythms of your prose, and the tone of your narrative voice, and the specificity of the details you choose to include, and the words you have your characters speak, and the particular 'slant' of your telling – your sense of what to withhold and what to reveal, what to emphasise and what to suggest – will come together to evoke in the reader a quite different experience from that induced by the original. You will in effect be creating your own vivid and continuous dream.

5. Write about what you used to know: remembering and place

A while ago in a charity shop I came across a scuffed little hardback called *Writers On Themselves*, a collection of essays broadcast by the BBC Home Service in the early 1960s by such literary luminaries as Rebecca West, Ted Hughes and Sylvia Plath (and such subsequent obscurities as Thomas Hinde, Richard Murphy and John Bowen). Each of the essays is interesting, but the best of them is the short introduction, written by the art critic Herbert Read, who summarises one recurrent theme of the writers' recollections in this way:

> What most of these writers describe is not a psychological process (the process of writing), but the occasion, particular or general, of their first awareness of a vocation. It was usually what William Sansom calls 'a flash of childhood memory', supporting a general theory put forward by an American psychologist (Ernest Schachtel) which maintains that all creative energy in the arts springs from this desire to recall the images and intensities of feeling that lie hidden behind the veil of childhood amnesia. The ancients thought that the Muses were the daughters of Memory, and all writers would agree that their moments of vision are a rending of this veil. For childhood we may sometimes substitute a difficult adolescence, or even traumatic experiences of war and love, but most psychologists agree with Wordsworth, that the child is father to the man, especially when his mind searches the memory for significant images.

When Read talks here of 'the ancients' and 'the daughters of Memory' he is referring to a genealogy of the Greek gods found first in Hesiod and later given expression in Plato's *Theaetetus* (among other places), in which Socrates speaks of 'the gift of Memory, the mother of the Muses'.

There are nine of these Muses, nine golden-haired daughters of Zeus and Mnemosyne (or 'Memory'), with their hearts 'set upon song and their spirits free from care'.[1] But it isn't only the Muses for whom Mnemosyne is celebrated. She is credited too with the creation of words, or of language, which made possible the narrative poems that were inspired by her daughters – a connection between recollection and storytelling that would have seemed crucial in a largely illiterate age, where the poet, a travelling minstrel, had to learn his lyrics by heart in order to recite them aloud.

The connection is one that is often revisited – by 'moderns' as much as by 'ancients' – and especially where it relates to the 'images and intensities' of childhood. For many writers, their earliest experiences are not simply a resource for their writing, but the very source of it, the place from which it all springs. And like the unconscious, perhaps, that spring is inexhaustible. Flannery O'Connor, for instance, puts it even more plainly than Wordsworth: 'The fact is that anybody who has survived his childhood has enough information about life to last him the rest of his days.'

Of course a word such as 'survive' casts a certain Southern Gothicky gloom over this remark, which seems to suggest that childhood is mainly a place of menace and risk. But there is a sly irony here; with Flannery O'Connor there frequently is. And in this instance she is countering the notion that writing shouldn't be taught in universities, given that the decorousness of college life (such as it was in the early 1960s) is too remote from the realities of uncloistered experience, the stuff of real life. Her response to this is to insist, once again, that 'real life' – that great abstraction – is to be found in 'what can be seen, heard, smelt, tasted, and touched'; it is to be found in the close observation of the world as we find it. And so she goes on to say, 'If you can't make something out of a little experience, you probably won't be able to make it out of a lot.' Which chimes nicely, perhaps, with the spirit of these famous lines by William Blake in 'Auguries of Innocence':

> To see a World in a Grain of Sand,
> And a Heaven in a Wild Flower,
> Hold Infinity in the palm of your hand,
> And Eternity in an hour.

---

[1] Some of this information about the Muses comes from this website: http://www.theoi.com/Titan/TitanisMnemosyne.html

For the writer, in other words, a childlike receptiveness to experience (however 'little') is vital. But so too is an ability to recall the lost experiences of the childhood we actually enjoyed or endured. And in order for those experiences to seem universal, we must – paradoxically – focus upon what is most local and particular about them.

Sometimes our recollections may seem effortless, even involuntary. A whole world of experience may appear to return in an image, a snapshot in the mind, perhaps just when we're least expecting it. Occasionally the prompt may be a sound, a smell, or even – like the tea and madeleine cake that give rise to Proust's *Remembrance of Things Past* – a taste.

At such moments we may feel, however fleetingly, that we have been touched by the fluttery muse of inspiration that Stephen King is so suspicious of in *On Writing*. But equally often our remembering is going to require an effort of will – we may have to descend with King's 'basement guy' in order to root around in the half-buried lumber of the almost-forgotten – and this idea that the stuff of our fictions is to be found 'down below' rather than 'up above' is one that frequently appears in writers' accounts of their own writing: for instance in *The Red Notebook*, where Paul Auster says:

> . . . the material that haunts me, the material that I feel compelled to write about, is dredged up from the depths of my own memories. But even after that material is given to me, I can't always be sure where it comes from.

The curious mixing of metaphors that Auster performs here, insisting both on the 'grunt labor' that King describes, and on something altogether more ghostly and mysterious, is perhaps indicative of the dual nature of our memories, which both haunt us, because they seem to represent something forever lost to us, and yet remain very present and real to us, the ground upon which our sense of ourselves is constructed. Elsewhere in his introductory essay Herbert Read uses the phrase 'to penetrate the veil of oblivion', and what I find most interesting about this is not so much the repeated idea of the gauze of forgetting that separates us from our past (which, to return to a theme of Chapter 4, might also be the cloak of familiarity that separates us from what is going on around us in the here-and-now), but the implication that writing is an effort of retrieval or rescue, that something has sunk into oblivion, or has been lost to us, and that the purpose of writing is to return this 'something' to us.

Occasionally that something may be our sense of ourselves. Occasionally it will be our sense of where we have come from. And in either case, I suspect, we will write in order to rescue ourselves from oblivion, or because we'd be lost to ourselves if we didn't. Our identity may depend on it.[2]

I'll come back to this notion shortly, but here in the interim is a sequence of five exercises that explore the theme of lost things and their relation to personal identity, the first of which derives from a suggestion in Beth Joselow's book *Writing Without the Muse*, which I mentioned in Chapter 3. Each of the exercises may take a little while, and I would suggest that you attempt them in order, tackling one a day, or perhaps one a week.

---

21. Lost things

All of us will have lost some small thing in our childhood that meant a great deal to us.[3] It may or may not have been valuable in itself. But it was precious to us. Think of that thing, and try to describe it in all its particulars.

Describe, too, its special importance to you, and how you came by it. Then describe the circumstances surrounding its loss. Possibly you

---

[2] One implication of this is that we may write not so much because it is 'therapeutic' to do so, but because it would be un-therapeutic *not* to. The following quotations may give a sense of what I mean here. Paul Auster in *The Red Notebook*: 'I often wonder why I write . . . It's an activity I seem to need in order to stay alive. I feel terrible when I'm not doing it. It's not that writing brings me a lot of pleasure – but not doing it is worse.' Jorge Luis Borges in *The Paris Review*: 'I know that I can't get along without writing. If I don't write, I feel, well, a kind of remorse, no?' And Joyce Carol Oates, also in *The Paris Review*: 'I feel somewhat at a loss, aimless and foolishly sentimental, and disconnected, when I've finished one work and haven't yet become absorbed in another.'

[3] My lost object would be a small plastic dog that I bought with my pocket money when I was nine or ten. It was small enough to fit in the palm of my hand, and I immediately lost it on a playing field close to my home. The field was the size of two football pitches, and when I realised I'd lost the dog I searched that field for hours, until it became too dark to see. At first my search was instinctive, but then I became more methodical. Slowly I walked the full length of the field in a straight line, beginning at its perimeter. Then I turned round, took one pace to the right, and walked the full length of the field in the opposite direction. Then I turned and walked the full length of the field again, then turned and walked it again, then turned and walked it again. I didn't find the dog, but the loss of it haunted me for months, and occasionally I continued to search for it. The search still recurs in my dreams. And much as I now marvel at that toy's importance to me, I marvel much more at that boy, searching so methodically and diligently. His *doggedness* describes something of my relationship to writing, I think.

searched for it. Or perhaps you knew where it had gone and knew that you couldn't retrieve it.

Describe how you felt about its loss, both at the time and afterwards. And try to recall not just the object, but the child who owned and lost it, the child you used to be.

---

22. Lost lands

Think of yourself as a child of eight or nine or ten, and think of the place you called home at that time. Think of your bedroom, and describe it in detail, as if you have just woken up there. Try to write this description in the voice of the child you once were.

What is your bed like? What is on the walls, the ceiling, the floor? What other furniture can you see? Some of the objects around you will hold particular associations: what are they? Use all of your senses. What can you see through the window, what noises can you hear?

Get dressed, and then open the door. Something is happening. Describe this in detail.

Now think of some other place that you often went to at that age, either a home from home, or some refuge from home. Set off for that other place, either alone or in company. Describe that journey in detail.

---

23. Lost selves

As we grow older we change, and hope that we change for the better. But many of us, however old we are now – whether sixteen or sixty – will sense that we have also left some part of ourselves behind. It could be innocence, a sense of wonder. It could be self-confidence, fearlessless, a sense of adventure . . .

Think of the child you described in the previous exercise. Write a list of half a dozen attributes that characterised you when you were that age.

Choose one of those attributes (one that you feel you no longer possess) and try to describe a time or situation when it was most evident. Then attempt to account for how it came to be lost.

24. Lost loves

We say of someone who has suffered a bereavement that they have 'lost a loved one'. Where once there was a person, now there is an absence.

Think of a person that you have lost, not necessarily because they have died. They were part of your life, and now they are not, for whatever reason.

Describe a time when you were together. This can be a fleeting moment, a particular incident, or a longer passage of time.

Now imagine a scene in which you come back together. Represent this as a conversation: what do you say to each other?

25. 'Lost'

Select the writing you produced for *one* of these exercises. Now attempt to convert this autobiographical material into a short story called 'Lost', written in the third person ('he' or 'she', not 'I'). As far as the material will allow, attempt to organise your story in the form of a series of scenes, using dialogue and precise sensory detail. Imply as much as you state, withhold as much as you reveal. Tell all the truth but tell it slant.

As the second exercise in this sequence may illustrate, the relationship between writing and remembering often also invokes a third term, which is 'setting', or 'place', and especially the place we used to call home. This connection is neatly expressed by the Croatian-American writer Josip Novakovich in his book *Fiction Writer's Workshop*, where he describes the effect on his imagination of migrating to America at the age of twenty, after which the lost landscapes of his upbringing in Croatia became the primary source (and subject) of his fiction and travel writing, to the extent that he would now sooner describe his work as being 'topographical' than 'autobiographical'.

The Polish-Canadian writer Eva Hoffman explores this theme further in her short essay 'The Uses of the Past',[4] in which she outlines her own experience of migration – from Poland to Canada, and so to a new language (as well as a new name) – at the age of thirteen. For the migrant, she suggests, this 'rupture of exile' creates an 'internal rupture' after which one's reality becomes starkly divided between the past and the present (with all the attendant dangers of sentimentalising and glorifying the past, or of demonising it as inferior and imprisoning). But while the urge to commemorate a 'familiar and longed-for home' is magnified by exile, she says, this yearning for imaginative return isn't unique to that condition. Even those of us who are not literally in exile – displaced from our homeland, the victims of history – may yet feel in some sense exiled from our childhood or from some other past phase in our life, dislocated by time and the momentum of personal history.

Hoffman illustrates this thought by quoting these words of Joyce Carol Oates:

> for most novelists the art of writing might be defined as the use to which we put our homesickness. The instinct to memorialize one's region, one's family, one's past is so strong that without it many writers would be rendered paralyzed and mute.[5]

This is, as Hoffman says, a 'striking formulation', and the key to its resonance lies in the suggestion that what distinguishes writers is not that they are prone to such 'homesickness' – most people are, whether migrants or not – but that they feel compelled to articulate it. The art of writing, in other words, is the means by which one both maintains a connection with what has gone before and gives expression to what one has become, and – if we think of the writer's blank page as being very like the future, a space in which the 'what next?' of our life is waiting to appear – guarantees the possibility of continuation.

[4] 'The Uses of the Past' is as much a talk as an essay and was delivered at a conference called *Writing Worlds* in Norwich in 2005 as a preamble to a larger conversation involving many writers from many different countries. In that larger conversation there are, intriguingly, as many similarities of experience as differences. The similarities relate, perhaps, to shared vocation, the differences to cultural background. But the main bone of contention concerns the propriety of using the traumatic reality of exile (exclusion from a homeland under fear of death or imprisonment) as a metaphor for something more universal and psychological (growing up).
[5] I haven't yet been able to locate the source of this 'striking formulation', though the twin themes of 'memorialization' and 'homesickness' are everywhere mentioned in Joyce Carol Oates's essays and interviews.

26. Departures

Picture the old-style destination boards at train stations and airports, the locations flipping rapidly over.

Perhaps in each of us there is a similar board, not just of locations but of people and incidents. The people may be significant to us – a grandparent, for instance – or the merest, briefest acquaintance. We may have visited the places only once, or we may have lived there for years. The events may be trivial or life-changing. But somehow they're etched into our memory and they return to us regularly, as fleeting images or lengthier daydreams, the board constantly changing, repeatedly flipping.

Take a few minutes to imagine your destination board, and begin to compile a list of the places, people and incidents that appear before your mind's eye. These are your headings, your points of imaginative departure.

When you have completed your list, asterisk the half dozen headings that are the most evocative for you. Now write a page or two in response to each of these headings. You are seeking to memorialise the places, people and incidents that define your internal landscape.

This may take several sessions. When you have finished, put this writing aside for a week or two, and when eventually you come back to it, cross out the sentences that seem laboured or long-winded, clichéd or imprecise. Rewrite your descriptions for clarity, economy and precision.

In writing about remembered people and places it can be especially difficult to avoid focusing on what was habitual or typical about them, and if my emphasis so far in this book has been on the avoidance of typicality in favour of the particular – stressing the importance of showing over telling, scene-building over summarising, particularising over generalising – that is because a tendency to telling, summarising or generalising is more common in beginning writers than not, and is the chief reason why so many first fictions fail to arrest the mind's eye or engage the reader's imagination.

To quote Flannery O'Connor once more: 'The eye will glide over their words while the attention goes to sleep.'

Consequently, when I read my students' work, I will often query an over-reliance on what I call the generalising tense, the use of 'would' (or 'used to') as a means of describing things that often, always, usually or sometimes happened in the past. (If a story is told in the on-going present, these generalisations tend to take the form of 'will' rather than 'would', the first sentence in this paragraph being an example.) Usually my response to this is to suggest that the student attempts to condense or merge these generalised events into a single event, and that this event be presented in the form of a dramatised scene. But the important word here is 'over-reliance', for as I remarked towards the end of the previous chapter, almost all successful narratives will alternate between 'scene' and 'summary' – both are required – and the generalising tense can be an essential means of summarising actions that occurred habitually or regularly and which it would be tedious or long-winded to represent (and then have to re-represent) in every particular.

The following is an example of the generalising tense in my novel *What I Know* (the theme is lost love) whose function is to give the flavour or mood of a fairly lengthy period of time in a fairly brief passage of narration:

> Sarah wasn't my girlfriend, though we spent many hours together, alone in my room, or hers, drinking wine in the park, playing pool, trailing from café to café in town. Sometimes, walking home from a pub after dark, she would tuck her arm under mine; sometimes we held hands. Lounging about on my mattress, our housemates downstairs in the kitchen or attending some meeting – and there was always some meeting – I would pillow my head on her lap; she might ask me to massage her back.

Here then is an exercise in summarising, whose focus is again childhood, and whose purpose is to reinforce an appreciation not only of the richness of memory as a resource for our writing, but of the different qualities and potential uses of summary and scene-building.

---

27. *Typical*

Think of a close friend from your childhood. This should be someone you can remember well, without too much effort. It might be someone you began to describe in the previous exercise. Contemplate the period of time that you were together. Try to identify patterns in your behaviour, the things you would often, always or usually do.

Now write an account of that period in the form of a generalised summary that is nevertheless specific in its details.

For instance, if I think of my best friend when I was ten, I might write:

> Most days that summer I would scrape open the heavy wooden gate to Lenny's back garden and knock on the door to his kitchen, and as

I waited for him to appear I would gaze at the flies circling over the breakfast bowls on the small table and wonder that they hadn't been washed yet, as ours always were. It was rare that I would go into his house, or talk to his mother. Always she would be wearing her dressing gown and smoking a cigarette, seemingly too worn-out to speak to us . . .

Even though I am describing 'most days' in this paragraph, the order in which I present the events takes the form of a typical day, beginning at the beginning. If I were to continue I would describe a morning spent wandering with Lenny around the local housing estate. At midday we would return to our homes for some food. Then in the afternoon we would go off to the woods, not returning till tea-time.

In similar fashion, try to keep your account both typical and chronological.

My friendship with Lenny ended when we had a fight over the ownership of a broken bicycle wheel. In our tussle for the wheel – which happened on the chalky white pavement across the road from his house – I bit him hard on the inner thigh. The next day his older brother brought him round to our back door and made him roll up one leg of his shorts to show my mother the teeth marks. Everything in my memory of this event is waist-high. I don't remember Lenny's brother or my mother from the waist up. I remember his brother's patched jeans and my mother's fluffy slippers; I remember Lenny's scrawny legs, and my teeth marks; I remember my struggle to avoid being spanked, and seeing Lenny's brother lead him away.

28. Untypical

As a continuation of the previous exercise, try to identify a specific incident when the nature of your friendship or relationship changed, whether for better or worse. Now write that incident as a fictional scene, avoiding any temptation to generalise or summarise. Nothing you describe this time should be presented as happening often, always, usually or sometimes. Everything is specific to the particular moment. Use concrete detail, especially in order to establish the setting. Use dialogue, too. And if you find that there are gaps in your memory – as inevitably there will be – then start making things up.

In stressing the importance of being able to 'make something out of a little experience', Flannery O'Connor is also emphasising the importance of invention, of making it up. Her advice, by implication, is not to rely on experience *as such*, but to fabricate to some degree, to embellish or exaggerate, distort and rearrange. Such is the nature of storytelling. But such is the nature, I'm sure, of any representational art form.

The poet Stephen Spender articulates something of the connection between experience (what you know) and invention (what you don't, yet) in his essay 'The Making of a Poem', which reflects on the relationship between memory and the imagination:

> It is perhaps true to say that memory is the faculty of poetry, because the imagination itself is an exercise of memory. There is nothing we imagine which we do not already know. And our ability to imagine is our ability to remember what we have already once experienced and to apply it to some different situation. Thus the greatest poets are those with memories so great that they extend beyond their strongest experiences to their minutest observations of people and things far outside their own self-centeredness.

Possibly underlying these remarks is an assumption that our memories are fixed and dependable, a stable body of remembered experience to which the imagination may be applied deliberately and consciously. But possibly the assumption is quite the opposite, that our memories are themselves in some sense invented, the products of our imagination. The following exercise, which I devised for an Arvon Foundation course, was premised on the former assumption, but has lately revealed to me the extent to which all our memories of childhood are in some degree 'false', not entirely (or even largely) made up, but nonetheless subject to all the usual degradations of time: bits will be missing, other bits jumbled up; the fabric will be threadbare in places, faded elsewhere. Whether or not we are writers, our memories will owe at least a little to our imagination. And as writers we should feel free to do with those memories whatever we wish, especially if they should start to falter or fade.

---

29. A place

Take a few moments to locate in your memory some small physical object that held a particular fascination for you as a child. You may have played with it, or simply held it, or merely looked at it (perhaps you were forbidden to touch it).

In my case it would be the tiny brass golfer in a floppy tam-o'-shanter and chequered plus-fours who stood on my grandparents' mantelpiece.

Ignoring the wider location, begin to describe this object. Imagine first that you are looking at it: how would you describe its appearance? Then pick it up: how would you describe the feel of it? Consider its size, shape, material, texture, weight. It may make a sound; it may even smell.

Now begin to pan out, as if your mind's eye were a camera. Describe the immediate location. This could be a shelf, a mantelpiece, a table, or the corner of a room. Is the surface patterned, varnished, coloured, reflective? Hard or soft? How does the light fall?

Pan out a little further and begin to describe the room, which should be empty of people. Is it spacious or cramped, tidy or cluttered? How is the space arranged? What do you see on the walls, the floor, the back of the door? Describe the furniture, the ornaments. How does the light fall?

My grandparents died some years ago, and when recently their lodger – my gran's brother, Uncle Ernie, who lived with them for most of their marriage – also passed away it fell to my brother and me to clear their house of furniture and ornaments that hadn't been moved in twenty, thirty, and sometimes forty years. I claimed the brass golfer as a keepsake. But he isn't at all as I remember him. His floppy tam-o'-shanter isn't floppy, and isn't a tam-o'-shanter, but something more like the tight-fitting cap of a schoolboy. He isn't wearing plus-fours, but full-length trousers. And they aren't chequered. In fact, the golfer is so smoothed by decades of polishing that he has no fine detail at all – no pattern in his clothing, no facial features. And he isn't a golfer, but clearly a caddy. My memory of him, in other words, is as much the product of my imagination as of any accuracy in my powers of recall.

Which is, I've come to appreciate, entirely as it should be. If the imagination is, as Stephen Spender insists, an exercise of memory, then memory is equally an exercise of the imagination, and 'the instinct to memorialize one's region, one's family, one's past' will always require an element of invention.

This inseparability of memory and imagination finds a correspondence of sorts in the indivisibility of setting and character or, indeed, of any of the other elements that cohere to create a successful work of fiction. The intention in this chapter, for example, was to explore the theme of remembering, yet most of the exercises are equally as concerned with setting, or place, and in discussing place I find I am drawn not only to revisit the themes of the previous chapter but to anticipate the themes of the next, which is about character.

Earlier, in discussing observational journals, I suggested that much of the material you gather will be 'the stuff of backdrop or setting'. But I also remarked that this material can lend something of 'the grain of the real' to your stories. And clearly there are two contradictory metaphors at work there. The first conceives of setting as if it were similar to stage scenery, very much in the background, somewhat static, while the second suggests that it is more akin to the fibres in wood, an inseparable, integral part of the whole (another, related metaphor might be that of the woof and weft of weaving, the threads being co-mingled, mutually dependent). And of course it's the second of these ideas that comes closest to the nature of fiction, in which all the elements interconnect, each functioning in relation to the rest.

Setting, for instance, is often conveyed through the eyes and emotions of a particular character, the description inflected by that character's voice. It is conditioned – or coloured – by point of view, and is in that sense as much an expression of psychology as it is of place, as we saw in relation to John Gardner's barn exercise, which forbids any direct statement of the father's bereavement but trusts that the description itself, in the particularity of its detail, will convey everything we need to know about his emotional condition.

On occasion the 'colouring' will be more explicit or emphatic, becoming, as David Lodge says in *The Art of Fiction*, 'a trigger for the effect John Ruskin called the pathetic fallacy, the projection of human emotions onto phenomena in the natural world'. Or it may work in quite the opposite direction, with a character's emotions being strongly influenced by setting, the weather, or some other 'phenomena in the natural world', which may induce fear, lethargy, dreaminess . . .

In the previous exercise you might have felt a degree of artificiality in being obliged to remember an object but not the person to whom it belonged, then a room but not the person who would usually inhabit that room. It can be difficult to separate person from place, and so you might possibly have pictured certain signs of recent habitation and included these in your description, suggesting that person in terms of their absence: a crushed cushion perhaps, a pair of slippers, a smouldering cigarette.

This final exercise, then, revisits the previous one, but requires you firstly to be more selective in your remembering and imagining, and to place more emphasis on character, including the character of the narrator, whose perspective is that of a child.

30. A person

Write a scene in the first person from the point of view of yourself as a child. The setting is the room you described in the previous exercise, and once again you should begin with close observation of a particular object, but this time you should also register the presence of another person. That person is not yet in the room. You can hear them – upstairs perhaps, in the next room, or outside in the garden. Write down a little of what they are saying, as if you are eavesdropping; just a few lines. Describe their voice. Now reach out for the object, and describe it. Perhaps you are forbidden from touching it? Describe your emotions. Do you remain alert to the presence of the other person, or do you gradually forget about them?

That person should at some stage come into the room. First of all you become aware of their feet. Describe their footwear. Allow your eyes to pan upwards, ending with their facial expression. They speak. Develop the scene as dialogue.

In all of this be precise but economical. Use the child's perspective to colour your description. Draw on your memory. But freely embellish the memory.

Later you may want to come back to this piece of writing and attempt to convert it into third person ('he'/'she') as a way of distancing it even further from yourself. You may then want to embellish it even more freely. You may want to allow your imagination to take over completely.

6.　Write about who you know: character

When she was asked in 2001 whether she thought that writing could be taught, the Booker Prize-winning novelist Pat Barker replied: 'What you do with a young writer is to recognise the note in their voice when they are on song for the first time and applaud.'

Which is to say: 'no' (though diplomatically 'no').

In one sense Barker's response expresses, albeit mildly, a scepticism shared by many writers (and almost all literary journalists), regardless of whether or not they have themselves benefited from or taught on a writing course. Writers, so the argument goes, must find their own way – and their own 'voice' – and the role of the teacher is not to offer instruction but suggestion and, ideally, confirmation.

I wouldn't necessarily disagree with this. It's a theme I shall return to in Chapter 12, when I consider the nature and function of the Creative Writing workshop, and it points to something I suspect will be found in every writer's 'back story': the presence, somewhere early on, of a teacher, mentor or supporter who not only applauded her, but first took the trouble to listen to what she was saying. In Pat Barker's case – as she goes on to acknowledge – that person was Angela Carter, who taught her on an Arvon Foundation course in 1978.[1]

---

[1] Angela Carter not only encouraged Barker to write about what she knew – the working-class milieu of her upbringing in the north-east of England – but introduced her to Virago, who would later publish her first novel *Union Street*. Several years later Angela tutored me on the Creative Writing MA at UEA, where she offered similar advice at a point when I was certainly not 'on song' or worthy of applause: quite the opposite. I was at the time attempting to imitate J.G. Ballard and her advice that I should write from my own experience was timely and – as for Pat Barker – productive. The next thing I wrote – a short story called 'Redundant' – was set in an industrial new town at a time of high unemployment and was the first thing I published.

In my own case, not untypically, it was an English teacher in secondary school. The 'confirmation' I received from Tony Drane, however, was not of my abilities as a writer of fiction, since I didn't attempt to write any fiction until after I'd left school. What he recognised, I think, was an unusual engagement with the inner lives of the books we were studying and, in my essays on those books, some natural facility for the language, perhaps even the beginnings of a 'voice'. Crucially, I now see, he provided me with my first serious reader and allowed me to experience something of the intoxication that all writers must feel in shaping sentences to impress or entertain others, and in this regard one unusual, extracurricular exercise stands out. While studying James Joyce's *A Portrait of the Artist as a Young Man*, he set us the task of attempting our own self-portrait, an extended essay in self-scrutiny, an exercise in representing ourselves on the page. My offering ran to sixteen hand-written sheets of foolscap; his numbered annotations ran to four pages more, and it was this generosity of response, as much as the initial exercise in self-exploration, that proved 'formative' to me as a would-be writer: it sounded like applause.

I was reminded of this exercise – and prompted to begin using something like it in my teaching – when I came across another little book in a charity shop, a Penguin Classics edition of the *Maxims* of the Duc de La Rochefoucauld, a seventeenth-century French courtier and soldier. Initially I was drawn by the aphorisms – the maxims – that make up the bulk of the book ('We only blame ourselves in order to be praised', 'We are never as unhappy as we think, nor as happy as we had hoped', etc.), but it is the short description of himself with which the maxims are prefaced – the *Portrait de La Rochefoucauld par lui-même* – that I've since found the most interesting, and the most useful in the Creative Writing classroom.

In this sketch the courtier confronts himself in a mirror and attempts to give a straightforward account not just of how he appears to his own eyes, but how he suspects he must appear to others, and what he considers to be the true nature concealed by his exterior. As the translator's introduction explains, among the habitués of fashionable Parisian salons in the mid-seventeenth century, the composing and discussion of such 'moral portraits' – also, intriguingly, known as 'characters' – was a popular parlour game. These 'characters' were written to be shared, and applauded.

Here is a little of La Rochefoucauld on his physical appearance:

> I am of medium height, well set-up and proportioned, my complexion dark but fairly uniform; my forehead is lofty and reasonably broad, eyes black, small and deep-set with thick, black, but well-shaped brows. I should be hard put to it to say what sort of nose I have, for it is neither flat nor aquiline, fleshy nor pointed – at least I do not think so – all I know is that it is big rather than small and comes down a little too low.

It might be objected that this description lacks particularity or vividness, that it's all a bit middling. Certainly it lacks any of James Joyce's sharpness of eye or expression in *A Portrait of the Artist*. But it does at least fulfil La Rochefoucauld's promise to present himself 'in plain terms' and allows him to continue into a consideration of what his outward appearance might signify in terms of his personality:

> My hair is dark and naturally wavy, thick and long enough for me to claim to have a fine crop. My expression has something melancholy and aloof about it which makes most people think I am supercilious, though I am nothing of the kind.

To which it might then be objected that this rejection of the accusation of superciliousness does actually sound rather supercilious. And while it's all too easy to patronise the past or judge it by our own standards, it's hard to avoid the impression of snobbery and arrogance that persists throughout La Rochefoucauld's self-portrait. We might also find ourselves wincing, for example, when he goes on to remark that he isn't easily touched by pity since pity has 'no place in a noble soul' and should be left to 'the common people' because they, apparently, 'never do anything because of reason and have to be moved to action by their emotions'. But La Rochefoucauld's intention is to give an honest account of himself, of his failings as well as his attributes – even if this reveals more of himself to posterity than he can possibly know or control. And his self-criticism does appear genuine:

> I am very reserved with strangers and not remarkably forthcoming even with the majority of the people I know. It is a failing. I realise that, and I will leave nothing untried to cure myself, but as a certain sullen expression on my face helps to make me look even more reserved than I am, and as it is not in our power to rid ourselves of a forbidding expression due to the natural arrangement of our features, I think that when I have corrected myself within I shall still keep unfortunate signs without.

In terms of characterisation, there are two important points to be made here. Firstly, however much we might want to 'read' a personality in terms of a person's outer appearance, there will often be a disjunction between how he seems to us and how he actually is: an ugly face doesn't necessarily indicate a foul temperament, nor a beautiful face a serene one.[2] Secondly, a person's

---

[2] I'm slightly nervous of using a phrase like 'actually is'. People are nothing if not inconsistent – foul-tempered now, serene in a little while. But their temperament is only rarely a consequence of their appearance, just as their appearance is only rarely a product of their temperament.

social being will often be a persona, whether successful or not, whether wholly conscious or not; it will be an attempt to disguise what is within, or merely to present a version of oneself – a 'character' – that is pleasing to others. This awareness of the potential disparity between the inner and outer person can be exploited to great effect in our fictions. And a good place to begin exploring the nature of that disparity is with the image we present to ourselves in the mirror.

---

31. A Portrait of Yourself as You Are Now

You are going to write a self-portrait in the manner of the Duc de La Rochefoucauld.

He begins by describing himself physically 'in plain terms' as he appears in the mirror. He also acknowledges what his appearance suggests about his temperament.

Take fifteen minutes to describe yourself plainly but accurately as you appear to yourself in a mirror or as you might appear to someone across a room.

What does your appearance suggest about your temperament? Are there aspects of your appearance that have associations or a history – a scar, perhaps; eyes that resemble your father's?

La Rochefoucauld goes on to give an account of 'such good qualities as he may have' and 'such defects as he certainly possesses'. Write for fifteen minutes on what you consider to be your best qualities and your worst defects.

Towards the end of his self-portrait La Rochefoucauld tells us that he is 'scrupulously polite with women' and goes on to describe how he behaves towards them and how he thinks he might behave were he to fall in love.

Whether you are male or female, take fifteen minutes to describe how you think you behave, generally speaking, in the company of women. Do you behave differently in the company of men? Describe how your behaviour is different.

Think finally of someone you recently wanted to impress. Describe a specific occasion. How did you behave? How did you feel? How did you hope to come across? How do you think you actually did come across?

While this exercise stresses an awareness of the gap between appearance and actuality, and so opens up the possibility of some depth or complexity in our presentation of character, it also depends quite heavily on what we know best – ourselves – and so permits only limited scope for the involvement of the imagination. In the exercises that follow there will be more opportunity for the invention of characters very unlike ourselves, though these may also sometimes appear in the guise of the first person, the seemingly autobiographical 'I'.

This is of course one of the standard fictions of fiction, that the tale being told is the 'true story' of the first person narrator. It's a central conceit in the origin and rise of the novel, as the critic and academic John Mullan notes in his book *How Novels Work*:

> The English novel begins with the first person. The first word of what is usually taken to be the earliest novel in English is 'I'. 'I was born in the Year 1632, in the City of *York*, of a good Family [. . .]' This is the opening of Daniel Defoe's *Robinson Crusoe*, published in 1719. *The Life and Strange Surprising Adventures of Robinson Crusoe* was, according to its original title page, *'Written by Himself'*. Robinson Crusoe was supposed the author as well as the hero. The novel includes a preface, purportedly penned by the editor of Crusoe's autobiography, but nowhere did Defoe's name appear on the first edition. All of Defoe's subsequent novels were, similarly, fictional memoirs.

The semi-autobiographical and the seemingly autobiographical are not then to be disparaged as lesser forms of invention or characterisation. It may be argued in fact that the first person 'I' allows the fullest exploration of character in that it allows the fullest access to the secret heart of another – an intimacy that is usually denied us in real life, even with those to whom we are closest (perhaps especially with those to whom we are closest). The novelist Nina Bawden has said: 'You know people better in a novel than in real life because you know what people think – not just what they *say* they think.' Which is to echo the sentiment of these words of E.M. Forster in *Aspects of the Novel*:

> In daily life we never understand each other, neither complete clairvoyance nor complete confessional exists. We know each other approximately, by external signs, and these serve well enough as a basis for society and even for intimacy. But people in a novel can be understood completely by the reader, if the novelist wishes; their inner as well as their outer life can be exposed. And this is why they often seem more definite than characters in history, or

even our own friends; we have been told all about them that can be told; even if they are imperfect or unreal they do not contain any secrets, whereas our friends do and must, mutual secrecy being one of the conditions of life upon this globe.

It is often argued that the reader can only be told all there is to be told about a character so long as the writer knows everything there is to be known about him, and then some. The question of what to reveal and what to conceal will certainly follow, but first the writer must be privileged with all the secrets, whether or not these are to be shared. And not only the character's secrets, but such humdrum information as the colour of his toothbrush, his underwear, his wallpaper, none of which need ever actually be mentioned on the page. I'm not wholly convinced by this: my own characters tend to remain a bit of a mystery to me, and what goes down on the page is usually all there is. But even so, one sure means of discovering more about a person – even a made-up person – is to ask him a question, preferably several, even as many as twenty . . .

If the previous exercise required you to scrutinise someone you know very well, this next requires you to examine the face of someone you will never have met and to imagine his or her replies to a series of questions, some more searching than others.

---

32. Twenty questions

If you haven't already been doing so, gather together some magazines (newspaper supplements are good, celebrity glossies less good) and begin to compile a collection of photographs of ordinary people. Snip off and discard any captions. You want your people to be anonymous.

Choose one of these photographs Study the person's face, posture, the clues in their clothing and setting. Then answer the following questions in the first person.

You should attempt to write the answers as one continuous paragraph, rather than a set of one-line replies. Certain of the answers may be strung together as a single sentence. For instance, the first three questions are these: *What is your name? How old are you? What do you do for a living?* To which the response might be: *My name is Arthur Battle and I am sixty-four years old this year, which is far too old to be cleaning windows for a living.*

These are the questions:

What is your name?
How old are you?
What do you do for a living?
Are you happy in your work?
What are your ambitions?
Do you live on your own or with others?
Do you have any pets?
What is your favourite smell?
How do you relax?
What is your most treasured possession?
What was the last thing you stole?
What do you most dislike about your appearance?
When were you last naked in front of another person?
Who was the last person to say that they loved you?
When did you last tell a lie, and why?
What keeps you awake at night?
What do you most regret in your life?
What is your proudest achievement?
What would you love to do that you haven't yet done?
What do you most fear?

We will return to this character later, in Exercise 37.

This is a variation on a widely-applied exercise whose form is fairly consistent but whose outcome will differ depending on the nature of the questions asked. Usually the aim is to produce a set of background notes from which you can develop a fully-fledged fictional character, and sometimes the aim is to flesh out a character you are already in the process of writing,[3] but in either case, the

---

[3] A related and frequently recommended strategy for novelists is to compile a card index file for each character – major and minor – detailing everything there is to be known about them – major and minor. I suspect there will be software that does the same thing. The novel that results may be no better than it would have been, but the novelist may feel less anxious or uncertain in the writing of it.

questions will rarely be more than a means to an end. In at least two[4] exceptional novels, however, something reminiscent of this exercise is incorporated into the body of the narrative.

William Maxwell, who died in 2000, was for forty years the fiction editor of *The New Yorker*, working with such celebrated authors as J.D. Salinger, John Updike and Eudora Welty, and was himself an accomplished writer of short stories and novels,[5] including *The Chateau*. This is, for the most part, a conventionally realist and psychologically subtle account of a young American couple's encounter with the other occupants of a dilapidated chateau in exhausted, impoverished, post-war France. But then after sixty pages or so the narrative is interrupted – to startling effect – by the insertion of such italicised questions as these:

> *What did he do, where was he, during the war?*
> *And who is she? Whom did he marry?*
> *And what was her childhood like?*
> *That's all very interesting, but just exactly what are these two people doing in Europe?*

The questions are disembodied. They might conceivably be the voice of Maxwell's imagined reader, who returns towards the end of the novel to pose a great many more questions, of a kind that anyone might want to ask of a story as it nears its conclusion. Here are some more of them:

> *Well, what happened to the money then?*
> *So the robbers got away?*
> *They never found that short circuit?*
> *Did they adopt the child?*
> *You are not asking me to believe that?*

[4] There is a third book on my shelves, to which my two examples may owe a debt of influence: the penultimate, 'Ithaca' episode of James Joyce's colossal masterpiece *Ulysses* is structured over sixty-odd pages as a relentless sequence of questions in the manner of a catechism or Socratic dialogue. Both the questions and the replies bear a somewhat chilly pseudo-scientific or bureaucratic aspect, and while there is humour, it is high-modernist humour based on wordplay, parody, irony: it's more 'fun' than fun, and doesn't much lend itself as an approachable model.

[5] In fact William Maxwell is so often mentioned as one of the overlooked or underestimated greats of twentieth-century American literature that the claims have become paradoxical: how can someone so often mentioned be regarded as overlooked? Or someone so often praised be regarded as underestimated? But perhaps both claims are true: many writers, myself included, admire and even revere him, but few of my students ever appear to have heard of him.

Presumably John Gardner would have frowned on such a 'conscious ploy on the part of the artist', given that these questions are so disruptive of *The Chateau*'s 'vivid and continuous dream' and force the reader into an awareness not just of the fate of the two young Americans but of 'the writer or the writing'.[6] But then it is perhaps salutary or instructive to be reminded from time to time of fiction's capacity for surprise, its potential for unruliness, even in prose as polished as Maxwell's. In other words, whatever rules this (or any other) guidebook might appear to be laying down, your ultimate success as a writer may well come in the breach of them. Or to put that another way, your capacity for creativity may first depend upon your learning the conventions, and then exceeding them.

Ali Smith is one contemporary writer who possesses the imaginative and technical brio to exceed most of the conventions. In her novel *The Accidental* she displays a kind of serious glee or determined exuberance that makes her equally as entertaining as she is challenging, and while the book is quite as humane and psychologically searching as *The Chateau*, it is more consistently audacious in its formal inventiveness. In one chapter, for instance, Smith deploys a 'Q&A gimmick' that is said to characterise the books written by one of her characters, Eve Smart, whose own method is to take 'the ordinary life of a living person who died before his or her time' and by a process of prompt and response to allow that person to tell 'his or her story as if he or she had lived on'. Thus the narrator of *The Accidental* is interrogated in the middle of a sleepless night by a disembodied voice that might, as in *The Chateau*, represent the book's imagined reader, but might equally be understood as a version of Eve herself, quizzing herself about herself.

Here is a brief run of questions that the narrator (or is it Eve?) actually refuses to answer:

> *It's a straightforward enough question, what did Eve believe?*
> *What did Eve believe?*
> *What credo did she live by?*
> *Well?*
> *What made her think?*
> *What made her write?*
> *What kept her motivated?*

---

[6] It gets more disruptive still. Occasionally too there appear italicised remarks by inanimate objects, for instance 'the dirt floor of the priory', 'the moss-stained fountain', 'the faded tricolor'. The chateau, we understand, has a mysterious life of its own, independent of history and of these people.

This 'Q&A gimmick' is used to telling effect in *The Accidental*, becoming something much more than a mere technical trick, and it does also suggest an interesting exercise for the Creative Writing classroom, a means by which you can create a fictional character while also attempting to structure a short story. As Ali Smith demonstrates, William Maxwell's device can be deployed in a manner that isn't necessarily disruptive.

---

33. Q&A gimmick

You are going to write a short story in response to a series of questions. The questions should be incorporated into the text. They are the voice of your imaginary reader. As you answer the questions you will be inventing a character. The first twelve questions are as follows. Write a paragraph or two in response to each.

Who is this woman?
And what does this place mean to her?
Was it always that way?
But is she sure she was right to come here?
Is she afraid that he won't?
How long since she last saw him?
On what grounds does she believe that?
So what has she brought with her?
Why does it matter so much?
What does she hope will happen?
And if it doesn't work out?
Is that him coming now?

Continue the story to its conclusion in this fashion, inventing your own 'reader's questions' from this point onwards.

Another exercise that finds an interesting correspondence in a published fiction – and which appears in numerous guises in Creative Writing guidebooks – is the next one, which seeks to reveal a person through their possessions and is very loosely based on a short story by the American author Tim O'Brien.

A Vietnam veteran, O'Brien has described his experiences during that war in a number of works, including a collection of twenty-two connected stories called *The Things They Carried* in which he consistently blurs the distinction between fact and fiction in pursuit of what he calls the 'story-truth' that communicates the emotional realities of combat in a way that mere 'happening-truth' (the presentation of verifiable facts) cannot. The book is in some ways a memorialisation of the men he fought alongside, and the now renowned title story takes the form of an extended list that describes the things his fictionalised comrades carry into battle, whether standard issue items such as helmets and boots, or personal effects such as letters, a girlfriend's stockings, a lucky pebble, or feelings such as grief and fear and shame.

In large part the technical interest of this story lies in its 'metafictional'[7] aspect – the deliberate questioning by the 'Tim O'Brien' character of the boundary between fact and fiction – but this device of using possessions to delve into personalities is particularly useful for the beginning writer, whether those personalities are to be tested in the extreme circumstances of war or by the more humdrum challenges of everyday existence.

My own version tends towards the humdrum.

---

34. *Notes towards a character*

In your notebook you will have been jotting down your observations of strangers in public places. You will have been noticing things about their appearance and manner that you find intriguing. Look through your notebook now and choose a person to develop as a fictional character.

Make a list of half a dozen objects you think this character might have on their person – in their bag, their pocket, their hand (e.g. a pair of silver spoons). Write a couple of lines about each of these objects, describing its significance. Write in the first person, in the voice of your character ('I').

Imagine this person has arrived home. Make a list of half a dozen aspects of their home (e.g. a fully-stocked bar in the living room).

Join each of the items in the first list to an item in the second list in order to describe a simple action (e.g. 'I place Father's old spoons on the bar in the parlour').

---

[7] Again it's interesting to consider this in relation to John Gardner's notion of the vivid and continuous dream. If metafiction is 'fiction about fiction' that purposely sets out to expose its own made-up-ness, how can it be that O'Brien's writing is nevertheless so affecting? Clearly there are ways of disturbing the dream that don't destroy the dream. Perhaps the nightmarishness of war is important here? Kurt Vonnegut's *Slaughterhouse Five* might be another example.

Now write 'because' after each of these six lines. Then explain the link more fully. (e.g. 'I place Father's old spoons on the bar in the parlour because always in the old days when we had a crowd in for a party, whether it was a wedding, a christening or a funeral, we'd have a drink and a sing-song and my old dad would play the spoons and get merry, then loud, and more often than not there'd be a bit of a ruckus, and I don't see why it should be any different now that it's his own funeral.')

You should have six paragraphs, six possible beginnings to a story. In each of these you will have begun to invent a character with a back-story, a life.

Choose one of the paragraphs, and continue on from this beginning. Develop your character from what you have written so far. Aim to reveal, in E.M. Forster's words, 'their inner as well as their outer life', leading finally to the revelation of their 'secret', which may be something they have been burdened with since childhood, or since last year, last month, or have perhaps only just discovered . . .

We will return to this character in Exercise 37, too.

The following exercise is another that takes its lead from 'The Things They Carried' and is one that I've used regularly on Arvon courses. Here it's offered slightly in passing, however, since it largely depends on my being able to present you with an envelope containing six items (and there being fifteen other students in the group to examine them).

---

35. Envelopes

In each of four large envelopes there are six small, everyday items.[8] These items might conceivably have come from someone's pocket or handbag.

The class should divide into four groups of four. Each group receives an envelope and examines the contents. Collectively, each group should invent a character based on the items contained in the envelope:

---

[8] To give an indication, Envelope One currently contains a disposable cigarette lighter, a potter's wooden tool, a pack of birthday candles, a phial of fake blood, a letter from an old folks' home, a heavy iron key.

Name:
Age:
Occupation, if any:
Current state of health:
Current state of mind:
Three physical attributes:
Three other characteristics – do they smoke, drink, go to church, like gardening, play sport, read *Hello!* etc.?
Finally, a recent life event, trivial or profound:

One person in each group should write up this information on a large (A3) sheet of paper. This person then introduces his or her group's character to the rest of the class.

The four sheets of paper describing the four characters should be displayed – along with the contents of the envelopes – for the duration of the writing course. Other exercises will incorporate these characters.

The immediate task is for each student to write a scene or short story in which two of the characters meet. They may be strangers or intimates, friends or enemies. The piece can be first or third person, but should be written from one character's point of view only.

At least one of the items from the main character's envelope should feature in this piece of writing. The other two characters should be given walk-on parts.

And should you happen not to be on a writing course, you can still attempt this exercise by gathering up from around your house (including the garrage if you have one, the garden, the greenhouse, the shed . . .) about eighteen small items. Pile these on a table. Shuffle them about fairly rigorously. Then take the six items furthest to the left and group them together: these belong to character one. The six middle items belong to character two. The six remaining items belong to character three. Write up a character profile for each. Attempt to write a scene or short story – as above – in which two of the characters meet and the third is given a walk-on part.

Clearly there are numerous methods for tackling the task of describing or revealing a fictional character. One approach is by means of physical appearance, as in the exercises with which this chapter began; another is by way of personal possessions, as in these two exercises. In Chapter 5, I pointed to the importance of setting or surroundings in influencing or reflecting the mood of a character; here I've suggested the fruitfulness of the 'Q&A gimmick'. Another common approach to illuminating a character is by way of the things that others say or think about them.

The potential shortcoming of each of these strategies, however, is that it can tend to produce a character sketch that is somewhat static, more descriptive than dynamic, possibly more superficial than searching. Each of them also depends on our gaining access to the inner person through what can be gleaned of them externally.

In certain types of story, of course, this may be entirely the point: it may be the author's intention to explore the limits to our understanding of others. But equally it may be the author's desire to represent a character from the inside, to reveal all there is to reveal of the personality behind the persona. And one fictional technique for achieving this is the interior monologue, a nice example being Dorothy Parker's short story 'But the One on the Right', first published in *The New Yorker* in 1929.

Although she came to disdain her own fame for wisecracking, which she described as 'simply calisthenics with words', Parker is probably best known now as a society wit – one of the founders of the so-called Algonquin Round-Table of writers, critics and actors who for ten years met daily in New York's Algonquin Hotel for luncheon and the exchange of acerbic *bons mots*. In this short story she depicts the struggle of a witty, caustic, but desperately bored 'Mrs Parker' to endure an exceptionally dull dinner party. The man on her left has nothing to discuss but the food (though the one on her right . . . she'll come to him later).

Here is Mrs Parker just after the first course:

Well, the soup's over, anyway. I'm that much nearer to my Eternal Home. Now the soup belongs to the ages, and I have said precisely four words to the gentleman on my left. I said, "Isn't this soup delicious?"; that's four words. And he said, "Yes, isn't it?"; that's three. He's one up on me.

At any rate, we're in perfect accord. We agree like lambs. We've been all through the soup together, and never a cross word between us. It seems rather a pity to let the subject drop, now we've found something on which we harmonize so admirably. I believe I'll bring it up again; I'll ask him if that wasn't delicious soup. He says, "Yes, wasn't it?" Look at that, will you; perfect command of his tenses.

Here comes the fish. Goody, goody, goody, we got fish. I wonder if he likes fish. Yes, he does; he says he likes fish. Ah, that's nice. I love that in a man. Look, he's talking! He's chattering away like a veritable magpie! He's asking me if I like fish. Now does he really want to know, or is it only a line? I'd better play it cagey . . .

And so it goes on, and if this appears somewhat mannered or stagey – more like a theatrical soliloquy than natural thought – or as if Mrs Parker is presenting herself to herself in the form of a persona, we do at least see the world through her eyes, refracted through her personality, and with all the immediacy of the on-going moment.

A less structured and seemingly less artificial means of representing a character's interior world is the 'stream of consciousness' technique associated with modernist writers such as Virginia Woolf, William Faulkner and James Joyce. Here the flux of an individual's experience is captured in all its randomness, fragmentariness and leaps of associative thought by way of an on-rushing flow of sometimes loosely punctuated and syntactically interrupted language that intermingles sensory impression, sudden digression and remembered connection (as well as the occasional collapse of the narrative thread).

The first page of Virginia Woolf's *Mrs Dalloway* offers one example of this, and is remarkable for retaining its immediacy and sense of interiority despite being written in the third person, past tense:

> What a lark! What a plunge! For so it had always seemed to her, when, with a little squeak of the hinges, which she could hear now, she had burst open the French windows and plunged at Bourton into the open air. How fresh, how calm, stiller than this of course, the air was in the early morning; like the flap of a wave; the kiss of a wave; chill and sharp and yet (for a girl of eighteen as she then was) solemn, feeling as she did, standing there at the open window, that something awful was about to happen; looking at the flowers, at the trees with the smoke winding off them and the rooks rising, falling; standing and looking until Peter Walsh said, 'Musing among the vegetables?' – was that it? – 'I prefer men to cauliflowers' – was that it? He must have said it at breakfast one morning when she had gone out on to the terrace – Peter Walsh. He would be back from India one of these days, June or July, she forgot which, for his letters were awfully dull; it was his sayings one remembered; his eyes, his pocket-knife, his smile, his grumpiness and, when millions of things had utterly vanished – how strange it was! – a few sayings like this about cabbages.

The opening to Ali Smith's earlier novel, *Hotel World*, consciously echoes *Mrs Dalloway*, and while it is highly stylised and considerably more 'worked' than natural thought, it does succeed in sounding convincingly like the tumult of a character's consciousness as she experiences the exhilaration of falling:

> Wooooooooo-
> hooooooo what a fall what a soar what a plummet what a dash into dark into light what a plunge what a glide thud crash what a drop what a rush what a swoop what a fright what a mad hushed skirl what a smash mush mash-up broke and gashed what a heart in my mouth what an end.
> What a life.
> What a time.
> What I felt. Then. Gone.

But perhaps the most famous example of stream of consciousness is Molly Bloom's vast and almost entirely unpunctuated soliloquy at the end of James Joyce's *Ulysses*. Molly is lying in bed as her husband Leopold sleeps beside her, having earlier in the day shared the same bed with her lover Blazes Boylan, and her tumbling thoughts are recorded in eight lengthy sections or 'sentences', the fourth and fifth of these sentences being interrupted by a fart:

> I feel some wind in me better go easy not wake him have him at it again slobbering after washing every bit of myself back belly and sides if we had even a bath itself or my own room anyway I wish hed sleep in some bed by himself with his cold feet on me give us room even to let a fart God or do the least thing better yes hold them like that a bit on my side piano quietly sweeeee theres that train far away pianissimo eeeee one more tsong that was a relief wherever you be let your wind go free who knows if that pork chop I took with my cup of tea after was quite good with the heat I couldnt smell anything off it Im sure that queerlooking man in the porkbutchers is a great rogue I hope that lamp is not smoking

Bearing these examples in mind, this next, somewhat lengthy exercise requires you to write an interior monologue and is structured as a series of shorter exercises deriving from those you will have attempted in previous chapters. Here the character to whom you are giving voice or expression is an artist's model, someone necessarily required to remain silent, and motionless, but whose mind will, as a consequence, be more than usually active. And if Dorothy Parker offers one model for rendering the inside of a character's mind, and James Joyce another – with Ali Smith and Virginia Woolf stylistically somewhere between – it may be that you want to remain, for now, nearer to the Parker end of the scale.

36. Still life

1. Begin with some automatic writing. The rules remain as they were in Chapter 3. You are free to write illegibly and ungrammatically, to be clumsy and clichéd, to repeat or contradict yourself, but you must write without pause for exactly fifteen minutes. Your theme is this: a recent event in your life, whether happy or sad, annoying or exciting, that you cannot stop thinking about.

2. For the purpose of teaching this exercise, I have a collection of post-cards of paintings. Each depicts an artist's model. Some are nude, some in costume; some are set against an imaginary backdrop, some are plainly posing in a studio. In the absence of one of my postcards, choose an illustration from a book of paintings. The picture you choose should contain only one model, shown more or less full-length, and it should not be a portrait of someone well-known.

3. Your aim is to write an interior monologue from the point of view of the model who is posing in the painting. So, for instance, if your model is dressed as a Shakespearean character, you would *not* write in the voice of the character but in the voice of the model, who may be getting quite hot in that costume. Alternatively, if the model is unclothed, you might consider whether he or she is 'nude' – i.e. self-confidently striking a professional pose, at one remove from his or her own body – or 'naked' – i.e. vulnerable, exposed, possibly embarrassed. (According to the art historian Kenneth Clark, the nude is a naked body 'clothed' in art.) Whether clothed or unclothed, 'in character' or simply submitting to the artist's anatomical scrutiny, consider the pose and expression and what it might reveal of the person: is your model anxious or at ease, sexually confident or vulnerable, engaging with the viewer or lost in his or her own thoughts . . . ?

4. Before you begin, you will need to amass some descriptive material. As we found in Chapter 5, setting is crucial; so too is the stuff of remembering. And as we explored in Chapter 4, the successful cre-ation of the vivid and continuous fictional dream depends upon the ability to convince through the senses.

    First think of an attic or an otherwise empty room. Imagine you are there. Write six separate lines on the sounds you can hear, whe-ther these are coming from outside or from downstairs, from another room or from the fabric of the building. Include any associations these sounds might have for you: e.g. an ice-cream van might remind you of a moment in your childhood; the creaking of a rafter might recall something sinister.

Now think of the art room at school, or an artist's studio that you have visited or know well, and write six lines on the objects, smells, colours and textures, etc., of the things you would find there.

Next imagine that you are the model, holding that pose, and write six separate lines on your physical sensations – whether you are cold, comfortable, itching, aching, whatever. Try not to write, for example, 'I am hot'. Try to show rather than tell: 'My skin prickles with sweat' or 'the air is shimmering above the calor gas heater'.

Now imagine the artist, and write six separate lines describing what you can see or hear of him or her. And again, show, don't tell: not 'he is scruffy' but 'he shambles across the room, his shirt tail hanging out'.

Finally, write six separate lines describing the view from where you are sitting or standing or lying. You might pick up on certain details about the room you are in, or notice something outside, seen through a window.

5. Read back through the lines you have just written. Choose one of them. If we were in a classroom, I would ask everyone in turn to read out their chosen line. But as we are not, you need only underline it.

6. This is your opening sentence. Your task now is to weave together as an interior monologue the various bits and pieces that you've just written, paying particular attention to physical sensations and the flux of your model's thoughts. You should also 'donate' or adapt the automatic writing with which you began this exercise: the 'recent event in your life' should become something your model might plausibly have experienced and be thinking about. You might also wish to donate or incorporate some lines from your observational journal.

7. You should aim to write three or four pages – around 1,000 words – and while it isn't necessary to create a story, only a character, so much the better if you can do both without doing damage to either.

Twice already in this chapter I have suggested that a distinction be made between 'persona' and 'personality'. The former may be understood as a façade, the presentation of a front, while the latter implies many more sides, or other aspects, including a hidden or interior dimension. A persona, we might say, is two-dimensional, a personality three- or even multi-dimensional.

Another way of expressing this is to distinguish between 'flat' and 'round' characters,[9] as E.M. Forster does in the lectures that are collected as *Aspects of the Novel*:

> Flat characters were sometimes called 'humours' in the seventeenth century, and are sometimes called types, and sometimes caricatures. In their purest form, they are constructed round a single idea or quality: when there is more than one factor in them, we get the beginning of the curve towards the round. The really flat character can be expressed in one sentence such as 'I never will desert Mr Micawber.' There is Mrs. Micawber – she says she won't desert Mr. Micawber, she doesn't, and there she is . . .

The great advantage that Forster finds in flat characters is that they 'have not to be watched for development', which is to say 'they are not changed by circumstances; they move through circumstances', and this allows them to be both memorable and easily recognised. They do their job on the page and they depart – and, crucially, they never surprise us.

By implication, then, a round character *does* need to be watched for development, and will change in response to circumstances, and will therefore be capable of springing surprises. The round character, in other words, has something of 'the incalculability of life about it', and in this regard it might be worth considering one further distinction, that between 'characteristics' and 'character'.

Characteristics may be understood as an assemblage of information about the outer, visible person, which will include her appearance, her mannerisms, her habits of behaviour and thought, all of which display some degree of fixity, typicality or 'calculability'.

Character, on the other hand, goes deeper, and is more dynamic. Character is associated not just with outward behaviour, but with the inner, moral choices and hidden psychological forces that govern it. Those choices may be complex; the forces may be contradictory. Character is never fixed or complete but always 'in process', and it is this dynamic aspect that most allows a person to come alive on the page and in the reader's imagination. A character's character, so to speak, is only fully revealed in response to events, but the nature of that response should never be obvious or predictable: it should never be 'calculable'.

---

[9] We should of course be wary of such simple and simplifying oppositions, these 'either/ors'. Always there will be a greyscale between the extremes of black and white, or – to be more colourful about it – always there will be a spectrum of possibilities: relative flatness, relative roundness.

In this sense, the most compelling form of 'what next?' in fiction is perhaps not related to the events – to the story as such – but to a character's moral and emotional response to those events. What grips and interests us is not so much 'story' as 'character'.[10] And indeed for many novelists these two terms are synonymous. Take, for instance, Henry James: 'What is character but the determination of incident? What is incident but the illustration of character?' Or, more straightforwardly, take F. Scott Fitzgerald: 'Character is plot, plot is character.'[11]

I will pursue the question of what constitutes 'plot' or 'story' when I consider 'structure' in Chapter 9, but here finally, for now, is an exercise that brings together two characters you have already begun to invent and requires you to create a situation – an event – that will test one or other or both of them.

---

37. Two characters

In Exercise 32 you were asked to gather together some magazines and to begin to compile a collection of photographs of ordinary people. For this exercise you will need a collection of photographs of locations, populated and unpopulated, rural and urban, indoors and outdoors.

Choose one of these pictures. This will be the setting for a short story in which two people come together: the character you invented in Exercise 32 ('Twenty questions') and the character you invented in Exercise 34 ('Notes towards a character').

Write in the third person ('he' or 'she') but from the point of view of just one of the two characters – that is, we will only see what that character sees, only know what that character knows.

Decide how well the two characters know each other before you begin, whether they are complete strangers, or lovers, or something somewhere in between.

Begin the story as your main character arrives at the location. Introduce the scene through their perceptions. Use all of the senses. Be

---

[10] I'm biased of course, and it ought to be conceded that genre fiction – which is far more popular than literary fiction – has a much higher tolerance of stereotypes and standard scenarios and tends to be far more plot-driven than character-driven. Genre fiction, we might say, is the natural home of the flat character.

[11] This is another much-quoted remark that has become something of a slogan in Creative Writing teaching but is nowhere given a source. Perhaps like Greene, like Carlyle, like Chekhov, Fitzgerald never really said it. Which doesn't mean it's not true.

particular, and be selective. Consider their state of mind: what are they thinking; what are they anticipating? Where have they come from? Have they hurried, have they perhaps been waiting outside? Have they arrived here by chance, or by arrangement?

This character sees the other character, whether from afar, or close to, whether in passing, or with a shock of recognition, whether with relief or excitement or puzzlement or fear: you decide.

Describe how the two characters come together. What do they do; what do they say? How do they behave? Describe the second character through the main character's eyes. Be attentive to facial expression, and to body language.

In Exercise 34 you gave your character a secret. Whether that character is your main character now, or your secondary character, what happens next hinges on that secret.

What happens?

7. Voices

Some time in the mid-eighties, as I was chaining my bicycle to the railings outside Norwich City Hall, I got into a conversation with another cyclist, a trim, pugilistic-looking fellow who told me he'd recently completed a charity bike ride of almost 900 miles that had taken him less than four weeks. He was nearly eighty years old. His name was Snowy Fulcher, and he was, he said, a 'lifelong health and fitness fanatic'. He had trained as a junior boxer in the back room of a pub during the First World War, and the lessons had cost his father a shilling and sixpence. On Friday nights a ring would be roped off in the bar for competitive bouts against the boxers of other pubs, and Snowy had won back his father's investment, first time out. Later he'd learned gymnastics in a boys' club organised by the city's chief constable to keep hooligans like himself, he said, away from the pubs.

Snowy told me a lot more besides, not just that afternoon but over the following two years, during which time – almost by accident – I became an oral historian, funded firstly by charities and then by the government to record the life stories of many other local people, whose recollections of the period beween the turn of the century and the end of the Second World War made me think repeatedly of the famous first line of L.P. Hartley's novel *The Go-Between*: 'The past is a foreign country: they do things differently there.'

When eventually the funding for this project ended I deposited the tapes and transcripts with Norwich library, and although something of the experience did find its way into the writing of my first novel *Pig*[1] (the narrator Danny

---

[1] I discussed in Chapter 1 some of the ways in which we avoid having to sit down and start writing. I mentioned putting *Pig* aside for a couple of days and failing to return to it for nine months. What I didn't mention was this project, which allowed me to postpone for

visits his grandfather in an old folks' home and listens to him reminisce), little of the period detail was directly useful to me. Recently, however, I've returned to this archive in an attempt to depict some of the textures of ordinary life on the 'home front' during the First World War, which is when my latest novel is set. And in re-reading the transcripts, and attempting to make novelistic use of some of the material, I've encountered a particular compositional problem. The archive contains a great many individual, characterful voices – each of them distinct, all literally *spoken* – but it can't provide me with the singular, authorial voice that might accommodate or alchemise them. I have encountered, in other words, the gulf between a natural speaking voice and the narrative voice of a novel.

Here is a sample of the narrative voice I've begun to arrive at (it describes a city-centre cattle market):

> Trading in the sale rings will go on until four but a good deal of business will also be sealed in the pubs, the prices agreed with a slap of licked hands and toasted with pints of the pissy government ale brewed as per War Office orders by Callard's of Riverside Road, the poor condemned animals then left unattended until the close of proceedings, some plainly distressed, and all of them naturally shitting on the hay-covered setts in their pens, so that in summer especially – on still, warm days such as today – the air on this side of the city will hum with fear and flies and the throat-gagging stench of the farmyard, even after the Corporation men have come on at five-thirty to begin sweeping and hosing the wide sloping expanse of standings and stalls, sending down hundreds of gallons of water to wash the excrement into the ditches and drains and swiftly out through the underground channels to the river, where the slick of effluent might briefly disturb the composure of the day-trippers returning from the coast on the pleasure steamer *Lord Nelson*, the deck packed with men in boaters and white homburgs, some in white suits, the ladies sheltering beneath the escalloped canopy, and the uniformed soldiers beside them all sporting clean dressings.

Other bits of research and some measure of imagination have fed into this paragraph, but one of the reasons I wanted to reproduce it here is because the details derive so straightforwardly from my interviews with Snowy. Like many boys at that time, Snowy earned pennies by helping drive the cattle to market; he also milked the cows on the sly when the farmers weren't looking. Here he describes the end of a typical market day:

---

over two years the point at which I would have to begin writing my novel. Transcribing tapes was a time-consuming and laborious process, but it involved typing, so it felt very *like* writing. It was the perfect displacement activity.

You used to come home with your shoes stinking. Well, you can just imagine what that must be like on the market. I mean, the whole of the place was full. Everywhere was full, from the top to the bottom. And in the summertime, the stink and the smell was impossible to imagine. And what they used to do – that all had to be off by dusk. And some of them would be left there. Because the farmer, if he'd had a good buy, he'd go in a pub and have a drink, until they kicked him out. Cattle would be standing there all that while – ain't had a drink, ain't had a bit of grub. Then they have to be driven back – there was no such thing as the RSPCA. What they used to do, as soon as that was finished, beginning to get dusk, they'd have the hose – the Corporation would send these hoses – and they'd be washing that all down. That was like a waterfall, all the manure and stuff going down there.

In *The Art of Fiction*, David Lodge describes quoted speech as 'the purest form of showing' because it allows fictional characters to exist on the page in all their particularity and individuality, without the author, as it were, speaking over them. At the opposite pole is authorial summary – 'the purest form of telling' – in which the characters' various voices are effaced by the dominating (or synthesising) voice of the narrator.

The two examples I've presented here are intended to represent these two poles, although I ought to offer a couple of caveats: firstly, of course, Snowy is not a fictional character; and secondly, there is some artificiality in using an interview to represent natural speech. An interview, after all, is more formal than normal conversation, more structured, more directed. And the main speaker – the interviewee – tends to be more thoughtful and considered, weighing his words, shaping his responses.

Even so, the sample of Snowy speaking does illustrate some common features of natural speech: the conversational tags ('Well', 'I mean'); the repetition ('the place was full. Everywhere was full'); the vernacular ('ain't had a bit of grub'); the ambiguity ('they' meaning variously, and not always clearly, the Corporation, the cattle, the farmers, the landlords); and the hesitation or self-interruption ('what they used to do – that all had to be off by dusk').

But there is another reason why I wanted to quote these two paragraphs in particular. Uniquely I still have a single page of transcript in which I attempted, experimentally, to transcribe a passage of Snowy's speech *exactly* as it was uttered. Why I wanted to do this, and why I thought to preserve the page, I can no longer remember. But here's a bit of it:

Your shoes – I mean . . . You never – you used to come home with your shoes stinking – that, er . . . Well, you can just imagine what they, er – what that must be like on the market. I mean, the whole of the place was full . . .

Everywhere was full, you know, from the top to the bottom – that was, erm
. . . And in the summertime, the stink – and the *smell*, that was impossible
to imagine. And, er, what they used to do – that all had to be off by dusk.
And, and some of them, well – they would be left there. They would be just,
erm – because the farmer, if he'd had a good buy, he'd, er . . . you know –
he'd go in a pub and have a drink, and, erm – until he, er, they kicked him
out . . . Cattle would be standing there all that while – ain't had a drink,
ain't had a bit of grub. Then, erm – they have to be driven back – there was
no such, er . . . RSPCA. There wasn't that then . . . And, er, what they
used to do, as soon as they, er – as soon as that was finished, beginning to get
dusk, they'd have the hose – the Corporation would send these hoses – and
they'd be, er . . . washing that all down. That was like a waterfall, well –
all the manure and stuff, all going down there.

Although my first example of Snowy speaking does reveal some of the
characteristics of natural speech, and the extent to which that differs from a
carefully worked authorial voice, this verbatim passage should demonstrate
the degree to which transcribed speech may actually be very far from the spoken
original. Genuine speech verges at times on the incoherent or frankly nonsensical, yet communicates often because of context, gesture, facial expression,
tonal inflection, the merest glint of an eye. Moreover, in a genuine conversation,
people interrupt each other, talk over each other, speak at cross purposes, fail
to finish their sentences. And so any written representation of speech – whether
in a novel, a newspaper, or an interview transcript – is likely to be considerably
tidied up, hardly ever a verbatim account. The 'white noise' and 'interference'
of natural speech will be filtered out; the jagged rhythms of natural speech will
be smoothed over. Fictional speech, we might say, is highly stylised speech.
The art is to make it *seem* natural.

---

38. Oral history

You will need a recording device that can pick up both sides of a conversation clearly, and has sufficient memory and power to record a lengthy
interview, and is designed to facilitate the stop-start playback (and
frequent rewinding) that transcribing requires.

All of us will know someone who has lived through interesting times,
and is perhaps an engaging or natural storyteller. Ask if you can interview them, whether about a particular experience or simply about their
memories in general, perhaps beginning in childhood.

Prepare your questions carefully. Keep them simple: one question at a time, not a bundle of several at once. And try to keep the questions open. Don't for instance ask, 'Did you have a happy childhood?' (answer: 'Yes'), but, for instance, 'Tell me about your first day at school.'

Be prepared to ask follow-up questions, prompted by the previous reply. And if a reply isn't clear, ask for clarification. Often an interviewee will wander off the point, or else answer in monosyllables. Allow this to happen. Some of the most interesting material comes in digressions. And if you do receive a monosyllabic reply, wait a while and say nothing. More will usually, eventually, follow.

Once you have the first of your interviews, attempt a verbatim transcript, typing every 'um', every 'ah'. You may find this hard going, and may not want to transcribe the entire interview in this way, so aim for two or three pages.

Once you have your sample of verbatim transcription, attempt a tidied-up version, being as faithful as you can to the original.

Then, finally, see if you can recast this tidier draft in the form of a monologue, as if your interviewee were telling a story rather than answering your questions.

With one of my interviewees in particular – Agnes Davey, a former cook to the Colman family (of mustard fame) – I produced so many transcripts, containing such a vivid and fluently remembered account of her upbringing in one of the impoverished, overpopulated yards in the oldest quarter of Norwich, that I was able to edit her interviews in the form of an autobiography which was published locally under her own name as *Hard Up Street*. This is one possible outcome of a series of oral history interviews. Another might be a compilation of various people's memories relating to a particular topic or locality or period of time. Another would be the selective quotation of passages in a more conventional form of history writing. Or else the interviews can be conducted solely in the spirit of novelistic research, with no expectation that they will ever be published in their own right.

Whatever the eventual use to which you put your recordings, for now it's sufficient merely to gain some insight into the requirements of representing speech on the page. And one alternative approach, with the same outcome in mind, is to be more surreptitious, or at least less structured, in order to capture something of the flow – which is often to say, the lack of flow – of a normal, informal conversation. The following is my variation on an exercise suggested in Josip Novakovich's *Fiction Writer's Workshop*:

---

39. Conversation

Record an informal gathering of your friends or family. It's important that everyone is relaxed, and the conversation spontaneous and natural. You may wish to be surreptitious, only revealing the presence of the recording device afterwards. It may be possible to announce the presence of the device from the outset, if you are confident that its inhibiting effect will quickly wear off.

Once you've completed your recording, begin as before by making a verbatim transcription. At times you may have two or three voices speaking at once. You may need to invent a method for representing this on the page.

Next, attempt to tidy up your first draft by editing out the mess and muddle. But consider as you make this edited version whether some aspects of natural speech should remain, in order to retain the feel of the real, the stumbling, sometimes rambling sense of authentic conversation.

As a final stage, use your edited version as the basis for a fictional conversation. Take things out, add things in, but write it as if it were taken from a short story or novel.

In order to complete the last part of this exercise you will need to employ one of the punctuation conventions for rendering speech on the page. The most common and familiar of these is illustrated by the playwright and novelist Michael Frayn in his short story 'He said, she said', which begins in this way:

'What was that?' he said suddenly.
She looked up sharply, frightened by the alarm in his voice.
'I thought I saw . . .' he began, then stopped. 'There they are again!' he said softly. 'Yes, and now there's two more of them.'

What the man is noticing – and this goes on for a little while longer – is the presence of inverted commas or quotation marks around his every utterance. Later he becomes irritated by the prevalence of speech attributions:

'*He said*,' he said, a few pages later.
'What?' she said.
'*She said*! There we go again! Didn't you hear it?'
'Oh, that. Yes. You always get that.'

'So who's saying it?' he demanded. 'Who's saying all this *she said* and *he demanded*?'

'Not me,' she shrugged.

The man and woman agree that there is hardly any need for these attributions, not *every* time they speak, and so the attributions disappear, which is fine for a while, but soon leads to a problem:

'They must have realised we could hear them.'

'Well, thank heavens for that!'

'Yes . . . Only . . .'

'Only what?'

'Well, this is rather silly, but I've forgotten which of us is which.'

'Which of us is which? That's easy. You just count back to the last *he said* or *she said*.'

'Oh, I see. Hold on, then . . . You, me, you, me . . . Or, just a moment, was it Me, you . . . ? No, no – I know – You, me, you, me, you, me, you, me . . . Good God – I'm *she*!'

There are alternative ways of formatting dialogue, of course, and I will come to these shortly, but here is a guide to the most orthodox method, as exemplified by Frayn's short story:

---

40. Formatting dialogue

- Speech is indicated by single quote marks (in America it's double):

    'I'm sure you've seen this before.'

- Speech within speech is indicated by double quote marks (in America it's single):

    'I said to them, "I'm sure you've seen this before".'

- All punctuation (commas, full-stops, question marks, etc.) that belongs to the speech act should come inside the quote marks:

    'Have you seen this before?' (not: 'Have you seen this before'?)

- If the speech is followed by an attribution (e.g. *he said*), then the speech should end with a comma, and the attribution should begin in lower case:

    'I'm sure you've seen this before,' he said.

- The attribution should begin in lower case even if it follows a question mark or exclamation mark:

  'Have you seen this before?' he asked.

- If the speech continues after the attribution, you may resume with either a capital or a lower case letter, depending on whether the speech continues as a new sentence or not.

  'I'm sure you've seen this before,' he said. 'It's a fairly common feature of fictional dialogue.'

- If you want to give the sense of an on-going utterance, the attribution should end with a comma:

  'I'm sure you've seen this before,' he said, 'because it's a fairly common feature of fictional dialogue.'

- Sometimes the attribution will come before the speech act. If so, the attribution should end with a comma, and the utterance should begin with a capital:

  He looked up and asked, 'Have you seen this before?'

- Alternatively, the attribution might end with a colon:

  He looked up and asked: 'Have you seen this before?'

- You don't always need an attribution. You can end the speech act with a full stop, and begin the next descriptive sentence with a capital:

  'I'm sure you've seen this before.' He put the book aside and looked out of the window.

- Sometimes you may want to interrupt an on-going utterance with a moment of description. Use dashes outside the quote marks:

  'I'm sure you've seen this before' – he put the book aside and looked out of the window – 'because it's a fairly common feature of fictional dialogue.'

- Each time you have a change of speaker you should begin a new paragraph, even if the utterance is only a single word long:

  'I'm sure you've seen this before,' he said, 'because it's a fairly common feature of fictional dialogue.'
  'No,' she said.
  'You haven't noticed?'
  'I don't think so.' She waited, then shrugged. 'Does it matter?'

A common anxiety among beginning writers is that they are being boring, and this anxiety finds expression at both the larger structural level and the smaller sentence level. The first-time novelist, for instance, might concoct a plot involving parallel or multiple storylines, told in alternating chapters, on the assumption that a single storyline is insufficiently interesting. The storytelling may then tend more towards summary than scene-building – the setting left sketchy, the characterisation skipped over – because the writer is anxious about dwelling too long in one place with one character and seeming too *slow*. For fear of seeming dull, or linguistically impoverished, the writer may embellish every sentence, pack every paragraph with superfluous similes, overemphasise every emotion. And related to this, there may be an oversensitivity to the repetition of 'said', coupled with a determination to make every attribution more expressive, every utterance more dramatic.

Thus we get alternatives for 'said' such as 'affirmed', 'asserted', 'asseverated'. Or else 'said' is coupled with intensifiers such as 'angrily', 'anxiously', 'aggressively'.

In truth, 'he said' and 'she said' can be almost as silent to the ear and as invisible to the eye as punctuation. They are no more 'boring' (or distracting) than commas. And while synonyms will sometimes work well ('he admitted'), and descriptive intensifiers will sometimes be necessary ('he admitted reluctantly'), often the dialogue itself will convey all that needs to be conveyed, without the requirement of additional commentary.

Part of the art of writing believable dialogue, in fact, may well reside in your ability to withhold more than you reveal, to say less than you mean: as in real speech, you may want your utterances to be ambiguous, teasing, or purposely enigmatic. This will permit your readers some room for imaginative manoeuvre. They can interpret the meaning of the dialogue as if they were participating. They can decide for themselves whether a character simply *said* something, or *admitted* it, or *asserted* it.

And of course, whether invisible or not, speech attributions are not required at every turn. A number of Ernest Hemingway's stories, for instance, are told principally through dialogue, the description kept to a minimum, the attributions sparsely applied. The following is a short passage from 'Hills Like White Elephants' in which a man and woman drink beer while waiting for a train. Their conversation is oblique, and appears to skirt around the possibility of the woman agreeing to have an abortion:

'Well, let's try and have a fine time.'
'All right. I was trying. I said the mountains looked like white elephants. Wasn't that bright?'

'That was bright.'
'I wanted to try this new drink. That's all we do, isn't it – look at things and try new drinks?'
'I guess so.'
The girl looked across at the hills.
'They're lovely hills,' she said. 'They don't really look like white elephants. I just meant the colouring of their skin through the trees.'
'Should we have another drink?'

Here we have just one instance of an attribution ('she said'), and while this may hardly be noticed on a conscious level, it will serve subtly to orientate the reader, as well as enhancing the rhythm of the prose (despite his apparent plainness, Hemingway is a consummate stylist, acutely attuned to the rhythms in his writing).

Pat Barker is similarly skilful at carrying a narrative through dialogue, and like Hemingway she uses orthodox punctuation. The following example from her novel *Regeneration* is interesting for its complete avoidance of attributions; Barker uses short descriptive sentences instead:

'By the way, your file arrived this morning.'
Prior smiled. 'So you know all about me, then?'
'Oh, I wouldn't say *that*. What *did* become clear is that you had a spell in the 13ᵗʰ Casualty Clearing Station in . . .' He looked at the file again. 'January. Diagnosed neurasthenic.'
Prior hesitated. 'Ye-es.'
'Deep reflexes abnormal.'
'Yes.'
'But on that occasion no trouble with the voice? Fourteen days later, you were back in the line. Fully recovered?'
'I've stopped doing the can-can, if that's what you mean.'

With these examples of Barker and Hemingway in mind, the following exercise requires you to 'translate' a largely descriptive narrative into conventionally punctuated dialogue, but with a minimal use of attributions.[2]

---

[2]   I've come across several variations on this exercise, but the original may be David Fine's, contained in Sue Thomas's excellent book *Creative Writing: A Handbook for Workshop Leaders*.

41. Dramatic twist

If you haven't already been doing so, gather together some copies of your local evening paper and look for interesting stories to snip out.

I have a collection of favourite clippings that I often use in class. In each of them the participants are quoted in brief, but the stories are mainly conveyed in the voice of the journalist. Here are three of the opening sentences:

> A lovers' tiff took a dramatic twist today after a young man scaled scaffolding at a city centre building site and threatened to kill himself.

> Two men who ran amok at a service station after a heavy drinking session have been warned they could be facing a stretch behind bars.

> Two employees of Shopacheck Financial Services were rescued by firefighters after they became trapped in a safe.

Select a story from your collection of clippings and attempt to rewrite it almost entirely as dialogue. Some description is permitted, but keep it to a minimum. Following the example of Hemingway, use speech attributions sparsely. Wherever possible, use short descriptive phrases instead, in the style of Pat Barker. Punctuate your dialogue in accordance with the guidelines above.

In *Hotel World*, Ali Smith uses very similar dialogue conventions, except for the complete absence of quotation marks. This is a common variation, but can cause difficulties when you want to include descriptive sentences in the middle of a character's speech: how is the reader to know when the description has ended and the speech has resumed? Smith gets around this problem by not interrupting any of her characters' utterances with description. Where she has description she places it on a separate line:

> Hello, Penny said. We're out looking at houses. Aren't you cold?
> The elderly lady wasn't wearing a coat. She told Penny she was looking for her cat.
> She's never been out this late, the elderly lady said. I just turned around and she was gone. It's not like her. I don't know what to do.

Don't worry, Penny said. Have you checked all round your house? She might be asleep in a cupboard or under a bed. Cats are very independent. They can look after themselves. Go inside, it's cold. She'll come home by herself. She's probably there now.
She's black and white, the elderly lady said. Have you seen her?
No, Penny said.

Out of context, the strangeness of this exchange may not be fully apparent. Penny is a journalist, but her mental state is somewhat unstable. She's inclined to misinterpret the world. Here, for no apparent reason, she's wandering through a housing estate with a homeless woman called Elspeth. Penny has yet to realise that Elspeth is homeless (or that she has just wandered off), and when she strikes up this conversation with the elderly lady she fails to realise that there isn't a cat, or that the elderly lady is senile. Nor does the elderly lady appear to listen properly to Penny. So we have a conversation in which the participants talk at cross purposes, neither quite understanding the other, neither quite communicating clearly.

All of which makes this an exemplary passage of dialogue, since speech in fiction tends to be most interesting when the characters speak at cross purposes, or don't quite mean what they seem to mean, or hide more than they show, or communicate more about themselves to the reader than they do to each other. Dialogue, in other words, often succeeds most for the reader where it most fails for the characters. And it's particularly interesting when it manages to signify on several levels.

In an interview with *The Paris Review*, the novelist Eudora Welty (who was, like Flannery O'Connor, associated with the 'Southern Gothic' tradition of American writing) describes something of the challenge of writing dialogue in her novel, *Losing Battles*:

> In its beginning, dialogue's the easiest thing in the world to write when you have a good ear, which I don't think I have. But as it goes on, it's the most difficult, because it has so many ways to function. Sometimes I needed to make a speech do three or four things at once – reveal what the character said, but also what he thought he said, what he hid, what others were going to think he meant, and what they misunderstood, and so forth – all in his single speech. And the speech would have to keep the essence of this one character, his whole particular outlook in concentrated form.

With Smith and Welty in mind, then, the next exercise requires you to write a passage of dialogue in which the speakers communicate obliquely (if at all) while revealing themselves on more than one level to the reader.

42. Cross purposes

Choose one of the following six subjects:

1. the new sculpture trail in the local park
2. the refurbishment of the town centre
3. the closure of the local swimming pool
4. the weather
5. holiday plans
6. last night's TV

Now write a minimum of two pages of conventionally formatted dialogue in which two characters talk about or around this subject. The subtext to their conversation, which influences what they say but cannot be stated, should be chosen from the following six possibilities:

a. they are competitive parents;
b. one of them has just achieved a great personal success, and the other is jealous;
c. one is having an affair with the other's husband or wife, and both are aware of the fact;
d. one of them is seriously ill;
e. neither likes or trusts the other, but they are required to get along because they are workmates, or neighbours, or related by marriage;
f. they are in love with each other but neither dares say so.

In common with Ali Smith, the Booker Prize-winning novelist James Kelman rarely employs speech marks, and while this is partly an issue of style – an avoidance of unnecessary punctuation – his principal reason is political: Kelman doesn't want there to be a separation between the dominating voice of his narrator and the vernacular voice of his characters. This passage from Lodge's *The Art of Fiction* may explain why:

One of the difficulties of writing truthfully about working-class life in fiction, especially evident in the well-intentioned industrial novels of the Victorian age, is that the novel itself is an inherently middle-class form, and its narrative voice is apt to betray this bias at every turn of phrase. It is hard for the novel not to seem condescending to the experience it depicts in the contrast between the polite, well-formed, educated discourse of the narrator and the rough, colloquial, dialect speech of the characters.

Kelman writes mainly about working-class Glaswegian experience, and not only does he refuse to enclose the vernacular speech of his characters in 'condescending' or segregating quote marks, but he often also allows the 'rough, colloquial, dialect speech of the characters' to determine his narrative voice. In the democracy of Kelman's prose, the voices of character and narrator are equal, as the following passage from his novel *How Late It Was, How Late* may demonstrate (the central character, Sammy, has lost his sight as a result of a two-day drinking binge that culminated in a 'doing' from the police; here he's sitting in a pub with another man, Tam):

What ye drinking?
I'll get it . . . Tam was onto his feet again. Sammy heard him walk off. It was a few minutes afore he came back; he kept his voice low when he spoke:
What is it gony be permanent? he said; the eyes and that?
Couldnay tell ye Tam.
Can ye no see nothing?
Not a thing.
Fuck sake.
The news is got round eh!
Aye . . .
Ye wonder how the fuck it happens but know what I mean! Sammy smiled.
Fucking carrier pigeons!
Aye I know. What ye been to a doctor?
Saw the cunt this morning . . . Sammy shrugged, swallowed the last of the first whisky, groped for the new yin and emptied in the drips. Cheers, he said.[3]

Like Woolf's *Mrs Dalloway*, Kelman's novel is a past tense, third person example of stream of consciousness, and so it might be argued that the narrative voice *ought* to be Glaswegian since it's so close to the character's inner world. Elsewhere in Kelman's fiction the fully vernacular voice is reserved for first person narrators, and this has become a fairly common feature of

---

[3]   As well as insisting on the equality of character and narrator, Kelman argues that there's no such thing as 'bad language'; there is only language. When *How Late It Was, How Late* won the Booker Prize not all of the judges agreed with him. One publicly denounced his novel for the 'crudity' of its language, as did several commentators in the broadsheets. For Kelman this only confirmed his view of a prissy middle-class, London-based elitism in British literary culture.

contemporary Scottish writing. Another example might be Mark McNay's debut novel, *Fresh*, where passages of first person 'Glaswegian' alternate with a third person 'Standard English'[4] voice in which only the speech is colloquial.

Here's an example of the first person vernacular in *Fresh*:

> The next day they gied us a map each and a pushbike and telt us to meet up in some cafe in the toon. It was alright coz Ah jumped in there quick and didnay get lumbered with a lassie's bike. Or a shopper. Me and Gambo managed to get teamed up the gether so we went for a wander in the country. We found a stream and it was that warm we thought we'd have a swim. There was clegs everywhere and Ah got bit to fuck but it was worth it.

And here's an example of 'Standard English' narration in *Fresh*, which contains colloquial, unpunctuated speech:

> The crowd thinned as they passed the bus shelter. He could feel Maggie's grip on his hand as they approached the bookie's. The door opened and a man stumbled out. He dropped a cigarette end on the pavement and stood on it. He tucked his paper under his arm and looked down the road. His face lit up when he recognised Sean.
> Alright wee man? How ye doin?
> Sean felt Maggie tug harder on his hand.
> No bad.
> We've no saw ye for a while. Gave it up have ye?
> Sean kept walking with the momentum of Maggie.
> Aye. It's a mug's game.

As David Lodge implies, the effort (however well-intentioned) to represent working-class experience truthfully will always be hazardous, particularly when it involves the representation of vernacular speech. The result may sound fake, or forced, or patronising. And this applies equally to those attempts to indicate not just class but age or region or ethnicity. In many cases, it may be enough to indicate the vernacular through judicious choice of diction (vocabulary) and careful arrangement of syntax (word order; sentence rhythm), while retaining Standard English spellings. That Kelman and McNay are able to succeed in writing phonetically is the result, firstly, of their both being literary stylists whose attention is always in part directed to the flow

[4] By 'Standard English' I mean the 'rules' of grammar as they are taught (or used to be taught) in schools, and the standardised spellings and definitions that are to be found in the Oxford dictionary, but also what is known as 'received pronunciation', or 'BBC English'. In other words, the minority form of English regarded by the majority as 'proper'.

of their prose, so that they rarely if ever sound forced, and secondly of the fact that they are writing from within the language and experience they describe. In terms of class, region and ethnicity, the language of their fictions is authentic rather than adopted.

---

43. Vernacular voices

We all come from somewhere, and that somewhere will speak its own variant of English. Some of those variants will constitute a dialect, having a distinctive vocabulary and grammar; some will be characterised simply by accent (even the educated middle-class speech of middle England has its own accent and can be represented phonetically).

In the previous exercise you chose from a list of six subjects and a list of six subtexts. Now choose a different subject and subtext from those same two lists, and again write a scene of at least two pages. But this time:

- include as much description as speech;
- write the description in Standard English, but write the speech phonetically, in the dialect or accent of your upbringing;
- don't use quote marks.

Then, as a final variation on this, choose two more subjects and subtexts from the same lists. Now write a scene of at least two pages entirely in the vernacular voice of one of the characters. In the manner of Kelman, there should be no distinction between narrative voice and spoken voice. Write everything phonetically.

The other main convention for rendering speech on the page is illustrated by the following short passage from James Joyce's *A Portrait of the Artist as a Young Man*. A dash (sometimes preceded by a colon) is used to signal the start of an utterance, any speech attribution comes after the first comma or question mark, and any description begins on a separate line:[5]

---

[5] Or not quite *any* description. Occasionally Joyce will add a descriptive gloss to a speech attribution – for instance: 'said Mr Dedalus, twirling the points of his moustache'. The potential difficulty here (as with any approach that avoids using quote marks) lies in establishing a clear enough boundary between dialogue and description, speech and narration. Joyce is quite good at it.

> – Simon, said Mrs Dedalus, you haven't given Mrs Riordan any sauce.
> Mr Dedalus seized the sauceboat.
> – Haven't I? he cried. Mrs Riordan, pity the poor blind.
> Dante covered her plate with her hands and said:
> – No, thanks.
> Mr Dedalus turned to uncle Charles.
> – How are you off, sir?
> – Right as the mail, Simon.
> – You, John?
> – I'm all right. Go on yourself.
> – Mary? Here, Stephen, here's something to make your hair curl.
>
> He poured sauce freely over Stephen's plate and set the boat again on the table. Then he asked uncle Charles was it tender. Uncle Charles could not speak because his mouth was full but he nodded that it was.

The scene from which this passage is taken unfolds over several pages and depicts a tense Christmas dinner that escalates into a furious row between young Stephen's father Mr Dedalus and his aunt (or 'Dante') Mrs Riordan, and while the adults express themselves clearly and sometimes vehemently on the subject of the Catholic church and Irish politics, they also speak by turns obliquely, ironically, sarcastically and euphemistically, and thereby manage to convey more to each other – and yet more to the reader – than the boy is quite able to comprehend. This, allied to Joyce's acute ear for the rhythms and idioms of natural speech, makes the episode a particularly good example of the potential for dialogue to function on several levels at once.

But there is something else here, too. The excerpt also allows us a glimpse of an alternative method for depicting dialogue. The sentence, 'Then he asked uncle Charles was it tender', is an example of indirect speech, which falls somewhere between the poles of quoted speech and authorial summary. It might easily have been rendered directly, in the voice of Mr Dedalus: '– Is that bird tender, Charles?' Or alternatively, the entire passage – and even the entire episode – might yet be converted to indirect speech, as follows:

> When Mrs Dedalus pointed out to her husband that he hadn't given Mrs Riordan any sauce, Mr Dedalus seized the sauceboat and apologised, jokingly asking Mrs Riordan to pity the poor blind.
> But Dante covered her plate and declined the offer, and so Mr Dedalus turned to uncle Charles instead, who declared himself right as the mail, after which John suggested that Mr Dedalus should go on and serve himself.
> Finally Mr Dedalus asked Mary if she wanted sauce, then poured some freely onto Stephen's plate, telling him it would make his hair curl.

Although I've retained much of Joyce's phrasing here, even a passage as short as this begins to lose the immediacy and vivacity that comes when the characters are allowed to speak, as it were, for themselves. Subtlety, too, is sacrificed, for we lose a sense of Mr Dedalus's forced geniality in response to Dante's buttoned-up austerity. What remains is not the event, but a report of the event, and this returns us to the distinction I explored in Chapter 4 between showing and telling, dramatising and summarising. Both are required, to differing degrees, and the balance between them will determine not only the complexity or richness of the scene, but the pace at which the narrative is allowed to unfold. And should an author wish to hasten that unfolding still further, then a straightforward summary might be offered instead:

> After Mrs Dedalus pointed out to her husband that he hadn't offered Mrs Riordan any sauce, Mr Dedalus asked each of his guests in turn if they would like some. All declined, and so he poured some onto Stephen's plate and returned the boat to the table. Charles, his mouth full, nodded when asked if the meat was tender.

As should now be clear, with the use of indirect speech the voice of the narrator begins to merge with those of the characters, whereas in this kind of summary the voices of the characters are almost entirely erased by the voice of the narrator. This final exercise allows you to explore these differences further:

---

44. In summary

Select a fairly lengthy passage of dialogue that you have written in response to one of the earlier exercises in this chapter (or, alternatively, use a short story such as Hemingway's *Hills Like White Elephants* that is written mainly as speech).

1. Rewrite this dialogue entirely in the form of indirect speech, in the third person (e.g. 'Mrs Dedalus pointed out . . . John suggested . . .').
2. Now rewrite it in the characterful voice of one of the participants (e.g. 'My dear wife pointed out . . . John kindly suggested . . .').
3. Now condense either of these rewrites in the form of a short summary of no more than eight lines.
4. Finally, rewrite your original dialogue in a way that combines elements of direct, indirect and summarised speech.

I began this chapter by attempting to draw a distinction between a natural speaking voice and the narrative voice of a novel.[6]

By 'natural speaking voice' I meant not just the way Snowy Fulcher, or any other person, might talk in real life, or the way in which his verbatim speech might be tidied up for the page so that it seems, paradoxically, more real (or at least more readable). I also meant the way in which the speech of a fictional character might be represented on the page so that it, too, acquires something of the feel of the real – and one obvious test of this is to adopt John Steinbeck's advice and 'say it aloud as you write it'. If it causes you to stumble, or sounds in any way wooden or stagey or forced, then it may need some finessing.

By 'narrative voice', meanwhile, I meant the storytelling voice that contains (or 'quotes') the individual voices of the various characters, and I offered the example of a paragraph from my novel-in-progress that is plainly not the speech of a protagonist; it is not the voice of a character who is participating in the story.

One clear indication that it doesn't belong to a protagonist is the absence of the first person pronoun, 'I'. But perhaps equally strong a signal is given by the somewhat inflated rhetorical style – the fact that it is all one sentence, and the clauses are written to a particular cadence, and it contains a fair amount of musical patterning (alliteration, assonance, half-rhyme). Additionally, the scope of the description – which roams from the sale rings to the pubs to the cattle pens to the underground channels to the pleasure steamer – suggests an omniscient 'god-like' perspective rather than the more limited awareness of, say, one of the ladies on the *Lord Nelson* or one of the farmers in the pubs.

This is not, however, to say that the narrative voice of a novel cannot adopt a more conversational style or be written as though penned by a protagonist. Consider, for instance, the beginning of J.D. Salinger's *The Catcher in the Rye*:

> If you really want to hear about it, the first thing you'll probably want to know is where I was born, and what my lousy childhood was like, and how my parents were occupied and all before they had me, and all that David Copperfield kind of crap, but I don't feel like going into it.

The attitude and personality expressed in this sentence is striking and memorable. It conveys a particular take on the world, a particular attitude or perspective on life. And it is written to a definite, conversational rhythm that will remain consistent throughout the novel (and become quite infectious). The voice belongs to seventeen-year-old Holden Caulfield, who is both the

---

[6] And not just the narrative voice of a novel, of course; this applies equally to short stories.

novel's main protagonist and its narrator. But Holden is, of course, an invention, the creation of the novel's author, J.D. Salinger.

We might say that Salinger 'ventriloquises' the voice of Holden Caulfield. And generalising beyond this, we might also say that the effort to assume the voice of a convincing, consistent narrator underpins the writing of any novel or story, whether or not it is conveyed in the first person, whether or not the style is as conversational as Holden Caulfield's.

The narrative voice of my novel-in-progress is no more my own voice than Holden Caulfield's is the voice of J.D. Salinger. It is the voice, as it were, of the novel, and the decisions taken in determining the nature of this voice (and in particular those concerning the narrative point of view) are arguably as crucial to the success of a novel or story as any concerning, for instance, the plot – which is where the concerns of this chapter on voice begin to shade into those of the following chapter on viewpoint.

8. Viewpoints

The Latin phrase *in medias res* ('into the middle of things') is used to describe a narrative that doesn't begin at the beginning but at some crucial point in the midst of the action. The beginning is then usually given in flashback. Here is the opening to my novel *Common Ground*, which offers a fairly low-key example of *in medias res*:

> The window shook in its frame and then the rain came. Ashley wrapped himself in a blanket and stood closer to the heater. He faced into the street. On the opposite kerb a red car had been abandoned beneath a shedding sycamore. With each damp gust of wind a shower of leaves fell to the bonnet and roof and stuck as if glued. The car was new, a model advertised everywhere on roadside hoardings, in bus shelters and train stations. It was designed for the city. The windscreen lay like a sheet of crazed ice across the front seats. The rear tyres were flat and the bodywork was dented. As he looked down, two girls paused on their way to the top of the street and pilfered what little remained to be taken – a cassette tape and window wipe, a bottle of oil from the boot. Twenty yards up the road they dropped all three in the gutter.
>
> He turned to Jay and said, 'I'll bet you fifty quid you're not.'
>
> 'You don't have fifty quid, Ashley,' she replied, and raised one knee to the height of her shoulder. She was sitting on the edge of their bed, carefully shearing her toenails with a pair of dressmaking scissors.
>
> 'I have employment,' he reminded her. 'I work.'
>
> 'Okay,' she shrugged, and for a moment she faced him. 'But I'm serious this time.'

Her gaze was direct, defenceless, and he felt a lift of excitement, almost elation. He sensed it was £50 lost, but would not admit it, feared his disappointment if she was mistaken. 'You're pregnant every other month,' he told her. 'You feel sick and you're pregnant, you forget your dates and you're pregnant, your period starts and you say you've miscarried. You owe me hundreds already.'

She didn't respond. The gas heater hissed softly in the silence between them, outside the rain eased and came stronger. He turned back to the window and watched a small boy straining to remove a wing-mirror from its bracket. 'So how do you know?' he asked finally.

'I keep crying,' she said.

'You do that anyway, Jay.'

'I feel nauseous,' she added. 'And miserable.' She dropped the scissors to the floor and heaped herself beneath the bedclothes. 'Constantly nauseous,' she said. 'And really fucking miserable.'

In this opening page and a half we encounter two characters in the midst of their on-going lives. There is no narrative preamble, no prior introduction to Ashley and Jay, no careful scene-setting, no immediate indication of time and place, and no announcement of any major themes or recent events. None of which is unusual. A great many short stories and quite a few novels will begin in this way, and a significant number of those will start with someone situated on some kind of threshold, some inbetween place. This may be at the moment of waking, poised between yesterday and today, the unconscious and consciousness, sleep and alertness. More dynamically, it could be at the wheel of a car, with the protagonist situated on the inside looking out, but also in a state of transition, placed on a journey between a past and a future, the already-known and the mystery of what is to come. Or else, less dynamically – as in this instance – the protagonist may be looking out of a window, whether at home or at work, or in some less familiar place.

As we read on, the narrative interest will move back and forth between a *here* and a *there*, and – without our being wholly conscious of it – several things will happen at once. We will gain our bearings in this fictional place, a sense of the setting, its dimensions, its atmosphere. We will become acquainted with a principal character and his point of view – not just his visual perspective, but his moral or psychological 'take' on events, his attitude towards what he sees. We will be introduced *via* this character to other characters, and so gain a sense of the important connections in this imaginary world. And we will begin to pick up on the main themes of the story, what it might be 'about', what the significant issues might be.

Here is an exercise in beginning a story along just these lines:

45. Something is happening out there

Write a scene in which you situate two characters in a room. This may be an office, a classroom, a bedroom, a portacabin, a prison cell; it may be wherever you like.

One of these characters is standing close to a window. We see everything through his or her eyes. The narrative point of view is third person: 'he' or 'she' (and 'they').

Begin the scene with what this character can see outside. Write in the grammatical past tense.

He or she remarks: 'Something is happening out there.' It may be humdrum or harrowing, amusing or alarming; it may be uncanny . . .

Now bring the attention indoors. Something is also happening in here. The two characters speak to each other. Then your main character turns back to the window.

Continue the narrative in this way, moving back and forth between outside and inside, interweaving description with dialogue. And once you have your first page, press on. See if you can develop this beginning into a story. Call it 'Something is happening out there'.

Point of view is commonly understood in grammatical terms, as if it were merely a matter of preferring one pronoun over another – whether 'I', 'you', 'he' or 'she' – which will determine whether the narrative is termed 'first person', 'second person' or 'third person' (each of which has a plural as well as a singular form, of course: 'we', 'you' and 'they').

Yet as I suggested towards the end of the previous chapter, the decisions taken in determining point of view will be among the most important a writer may take in the shaping of any fictional narrative. This is because they involve so much more than the question of who is telling the tale, and about whom – crucial as these two considerations may be.

Point of view, as ought to be obvious, concerns perception first of all, the issue of what can be *viewed* (or seen) and, by ready implication, what can't be seen. Related to this – as I emphasised in Chapter 4 – it will also concern what can and can't be heard, smelled, tasted or touched.

Perhaps a little less obviously, point of view defines the limits of what can be known or understood, both by the narrator and by the reader, and this will have major implications for the degree of suspense or mystery or simple human interest a story may generate. This question of 'knowability' will then raise the issue of 'reliability', since the narrator may appear to know more than she reveals, or may 'reveal' what turns out not to be true, or may appear to understand events rather less clearly than the reader does (in which case the reader will sense some higher, authorial intelligence, some other point of view above or behind the narrative point of view). In addition, in common parlance, to speak of having a point of view is to speak of having an opinion, whether or not this is openly expressed. Point of view will then imply a moral, ideological and psychological attitude towards the events being described, as was evident from the opening lines of *The Catcher in the Rye*, which I quoted in the previous chapter.

In what follows I do in fact intend to proceed by pronouns, taking first, second and third person narration in turn. But there is clearly a degree of complexity to the issue of point of view – more, indeed, than this initial survey reveals – and so it may be worth acknowledging one or two other considerations, a few further complexities, before we go on.

There is for example a temporal dimension, which will determine the grammatical tense in which a story is told, whether past, present or, in some cases, future. This will depend on whether the narration is related in retrospect – whether from a distance of many years or from some much closer vantage, offering fewer benefits of hindsight – or is simultaneous with the events being described – fully in the present moment, fully in the present tense – or is written in anticipation of events still to come. Each of these will again have implications for what can be known and what might be revealed.

The nature of our engagement with the fictional world will rest, additionally, on whether the narrator is inside or outside the events of the story; which is to say, on whether she is dramatised as one of the fictional characters or remains in some way impersonal and objective, an external commentator. Either of these two options will then entail further possibilities. The dramatised narrator may be a central character or merely a witness – an interested onlooker – while the external narrator will demonstrate a greater or lesser psychological distance on her characters, a greater or lesser degree of intimacy with their innermost feelings and thoughts.

Connected to this question of intimacy will then come the question of whether the narrator is able to see into the hearts and minds of all of her characters, or just a few of them, or just one of them. And even if she is able to penetrate to the inner lives of all of them, we may yet wonder if there is some small gap – some small degree of ironical distance – between the narrative voice and the assumed or implicit views of the author.

And finally – for this survey at least – whether internal or external, reliable or unreliable, limited or omniscient, the narrator may be more or less self-conscious, more or less inclined to draw attention to the fact that she is telling or writing a story; which is to say, she may be more or less inclined to address the reader directly, advertising a narrative point of view that is quite separate from the main character's point of view – and which may also, in some subtle measure, need to be distinguished from the assumed perspective of the author.

Perhaps unsurprisingly, a good many academic careers have been built on such considerations, narrative point of view being but one concern of the scholarly discipline of 'narratology'. Yet each of these issues is present, to some degree, in every novel and short story you will ever have read – and in general they do not present any obstacle to your understanding or enjoyment of those narratives. They are, indeed, central to the pleasure you may derive from them; they are part and parcel of the experience of the vivid and continuous dream.

My purpose, then, in offering this further account of the intricacies of point of view is not to intimidate or obfuscate, but to reveal to you something of your own sophistication as a reader. Most of us will read – and read fluently – without being aware of these issues or terms. We don't need to know we are reading a past tense, third person objective narration to engage with Ernest Hemingway's 'Hills Like White Elephants', or a present tense, first person protagonist narration to enjoy Ian McEwan's 'Last Day of Summer'.

However, if we are to attempt to emulate such narratives, it may help us to be aware of at least some of the terms, some of the issues. And principal among these – fundamental, in fact – is the distinction between 'who sees?' and 'who speaks?'

This is a distinction first made by the most distinguished and influential of the narratologists, the French structuralist scholar Gérard Genette. In his major work – *Narrative Discourse: An Essay in Method* – Genette identifies a confusion in most other accounts of point of view concerning 'the question *who is the character whose point of view orients the narrative perspective?* and the very different question *who is the narrator?*'

The difference between these two questions may be illustrated by returning to our extract from *Common Ground*, where clearly it is Ashley whose point of view orients the narrative perspective: it is Ashley 'who sees'. He is the one looking out of the window, and who turns and looks at Jay. We are not offered Jay's view of Ashley, or of the room, or of the street. More than this, it is Ashley who hears the window shaking in its frame, and the gas fire hissing. Conceivably, Jay also hears these things, but because the visual information is entirely filtered through Ashley's perceptions, we must assume that the aural information comes through him, too. And then there is the perceptual dimension that concerns a character's thoughts, feelings and reactions. Consider these two sentences:

> Her gaze was direct, defenceless, and he felt a lift of excitement, almost elation. He sensed it was £50 lost, but would not admit it, feared his disappointment if she was mistaken.

We are not permitted an equivalent insight into Jay's inner life. If we are to understand anything of her feelings and fears, this must be gleaned either from Ashley's observations of her demeanour, or from the things she says to him. In other words, she must vocalise her feelings to Ashley, and if he hears her, we hear her (and if he doesn't, we don't).

To adopt another term from Genette, we might say that the narrative is *focalised* through Ashley. Everything is mediated through his consciousness. But it is not Ashley 'who speaks'. If it were, the narrative pronouns would be different: not 'he' but 'I', not 'himself' but 'myself', and so on. It would look like this:

> The window shook in its frame and then the rain came. I wrapped myself in a blanket and stood closer to the heater. I faced into the street. On the opposite kerb a red car had been abandoned beneath a shedding sycamore . . .
>
> I turned to Jay and said, 'I'll bet you fifty quid you're not.'
>
> 'You don't have fifty quid, Ashley,' she replied, and raised one knee to the height of her shoulder. She was sitting on the edge of our bed, carefully shearing her toenails with a pair of dressmaking scissors.
>
> 'I have employment,' I reminded her. 'I work.'

In its original form, the opening to *Common Ground* is third person, past tense. To qualify this further, it is third person *limited*, because the point of view is confined to Ashley's perceptions alone. And so the answer to the question 'who speaks?' is not 'Ashley' but 'a third person (limited) narrator'.

In my revised form of this opening, meanwhile, the narration is first person, past tense. To qualify this further, it is first person *protagonist*, because the narrator is a central participant in the events he is describing. He is *internal* to the events of the story and – unavoidably – these events must be focalised through him. So the answer to the question 'who sees?' is again 'Ashley'. However, it would be wrong to say that the answer to the question 'who speaks?' is also 'Ashley'. Or rather, it would be wrong to say that it is 'the *same* Ashley'.

This is because the events are narrated in the grammatical past tense. We must therefore assume a delay between the time of the events and the time of their narration. Another way of expressing this is to say that there's a differ-ence between 'the time of the told' (the events) and 'the time of the telling' (the narration). In this instance the temporal gap is unspecified: it might be a few seconds; it could be several years. But whatever it may be, for Ashley to comment upon himself in the past tense he must, logically, be older than the Ashley he is describing. The two Ashleys are not, quite, identical.

This is a subtle distinction and, arguably, not a significant one. In numer-ous other first person narratives it will be much more meaningful, however, one example being L.P. Hartley's novel *The Go-Between*, which I mentioned in passing in the previous chapter.

Here the narrator, Leo Colston, is a man in his sixties – world-weary, some-what buttoned-up – who is prompted by the discovery of an old diary to recollect the events of a long-distant summer when, in his innocence and enthusiasm, he allowed himself to become the intermediary – the go-between – in an affair between an upper-class young woman, engaged to be married, and a local tenant farmer. This affair culminated in the suicide of the farmer, an outcome for which Leo has always felt in some way culpable. His recollections are therefore painful, and poignant, and this poignancy is made possible by the temporal gap in the narration, the distance between 'the time of the telling' and 'the time of the told'. In other words, the emotional complexity of the novel depends on its being written in the first person, past tense, and narrated from a position of regretful hindsight. It depends on there being a significant difference between 'who sees' (a schoolboy) and 'who speaks' (an old man).

It is almost inconceivable that L.P. Hartley might have envisaged a novel in which the Leo 'who sees' and the Leo 'who speaks' were one and the same, because this would have robbed *The Go-Between* of most of its power and resonance (not to mention its famous first line). To imagine a version of *Common Ground* in which the two Ashleys become identical is not so difficult, however. The narrative would simply need to be rendered in the first person, present tense. This, indeed, is the only way technically to collapse the gap between 'the time of the telling' and 'the time of the told', and in this case would result in the following:

> The window shakes in its frame and then the rain comes. I wrap myself in a blanket and stand closer to the heater. I face into the street. On the opposite kerb a red car has been abandoned beneath a shedding sycamore . . .
>
> I turn to Jay and say, 'I'll bet you fifty quid you're not.'
>
> 'You don't have fifty quid, Ashley,' she replies, and raises one knee to the height of her shoulder. She is sitting on the edge of our bed, carefully shearing her toenails with a pair of dressmaking scissors.
>
> 'I have employment,' I remind her. 'I work.'

Arguably this loses a little in tone; it loses, perhaps, the minimal element of poignancy – of time already gone – that makes any past tense narration seem to resonate. What it gains (though this, too, may be arguable) is a greater sense of immediacy. The following exercise asks you to collapse the temporal gap, and to change the narrative focus; it asks you to substitute poignancy, perhaps, for immediacy.

---

46. Something else is happening

You are going to attempt three variations on the scene (or first page) that you wrote in response to the previous exercise.

1. *'Who sees' remains the same; 'who speaks' is different.* While keeping everything else more or less the same, render the narrative into first person by carefully changing each of the pronouns (including the possessive pronouns, so that 'his' becomes 'my', etc.).
2. *'Who sees' is different; 'who speaks' remains the same.* Change the narrative point of view by rewriting the scene from the perspective of the other character, the one who isn't next to the window. The narrative should remain third person limited, past tense, but differently focalised.
3. *'Who sees' is different; 'who speaks' is different.* Finally, rewrite the scene so that it becomes first person, present tense, again from the point of view of the character who isn't next to the window.

Consider the subtle (and not so subtle) differences of effect created by each of these variations.

In this and previous chapters I've quoted passages from a number of first person narratives. Some are from short stories, some from novels. Some are past tense, some present. Some are more interior than others; some occur in novels that contain several viewpoints. But in each instance, what they have in common is that the narrator is an active participant in the events that he or she describes. Each of them offers an example of first person *protagonist* narration.

This is the most common form of 'I' narration. And the most common variation upon it is the first person *multiple* novel in which the storytelling passes from one protagonist to another (and then to another, and another, and so on). Perhaps the most famous example is William Faulkner's modernist classic

As I Lay Dying, which alternates the perspectives of fifteeen narrators across fifty-nine chapters, the longest chapter being just eight pages, the shortest being just five words. But while it might be assumed that the distinguishing feature of first person narration is that it brings us closer to the truth of a situation – the character is after all speaking on his own behalf, unmediated by any other person's point of view – what the first person multiple novel tends to reveal is the extent to which overlapping perspectives may actually contradict rather than corroborate each other. Because we are allowed several accounts of the same story, we gain a sense of the unreliability of any singular view – sometimes to subtly ambiguous effect, sometimes to starkly dramatic effect.

One powerful example of this is John Fowles's novel *The Collector*, which offers a minimal version of the 'multiple' narrative by alternating just two voices, representing two markedly different perspectives on a shared situation. Here the dominating voice belongs to socially awkward, possibly psychotic Frederick Clegg, who abducts an art student, Miranda Grey, on whom he has been spying for several years. An amateur lepidopterist, Frederick has always coveted Miranda as a rare and beautiful example of her genus, and he fantasises that she might come to admire him, too, if only she were to be given the opportunity. That opportunity arrives when he wins the football pools. He is then able to buy a large, isolated house with a basement, in which he 'collects' and imprisons Miranda.

Such is Frederick's self-justification, or self-deception, he insists on viewing Miranda not as his captive but as his guest. For the most part he treats her with great courtesy, even indulgence, but when she tries to escape he uses chloroform to subdue her, then seizes the opportunity to take some photographs of her in a state of semi-undress. Even this he contrives to present as an example of his restraint – 'it wasn't so bad; not many would have kept control of themselves, just taken photos, it was almost a point in my favour' – and he finds her subsequent treatment of him to be quite unreasonable:

> One day soon after, I brought in a plate of perfectly nice baked beans on toast and she just picked it up and hurled it straight at me. I felt like giving her a good clip over the earhole. About this time I was fed up with the whole thing, there didn't seem any point in it, I tried everything, but she would keep on holding that evening against me.

The Collector is written in three parts, with Frederick's narrative coming first and last, enclosing Miranda's. And while his account is related with hindsight, meaning that he's always aware of what is to come in the story, Miranda's narrative is presented in the form of a diary, meaning that she's always at the mercy of uncertainty, the unknowability of what is to follow.

For Frederick, the 'time of the telling' is some distance beyond the 'time of the told': all of these events have already happened, and so the Frederick 'who speaks' is able to place on the page what he hopes will be a favourable impression of the Frederick 'who sees'.

But Miranda is denied that liberty, among others. Her diary is imprisoned both within Frederick's narration, and within the 'time of the told'. The Miranda 'who sees' and the Miranda 'who speaks' are almost identical, and therein lies the horror of her situation: she is denied the possibility of hindsight.[1]

Despite Frederick's fantasies, he and Miranda could never be compatible. Social class divides them, sensibility, intelligence, self-awareness. But a large part of the tension and tragedy is created not by anything they say or do, but by something more technical than that: by the temporal disparity in their respective points of view.

---

47. Captors and captives

Here is a list of captors:

a bank robber estranged from his three children
a bodybuilder who was bullied at school
a female freedom fighter
a perfect gentleman
a girl with a dragon tattoo
a religious fundamentalist father
a woman with a history of breakdowns
a young man, just taking orders

Here is a list of captives:

an angry child whose parents are wealthy
a cleaner with a sick husband
the daughter of a fundamentalist family, unsure of her faith
a newly pregnant woman, out shopping
a once famous pop star
a soldier on leave from a war zone

---

[1] Or rather, she is allowed some very limited hindsight. She is able to reflect in her diary upon the events of the previous day, and of her life prior to her abduction. But what she cannot do is reflect upon the period of her imprisonment from a later place of safety.

a teenage girl in her best outfit, new shoes
a young woman in a massage parlour

Version 1: Choose one person from each list and write a first person narrative in two parts. Have both characters describe exactly the same event, in the past tense: first one, then the other.

Version 2: Choose one person from each list and write a first person narrative in short alternating sections. First one narrates, then the other, but they do not describe exactly the same event: they take it in turns to move the story on. Neither narrative should be 'aware' of the other. Both should be present tense.

Version 3: Choose one person from each list and write a first person narrative in three parts. The middle part should be from the point of view of the captive. It can be in diary form, but doesn't have to be. It must be in the present tense. The first and final parts should be from the point of view of the captor. These must be in the past tense. They should also be 'unreliable' to some extent: the captor is seeking to justify his or her actions.

One other interesting variation on first person narration,[2] which also serves to emphasise unreliability and the difficulty of penetrating to the truth of a person or situation, is first person *witness* narration.

Here the 'I' offers an account of something he has observed, usually at close quarters, usually as a minor participant, but adopting a perspective comparable to that of a third person narrator, his principal role being to describe and comment on the behaviour of others, albeit from a vantage that is internal to the events of the story. One classic example of this is F. Scott Fitzgerald's *The Great Gatsby*, in which the narrator, Nick Carraway, is drawn into the ambit of his charismatic and extravagantly wealthy neighbour, Jay Gatsby, who is introduced to the reader initially only by reputation and rumour. Gradually, over the course of the novel, the personality behind Gatsby's persona begins to emerge as Nick becomes increasingly involved – and implicated – in the complications of Gatsby's existence. To some extent Nick cannot help but be affected, and altered, by the events he describes, but the narrative interest remains far less about him than about the uncertainties surrounding the 'great'

[2] A further variation, which I don't intend to cover here, is first person *plural* narration, a rare phenomenon exemplified by Jeffrey Eugenides's *The Virgin Suicides*, in which the story of five long-deceased sisters – all suicides – is pieced together by a chorus of their admirers, a group of anonymous adolescent boys now grown to middle-age, who refer to themselves throughout as 'we' and 'us'.

Gatsby; it is far less about the first person 'I' than the process of unravelling the enigma presented by the third person 'he'.[3]

---

48. *Eye witness*

1. Look again at the list of captors in Exercise 47. This time imagine that you are an accomplice of one of these characters. Describe a scene after you have taken your hostage(s). Write in the first person as a minor participant, a secondary character. Your main interest is the behaviour and personality of the other person. Write in the present tense.
2. Now return to the list of captives. Imagine that you were taken hostage along with one of these characters, and that you have now been asked to describe what happened. You could be under police protection, giving evidence, or in a court of law, or speaking to a journalist, or simply writing a memoir of the event. Again, your main interest is the behaviour of others. Write in the past tense.

One of the main effects of first person point of view is to personalise and particularise a story and thereby draw the reader into a relationship of apparent intimacy with the 'speaker' and the world she inhabits. This relationship can take on a quality of directness and immediacy that isn't available to third person narration. And as we saw in Chapter 6, the use of the personal pronoun – the seemingly autobiographical 'I' – can appear to authenticate the tale as the 'true story' of the narrator. In many discussions of first person narration, in fact, the terms 'authentic' and 'truthful' are applied as near synonyms. But as we have seen, what lends authenticity to the account may be the very unreliability of the first person perspective; authenticity may be achieved by way of a failure to arrive at the truth, whether deliberate or otherwise.

---

[3] Another canonical example is Emily Brontë's *Wuthering Heights*, which has the additional interest (or complication) of embedding one first person witness narration – the servant Nelly Dean's – within a second, 'framing' witness narration – the neighbour Lockwood's. Nelly tells the story of Catherine and Heathcliff to Lockwood, who records it in his diary, along with his own present day observations of Heathcliff. Joseph Conrad's *Heart of Darkness* employs a similar device of nesting one narration within another. Here the framing narrator speaks in the first person plural – 'we' and 'us' – on behalf of a group of men on board a ship on the Thames, one of whom is Charlie Marlow, who begins to relate the story of his journey to the heart of the Congo, where he encountered the mysterious Kurtz, a man as charismatic as Gatsby and considerably more brutal than Heathcliff.

With *second person* narration, meanwhile, the main effect is not to person-alise but to universalise, while retaining much of the particularity of the first person account. The use of the second person pronoun – 'you' – cannot help but implicate the reader. Addressed directly in this way, the reader cannot help but participate imaginatively in the events being depicted. Narrator and reader become one; the experience is shared. And of course, because the reader is never specified, it could be anyone; it could be everyone.

One common mode of second person address with which we are all familiar is the imperative voice found in recipes, instruction manuals and guidebooks – including guidebooks like this one. This form lends itself particularly well to the short story, as exemplified by Peter Ho Davies's 'How to Be an Expatriate', in which the 'you' moves from England to America, becomes an academic, becomes a philanderer, marries and divorces an American wife, and gradually loses a sense of who he used to be. The story presents, in a way, a set of instruc-tions in how to go wrong:

> Tell your wife you've noticed you're spelling words like *realize* with a *z*. Stare at her blankly when she says, 'A zee? You mean a zed. A zee!' Ask her if she thinks you're losing your accent. Hear her say, 'I don't *think* so.'
>
> When people ask you where you're from, start to say, 'Originally?'
>
> Be wary of other British people. Avoid them at parties. Feign surprise when your colleagues introduce you to their British graduate students. Say, 'Oh, hello.' They look pale and half starved. Notice how bad their teeth are.

Many of the incidental details in 'How to Be an Expatriate' have something of the specificity of lived experience – the stuff of observational journals, per-haps – which creates a curiously dualled and contradictory effect: the narrative appears to be both universal *and* autobiographical, both generally applicable *and* highly individual. Of course, it is no more (or less) autobiographical than first (or third) person narration. And the effect of universality is no more than just that: an effect. But even as the depiction of this expatriate darkens – presenting a personality with whom we would not wish to identify – the insinuating power of the second person address draws us into a relationship of queasy intimacy with him. His actions and attitudes are also ours, since we are also, always, the 'you'.

This potential for insisting on an intimacy that may not be welcome is exploited to harrowing effect by Nancy Lee in her collection of linked short stories, *Dead Girls*. Stalking the margins of each of these technically startling narratives is the story of a recently captured serial killer: 'You are addicted to television news', the title story begins. 'The speculation, the body bags, the hopeful high school photos; dead girls, everywhere.' Gradually it emerges that the 'you' is a mother fearful that her only child may be among the victims, a prostitute and drug-addict long since lost to her parents. And so in addition to memories of the daughter's birth and her first day in kindergarten, we are presented with images of finding her 'at fourteen, in the garage with a boy, her panties clutched in a fist behind her back' and of meeting her 'in the bright light of the glass-walled treatment centre' just before her final disappearance. The body count reaches twenty-three, and as the story delineates the mother's hope and despair, it also describes the desolation of her marriage as she and her husband become estranged from each other:

> You and your husband have not had sex in over a year. You have thrown out your birth control pills, lubricants, anticipating that you will never have sex again. It is as if the two of you have been accomplices in an unspeakable crime and can no longer return to the backroom of its conception. You move around your house like cautious guests, clothing wrapped tightly, eyes averted.

But they do have sex again, violently, after the mother returns from a search of the red light district, where she has just witnessed a dismal transaction in an alleyway, a scene her own daughter will have enacted any number of times, and while the violence in this case is redemptive, a release from numbness and a means of connecting again with her husband, it is also unavoidably disturbing, because of course the mother is never actually a 'she': she is always a 'you', and so we are compelled to share in her grief, and the pain she inflicts on herself.

---

49. You

1. In Chapter 5 you completed a sequence of exercises (21 to 25) that drew on autobiographical material to explore the experience of loss. Revisit one of these pieces now and attempt to rewrite it in the second person, present tense.
2. Select a favourite short story or the opening pages of a favourite novel that is written in the first person. Attempt to render this in the second person, too.
3. Whether drawing on experience or imagination, write a scene or short story in which the 'you' brings about the end of a relationship, whether deliberately or by neglect. Write this scene or story in the manner of 'How to Be an Expatriate', almost as if it were a set of instructions. Note that not all of the sentences need be instructions. Some may be observations and statements. Write in the present tense. Keep the details specific, fully particularised.

To some extent, the 'you' in both 'How to Be an Expatriate' and *Dead Girls* is similar to the more formal 'one', a means of distancing the 'I' from itself by means of a pronoun. In the former story the motivation for this distancing may be self-disgust; in the latter it's something more complex, a form perhaps of self-protection.[4] But in both instances the 'you' is the main protagonist in the events of the story, as fully involved as any first person narrator. The 'you', in Gérard Genette's terms, is *'the character whose point of view orients the narrative perspective'*. The narrative is entirely 'focalised' by the 'you'; it is the 'you' 'who sees'.

If I labour this point it is because there are two varieties of second person address that are arguably more common, and equally as interesting, but which do not constitute second person point of view. In the first of these, a first person narrator addresses the reader directly as 'you'. In the second, a first person narrator addresses another character as 'you'.

A straightforward example of the first possibility is encapsulated in one of the most famous lines in English literature – 'Reader, I married him' – which occurs in the final chapter of Charlotte's Brontë's *Jane Eyre*, a book that was considered somewhat scandalous at the time of its publication in 1847 for allowing a mere governess so individual and forthright a voice. A more ambiguous example, meanwhile, is to be found in *The Catcher in the Rye*, where the person 'who speaks' and the person 'who sees' are clearly one and the same: Holden Caulfield is a first person narrator. And he addresses an unspecified 'you' ('If you really want to hear about it . . .'). But while we might assume (as I tend to) that this 'you' is the reader, someone external to the world of the fiction, it is equally possible (since Holden is currently residing in a psychiatric institution) to suppose that he is addressing an unnamed, unseen psychiatrist, someone internal to the world of the fiction.

A less ambiguous example of a narrative addressed to someone internal to the fiction is offered by Marilynne Robinson's Pulitzer Prize-winning novel *Gilead*, which takes the form of a series of letters written by an elderly pastor to his seven-year-old son in the hope that one day the boy will be able to read them and so come to know and understand his father, who will long since have passed on. It begins:

[4] Second person is a notoriously difficult form to sustain over the length of a novel – partly, perhaps, because it may come to feel hectoring. One much-cited exception is Jay McInerney's *Bright Lights, Big City*, which describes the drug-fuelled existence of a disaffected fact-checker on a prestigious New York magazine. Here, too, there is self-disgust and self-protection: his frenetic lifestyle is ultimately revealed to be a means of numbing the pain of his mother's death and his recent divorce. A key critique of the yuppie values of the 1980s, the novel is additionally interesting because the 'you' comes to sound a little like an accusation of the age.

I told you last night that I might be gone sometime, and you said, Where, and I said, To be with the Good Lord, and you said, Why, and I said, Because I am old, and you said, I don't think you're old. And you put your hand in my hand and you said, You aren't very old, as if that settled it. I told you you might have a very different life from mine, and from the life you've had with me, and that would be a wonderful thing, there are many ways to live a good life. And you said, Mama already told me that.

Gilead is only loosely an epistolary novel. The pastor himself refers to 'these letters', and makes passing reference to the passage of time, but adopts none of the formal conventions of date headings, salutations, and so on. And of course he receives no letters in reply. In common with all epistolary novels, the 'you' is very much present in the heart and mind of the 'I', and is entirely internal to the fictional world, while remaining physically absent at the time the letter is written. But without the formal conventions, the narrative in *Gilead* becomes in effect an imaginary (if one-sided) conversation, and possibly takes on an additional strangeness and power because of that.

---

50. *You, too*

Return to the lists of captors and captives in Exercise 47. Chose one person – either a captor or a captive – and write a first person narrative in which this person explains him- or herself to someone else, an absent 'you'. That 'you' may be the reader, someone external to the fiction. Or it may be a significant other person in the narrator's life, someone internal to the fictional frame, but physically absent. This could take the form of a letter, or an imaginary conversation, a monologue. It isn't necessary to include the scenario of hostage-taking.

I suggested earlier that point of view does not simply define the limits of what can be seen, but has significant implications for what can be known or understood. In the case of first person narration, the reader can only see what the 'I' sees, and only know as much as the 'I' chooses to reveal.[5] Similarly with

---

[5] This is to put it somewhat simplistically. The example of Frederick in *The Collector* alerts us to the possibility of authorial irony: implicit in the characterisation of Frederick is another, higher point of view, which appears to be John Fowles's critical or satirical perspective upon him.

second person narration, the reader can only see what the 'you' sees and know what the 'you' knows. With third person narration, meanwhile, the common assumption is that there are no limits on what might be shown or known; third person is very often taken to mean omniscience.

In the fully omniscient short story or novel the narrator is able to know everything about everyone – perhaps better than they know themselves – and is able to shift from one character's thoughts and feelings to another's with relative ease (the main constraint, in fact, may be one of technique, the author's ability to manage the 'choreography' involved in this movement from one mind to the next). In addition to this unlimited access to the characters' inner lives, the omniscient narrator can range freely in space and time, visiting locations before the characters arrive, lingering after they have departed, revealing what may be in store for them, and remembering what they may have forgotten.

The fully omniscient narrator is god-like, in other words, possessed of an apparently infinite authority over the world of the fiction, in the same way, perhaps, that the imperial powers of the nineteenth century – the age most closely associated with the third person, omniscient novel – exercised a temporal authority over much of the globe, when all lands seemed conquerable, all peoples knowable (at least, from a European perspective). The decline of both religious faith and imperial self-confidence in the West accounts, perhaps, for the relative rarity of the fully omniscient novel in our more doubting, sceptical, post-colonial age. And possibly, too – if this isn't too speculative – it is the growing self-confidence of the formerly colonised that accounts for one of the most striking novels to emerge at the end of the twentieth century, Vikram Seth's *A Suitable Boy*, which is set in newly independent India and appears quite anomalous in its Victorian bulk and omniscient self-assurance.

Opening Seth's novel at random, we find this paragraph on page 67 of its 1,474 pages:

> Arpana got down reluctantly from the bed and made her way to the door. She toyed with the idea of saying, 'I'll tell Daddy!' though what she could have complained about was left unformulated. Her mother meanwhile was once again sleeping sweetly, her lips slightly parted, her long black hair spread across the pillow. It was so hot in the afternoon, and everything tilted her towards a long and languorous sleep. Her breasts rose and fell gently, and she dreamed about Arun, who was handsome and dashing and covenanted, and who would be coming home in an hour.

Besides being allowed access to the thoughts of three-year-old Arpana and the dreamlife of her mother Meenakshi, elsewhere in this chapter we will be privileged with an insight into the inner life of Meenakshi's husband, Arun, and of his mother, Mrs Rupa Mehra. Over the course of the novel, these and dozens of other characters will be granted a point of view, among them servants and government officials, children and captains of industry. Additionally, dozens of others will appear on the page without being granted a point of view, and in this, as in so much else, *A Suitable Boy* conforms to the conventions of the great novels of the Victorian age, which were similarly selective in their omniscience. Infinite knowledge might otherwise result in novels of infinite length, and diminishing interest, since the success of any fiction will depend as much on what is withheld or concealed as on what is revealed.

Another, more recent Indian novel is Anjali Joseph's *Saraswati Park*, which is a good deal less expansive – or encyclopaedic – than *A Suitable Boy*, but no less self-assured in its omniscience, and no less delicate in its observations. Here in suburban Bombay we find three principal characters: Mohan, his wife Lakshmi, and their nephew Ashish. Other characters illuminate the page, but only these three are privileged with a point of view. For the most part, however, this point of view is confined, for the duration of each successive chapter, to one or other of the three principals.

Thus, in one chapter, the narrative will be focalised entirely through Mohan:

> Lakshmi, sitting on the bed and plaiting her hair, was silent. Her expressions these days were bruised, as though she existed under a perpetual affront.
> 'Will you come with me?' he asked.
> She shook her head, and began to tie a thread round the end of the plait. He noticed, incongruously, the grey hairs at the side of her head, and that she looked like a little girl in her printed nightdress.

Then, in another chapter, the narrative will be focalised entirely through Lakshmi:

> Mohan's breathing and his gentle snoring continued. In the first part of the night he slept on his back; she regarded his unmoving bulk under the sheet while the fan whirled hectically. The usual sighs, followed by the gravelly exhalation every third breath, were at first reassuring; soon after, they began to irritate her. Slightly later, everything oppressive in the room and the world . . . which might have been minor at another time of day, seemed to emanate from the serene, infuriating exhalations of the figure next to her. She got up and adjusted the fan. There was no satisfactory setting for it. When at a slower speed, it nearly forgot to turn, but at a medium it flew into a frenzy.

It is in fact the couple's nephew Ashish whose point of view predominates, but the novel is never exclusively his, and in this respect *Saraswati Park* occupies a position of relative omniscience – if that is not too much of a contradiction in terms – being some distance from the pole of god-like omniscience, but falling just short of what is perhaps the most common form of restricted omniscience: third person *limited* narration, in which the narrator appears to know everything about one character only, while sharing that character's restricted understanding or knowledge of every other character.

As I remarked earlier, the passage from *Common Ground* with which this chapter began is an example of third person limited narration. Flannery O'Connor's short story 'A Stroke of Good Fortune', which I quoted in Chapter 4, is another. James Joyce's *A Portrait of the Artist as a Young Man* is a third. And while in each of these instances it is the central character 'who sees' and an anonymous third person narrator 'who speaks', the narrative voice is additionally inflected or coloured by the personality or psychology of the central character, as may be illustrated by Joyce's *A Portrait*, which famously follows the development of Stephen Dedalus from infancy to young adulthood. This novel begins:

> Once upon a time and a very good time it was there was a moocow coming down along the road and this moocow that was coming down along the road met a nicens little boy named baby tuckoo. . . .
>   His father told him that story: his father looked at him through a glass: he had a hairy face.

By the end of the novel, however, we have come to know Stephen as a lovelorn, poetical, somewhat pretentious undergraduate:

> Towards dawn he awoke. O what sweet music! His soul was all dewy wet. Over his limbs in sleep pale cool waves of light had passed. He lay still, as if his soul lay amid cool waters, conscious of faint sweet music. His mind was waking slowly to a tremulous morning knowledge, a morning inspiration. A spirit filled him, pure as the purest water, sweet as dew, moving as music.

This merging or alignment of the neutral, external voice of the narrator and the more characterful, internal voice of the protagonist is an example of 'free indirect style', which is a technique by which an author is able to achieve some of the immediacy and personality of first person narration while maintaining the authority and flexibility of third person. In effect, it closes the gap between the third person narrator and the inner life of the character, and thus between the reader and the character, a gap that is sometimes termed 'psychic distance', not least by John Gardner, who provides this useful explanation in *The Art of Fiction*:

> By psychic distance we mean the distance the reader feels between himself and the events in the story. Compare the following examples, the first meant to establish great psychic distance, the next meant to establish slightly less, and so on until in the last example, psychic distance, theoretically at least, is nil.

> 1. It was winter of the year 1853. A large man stepped out of a doorway.
> 2. Henry J. Warburton had never much cared for snowstorms.
> 3. Henry hated snowstorms.
> 4. God how he hated these damn snowstorms.
> 5. Snow. Under your collar, down inside your shoes, freezing and plugging up your miserable soul . . .

In practice, of course, it frequently happens that the psychic distance narrows and widens continuously. A novel might well begin, 'It was winter of the year 1853. A large man stepped out of a doorway.' And then within a few lines we might plausibly encounter the sentence, 'God how he hated these damn snowstorms.' Consider again, for example, these opening lines from Virginia Woolf's *Mrs Dalloway*:

> What a lark! What a plunge! For so it had always seemed to her, when, with a little squeak of the hinges, which she could hear now, she had burst open the French windows and plunged at Bourton into the open air. How fresh, how calm, stiller than this of course, the air was in the early morning; like the flap of a wave; the kiss of a wave; chill and sharp and yet (for a girl of eighteen as she then was) solemn, feeling as she did, standing there at the open window, that something awful was about to happen . . .

The first two phrases in this instance are free indirect style, largely internal to Mrs Dalloway's mind, whereas the sentence beginning, 'For so it had always seemed to her . . .' is much more the external voice of the narrator, much less the voice of the character. Woolf begins very 'close', then immediately widens the psychic distance, only to narrow it again in the very next sentence: 'How fresh, how calm . . .'

The stream of consciousness technique associated with Woolf (and Joyce), and which is partially exemplified here, corresponds to John Gardner's fifth variation on psychic distance, in which the gap between reader and character is, 'theoretically at least', nil. Should Gardner's first example be sustained for the length of a story, meanwhile, we would have the maximum gap, corresponding to third person *objective* narration, in which the narrator sees and hears only as much as is seen and heard by the characters, but does not have access to their thoughts and feelings, and maintains a strictly neutral attitude towards them.

Third person objective narration depends, we might say, upon the absence of free indirect style, which might be illustrated by Ernest Hemingway's 'rigorously impersonal'[6] short story 'Hills Like White Elephants', which I quoted in the previous chapter. This story concludes:

> He picked up the two heavy bags and carried them around the station to the other tracks. He looked up the tracks but could not see the train. Coming back, he walked through the bar-room, where people waiting for the train were drinking. He drank an Anis at the bar and looked at the people. They were all waiting reasonably for the train. He went out through the bead curtain. She was sitting at the table and smiled at him.
>
>   'Do you feel better?' he asked.
>
>   'I feel fine,' she said. 'There's nothing wrong with me. I feel fine.'

It might be argued that the word 'reasonably' in this passage lacks a degree of impersonality, brilliant though it certainly is. The perception that the other people are waiting 'reasonably' might be the character's, or the narrator's; either way, it is subtly expressive of a perspective that is evaluative and therefore lacking in neutrality or objectivity. This is to split hairs of course, but it points towards the possibility of greater, more glaring inconsistencies. Hemingway might have given us the private thoughts of one of the people waiting in the bar-room, for example, if only for a sentence or two. He might have shifted momentarily to first or second person, or to Joycean stream of consciousness. Such departures can work. As David Lodge points out in *The Art of Fiction*, 'there is no rule or regulation that says a novel may not shift its point of view whenever the writer chooses'. But these departures need to be justified; they need to be done 'according to some aesthetic plan or principle' or else the author's authority over the fiction may be lost, along with the reader's engagement.

All of which is to say, whatever type of narrator you choose, he or she or it will be your reader's only guide into the world of your fiction. Without the narrator, in fact, there can be no access to your fictional world. It is therefore

---

[6] The phrase 'rigorously impersonal' is Wayne Booth's in *The Rhetoric of Fiction* (1961), and is used about another Hemingway story, 'The Killers'.

crucial that the reader has confidence in your narrator, and key to establishing that confidence is consistency. Every novel and short story will establish the terms of its own reading; it will create its own 'rules', its own 'regulations'. But once established, those rules need, above all, to be consistently followed.

---

51. Third, and finally

Look again at the list of captors and captives in Exercise 47. This time choose four of them. You may want to retain the hostage-taking scenario, or imagine some other context in which the four are brought together: an AA meeting, a board meeting, a wedding reception, a dinner party, the aftermath of an explosion, the build-up to a confrontation.

1. Write a scene in the third person omniscient, in which the point of view passes freely from one character to another, as in *A Suitable Boy*. Allow us access to the inner world of each of your four characters. Inform us, too, of something they cannot know, something that may be in store for them.
2. Write a scene in the third person limited, from the point of view of one of these four characters, in which we are privileged with full access to this person's interior world, but can only speculate on the thoughts of the other three characters. Modulate the narrative so that it widens and narrows the psychic distance, verging at times on stream of consciousness.
3. Re-write one of these previous two scenes in the third person objective, describing only as much as your impersonal, objective narrator can see of the four characters' behaviour.

9.   Middles, ends, beginnings: structure

If I were coming into a classroom at this point, rather than the start of this chapter, I would begin by dividing my students into groups of three, and then, before any other discussion, I would set them this task (which of course you can attempt on your own, before you read on):

---

52.   Story vs plot

Within your group discuss the terms 'story' and 'plot' and attempt to come up with:

a.   a one-sentence definition of 'story'
b.   three characteristics of a story
c.   a one-sentence definition of 'plot'

   The middle person in each group is the scribe. After fifteen minutes, report your conclusions to the rest of the class.

Although the discussion that follows will be different each time, almost invariably two things will emerge from this exercise: a certain confusion about terminology – with some saying 'story' when others mean 'plot' – alongside a general agreement that any story (or perhaps I mean plot?) will have a beginning, a middle and an end.

Certainly this has always been my own assumption, and were I to attempt my own single-sentence definitions I might describe a story as 'a sequence of connected events having a beginning, middle and end', and a plot as 'a sequence of connected events having a beginning, middle and end, though not necessarily in that order'.[1]

The notion that there should be a beginning, middle and end is both ubiquitous and ancient and derives from Aristotle's *Poetics*, which precedes the emergence of the literary novel by two millennia, and is concerned primarily with the structure of Athenian tragedy as 'performed by actors, not through narration'. In other words, the *Poetics* is more about storytelling on the stage than on the page, though much remains applicable beyond the bounds of ancient Greek theatre.

Aristotle's treatise is brief, but complex, and suggests that tragedy is comprised of six elements: 'plot, character, reasoning, diction, song and spectacle'. Only the first of these need concern us here, though it may be worth noting in passing that the six elements are presented in order of importance, forming a definite hierarchy, with character entirely subservient to plot. This is to take a somewhat different view to many novelists, of course, including (as we saw in Chapter 6) Henry James and F. Scott Fitzgerald, for whom plot and character are seen as being so entangled as to be virtually indistinguishable. 'Character is plot, plot is character', Fitzgerald (reputedly) said, whereas for Aristotle, 'the plot is the source and (as it were) the soul of tragedy; character is second'.

What might be meant by 'plot' in the *Poetics* is defined in one translation as 'the organisation of events', and in another as 'the arrangement of the incidents'. In either case, this is to imply that 'story' is the natural chronological order of the events or incidents as they would have occurred in 'real life', before the shaping hand of the storyteller succeeded in turning them into a plot.

For Aristotle this plot must have 'completeness', by which he means that the beginning, middle and end must have a necessary and plausible connection and must form a self-contained whole. Within the compass of the play, the beginning should not be the consequence of anything else; rather, the beginning should *have* certain consequences. These will be described in detail in

---

[1] I've borrowed this last phrase from Flannery O'Connor, who says in *Mystery and Manners*: 'A good short story should not have less meaning than a novel, nor should its action be less complete. Nothing essential to the main experience can be left out of a short story. All the action has to be satisfactorily accounted for in terms of motivation, and there has to be a beginning, a middle, and an end, though not necessarily in that order.'

the middle, and while plots may be simple or complex they will always involve a change or reversal or a coming to awareness of some sort. The ending will then offer a satisfying sense of closure or resolution to all that precedes it, and will not lead to any further events beyond the scope of the play.

Malcolm Heath, the translator of the 1996 Penguin edition of the *Poetics*, summarises this nicely in his introduction:

> Consider by way of illustration a simple story: 'Bill strangled a cat. Ben strangled a cat.' This is not a 'complete' plot in Aristotelian terms. The two events have no necessary connection. So let us try again: 'Bill strangled Ben's cat. So Ben strangled Bill's cat in retaliation.' This is better: we can now see how the two events hang together; the series of events is connected. But is it self-contained? Why did the cat-strangling start in the first place? And was that the end of it? Let us try once more: 'Bill thought that his cat was going to lose to Ben's in the cat-show. So he strangled Ben's cat. Ben strangled Bill's cat in retaliation. They never spoke to each other again.' Now the story, connected and self-contained as it is, does satisfy Aristotle's criteria.

In screenwriting terms, Aristotle's conception of plot is sometimes represented as the 'three-act linear structure': set-up, development, pay-off. It is also often rephrased in terms of a five-stage sequence: situation, complication, crisis, climax, resolution.

In both of these schemes, far greater emphasis tends to be placed on the importance of character, and on the importance to the main character's fortunes of some form of conflict, whether internal (a dilemma) or external (a threat). The beginning will remain, by definition, what comes first, and in most narratives this will mean the introduction of the main protagonist, situated in a time and place, a setting. This is our 'set-up' or 'situation'. The protagonist's dilemma may be there from the outset; alternatively some catalyst, some 'inciting incident', will create a conflict that the protagonist must respond to. This will be our 'complication'. The middle will then describe the challenges that follow on from this dilemma or complication. This will be our 'crisis' (or more likely 'crises') and will usually take the form of a series of logically connected events that will involve a transformation or 'development' in the protagonist's fortunes, for better or worse, as well as some degree of change or development in the protagonist's character, for better or worse. This sequence of events will often involve a series of surprises, or reversals, which will build along an incline of rising action and tension and culminate in the narrative 'climax'. The ending will then offer a logical, plausible and organic conclusion to all that precedes it. This will be our 'pay-off' or 'resolution'.

53. *Diagnostics*

Some of the exercises you've attempted in previous chapters will have resulted in full-length short stories, for instance:

25. 'Lost'
33. Q&A gimmick
36. Still life
37. Two characters
41. Dramatic twist
45. Something is happening out there
49. You

You may well have written other stories, too, whether in response to exercises or not.

Look through your collection of stories now and select two of them: the one you are most satisfied with, and the one you are least satisfied with.

Write a plot précis for each of these two stories. This should be a straightforward list of what happens when and to whom. Then analyse these plot summaries in terms of Aristotle's *Poetics*:

• Is there a definite beginning, middle and end?
• Is the story complete and self-contained?
• Do the events have a causal connection?
• Is there a change or reversal or a coming to awareness of some sort?

Now consider each of your two stories in terms of the five-stage sequence: situation, complication, crisis, climax, resolution:

• Does your beginning situate your main protagonist in a definite time and place?
• Does your protagonist have a dilemma?
• What is the 'inciting incident' that creates a complication?
• What are the events that follow?
• Are these events causally connected?
• Do they involve conflict? Is this conflict internal or external?
• In what ways does your protagonist change or develop?

- Is there a definite narrative climax?
- What is the resolution?

There are any number of reasons why a story might not work. One of them is structural, and might be identified by this kind of analysis. Perhaps the story you find the most satisfying will conform to most of these criteria? Perhaps the story you find the least satisfying will not?

The *Poetics* is widely accepted as an example of literary theory that is readily applicable to the Creative Writing classroom. Much other 'critical' writing – especially contemporary literary theory – is presumed not to be so helpful, however. This is despite the exponential growth of Creative Writing as a discipline in academia, and despite the increasingly commonplace coupling of the 'creative' and the 'critical' in course descriptions, and the now widespread acceptance that creative and critical thinking are not entirely separate activities. Part of the reason for this may be that most actual writers of poems and plays, novels and stories will feel somewhat uncomfortable with the institutionalisation of what they do. Those who actually teach in the institutions may feel especially uncomfortable with the institutionalisation of what they do. And this institutionalisation will be symbolised, in part, by the encroachment of literary theory into the more practice-based, experiential 'discipline' of Creative Writing. Some writers – as I once did – may even consider themselves to be in flight from 'the critical', by which I mean the high-end literary theory that emerged as a swarm of *isms* in the sixties and seventies and had its heyday in the eighties, when I was a student.

As an undergraduate I studied Shakespeare, of course, and Tolstoy, and Dostoevsky, the Brontës, Conrad and Joyce, Lawrence, Eliot and Pound. I studied others besides, but the deities of my BA were not dramatists, poets or novelists; they were French-speaking theorists: Barthes, Althusser, Foucault, Lacan, Derrida. And I was an enthusiast, almost an evangelist. I committed myself to learning the languages of structuralism and poststructuralism; I dizzied myself on the difficulties of deconstructionism. Yet when I came to write my first stories I found them to be of no help to me; worse, they were a positive hindrance.

In simple terms, my sensibility was that of a literary realist, and the thrust of these theories was profoundly anti-realist. The 'real' was illusory – an effect of language – and so too was the 'I' who attempted to write about it. Self and society were 'ideological constructs'. All was 'text', or 'processes of signification'.

And the Author, as Roland Barthes had proclaimed in an essay of 1968, was dead.[2]

I was beguiled by much of this, but it was only as I began to forget or reject it that I felt able to find myself as a writer. Any attempt to write about what I knew was doomed, I came to realise, so long as I held to the view that 'I' did not exist and that my reality was not actually knowable.

Latterly, however, I have begun to make my way back to some of the key concepts I learned as a student, in part because my day-job in academia requires me to have at least a passing acquaintance with the canon of criticism, but also because certain of those concepts are of genuine help to the writer, in particular those that might be termed, broadly, 'narratological'. In the previous chapter, for instance, I drew on some of the important distinctions made by the narratologist Gérard Genette in his study of point of view. In Chapter 4 I introduced the concept of defamiliarisation, which I'll revisit in the next chapter and which is a cornerstone concept of the school of Russian Formalism.

Genette may be counted among the structuralists. In his analysis of Proust's *À la Recherche du Temps Perdu* he sought to identify and describe the codes and conventions that may be said to define all narrative fiction. By concentrating on the example of this one particular work, he sought to illuminate more general rules, the underlying system (or structure) that permits any novel to work as a novel.

The Russian Formalists – active from about 1915 until roughly 1930 – were significant precursors of structuralism who similarly sought to identify what made literature 'literary'. This meant that they, like Genette, paid particular attention to matters of form and technique – and important among them was Boris Tomashevsky, whose relevance to this chapter derives from his essay, 'Thematics', a study of narrative structure that is strongly reminiscent of Aristotle's *Poetics*.

Tomashevsky, too, makes a distinction between story and plot. The former is principally concerned with chronology and causation, and 'the weaker the

---

[2] In announcing the death of the Author, Barthes was writing figuratively. He meant a particular concept of the Author (hence the capital A) rather than individual, empirical authors. After all, he himself was an author and very much alive when he wrote those words. What he meant was that we couldn't take the author as the sole source of a work's meaning. The reader had a role, too. And the social and historical context will produce different readers, and different readings, at different times. This wasn't such a new idea, just expressed more provocatively than previously.

causal connection,' he says, 'the stronger the purely chronological connection'. Plot will include many of the same events, but whereas a story is obliged to be faithful to the 'real life' sequence of events, the plot will be an entirely 'artistic creation' that will necessarily rearrange those events. It may also introduce elements that are designed to mislead or incidentally entertain the reader, elements that are not strictly necessary to the telling of the story but which have some aesthetic justification. These are often, in fact, what makes the work 'literary'.

For Tomashevsky, too, there will be a beginning, middle and end, and the situation we encounter at the beginning will usually be static, a state of harmoniousness. Sometimes this initial situation will be presented in the form of an ordered 'exposition', a survey of the principal characters and their interrelationships. Sometimes, as we saw in the previous chapter, the beginning will present us with the characters *in medias res*, and the 'exposition' may then be deferred, often in the interests of suspense. The introduction of some complication – otherwise known as the 'exciting force' – will act as a spur to the development of the plot,[3] which 'may generally be understood as a progress from one situation to another, so that each situation is characterized by a *conflict* of interest, by discord and struggle among the characters'.

Two things in particular are important here – that the plot will involve a sequence of different situations, and that each of these situations will be defined by the nature of the interrelationships between the characters:

> For example, the hero loves the heroine, but she loves his rival. We have three characters: hero, heroine, rival. . . . Also typical are situations in which the characters are related by opposition, in which different persons want to change a situation by different means. For example, the hero loves the heroine and she loves him, but the parents prevent their marriage; they try to marry, but the parents try to separate them.

The emphasis that Tomashevsky places on character is also important. In common with E.M. Forster's distinction between flat and round characters, Tomashevsky identifies 'static' and 'dynamic' characters, the former remaining 'exactly the same throughout the development of the story' while the latter undergo significant changes, with their journey, and their crises, constituting

---

[3] Maddeningly, for me, having made his distinction between story and plot, Tomashevsky (or his translator) then proceeds to use the term 'story' throughout. For consistency I've substituted 'plot' where actually he says 'story'.

the substance of the narrative. These crises will usually reach a climax just before the end, which Tomashevsky calls the 'antithesis'. The 'exciting force' is meanwhile the 'thesis', and the ending or resolution the 'synthesis'.

The following exercise takes its lead from Tomashevsky, and while it does – more than any other exercise in this book – depend upon there being a classroom of students, its relevance may also be tested against the next short story you write.

---

54. Beginning middle end

We're going to write some short short stories along the lines described by Boris Tomashevsky.

Each person should begin with a fresh sheet of paper.

Everyone writes the beginning of a story. This should establish an initial situation of harmoniousness. There should be at least two characters, who may be introduced *in medias res*. This beginning should be no more than six lines. It must be legible.

Everyone passes their sheet to the left. Everyone reads the sheet they've received and adds a second paragraph. This should introduce a complication, an 'exciting force', our 'thesis'.

Everyone passes to the left, and receives from the right. Everyone now writes three paragraphs describing what happens in response to the complication. Each of these paragraphs should present a new situation, and each new situation should be brought about by some form of conflict.

Everyone passes to the left, and receives from the right. Everyone now adds one more paragraph that brings the sequence of events to a climax, our 'antithesis'.

Everyone passes to the left, and receives from the right. Everyone adds one final paragraph. This should bring the story to its end in a single short paragraph that offers a sense of narrative closure. This is our 'synthesis'.

Some of these stories are read out and discussed.

In the distinction that Tomashevsky draws between story and plot, there are three crucial elements: chronology, causality, and the arrangement of the parts. In E.M. Forster's *Aspects of the Novel*, written at much the same

time as 'Thematics', and in quite another world,[4] a similar understanding
is offered:

> We have defined a story as a narrative of events arranged in their time-
> sequence. A plot is also a narrative of events, the emphasis falling on causal-
> ity. 'The king died and then the queen died' is a story. 'The king died, and
> then the queen died of grief' is a plot. The time-sequence is preserved, but
> the sense of causality overshadows it. Or again: 'The queen died, no one
> knew why, until it was discovered that it was through grief at the death of the
> king.' This is a plot with a mystery in it, a form capable of high development.
> It suspends the time-sequence, it moves as far away from the story as its
> limitations will allow. Consider the death of the queen. If it is in a story we
> say: 'And then?' If it is in a plot we ask: 'Why?' That is the fundamental
> difference between these two aspects of the novel.

The 'fundamental difference' identified by Forster is waspily illustrated by
Margaret Atwood in her short story 'Happy Endings', a 'metafiction' that is as
much about the writing of a story called 'Happy Endings' as it is about the
characters contained within it, and is, by extension, as much about writing in
general as about writing this particular story. Here is the beginning:

> John and Mary meet.
> What happens next?
> If you want a happy ending, try A.

'A' is the first of six alternative narratives about John and Mary that constitute the middle of the story, after which Atwood offers this ending:

> The only authentic ending is the one provided here:
> *John and Mary die. John and Mary die. John and Mary die.*
> So much for endings. Beginnings are always more fun. True connois-
> seurs, however, are known to favour the stretch in between, since it's the
> hardest to do anything with.
> That's about all that can be said for plots, which anyway are just one
> thing after another, a what and a what and a what.
> Now try How and Why.

---

[4] Forster was invited to present the annual Clark Lectures at Trinity College, Cambridge
in 1927. Each of the eight chapters in *Aspects of the Novel* represents one of these lectures.
Tomashevsky was a member of the Moscow Linguistic Circle in the early years of post-
revolutionary Russia. He wrote 'Thematics' in 1925. It wasn't translated into English
until 1965.

Just to complicate things slightly, what Atwood calls 'plot' in this instance is precisely what Forster and others call 'story' – the chronological sequence of events that answers the question 'And then?' But Atwood and Forster do in fact mean much the same thing; the difference between them is terminological rather than conceptual. And so we might say that while stories are 'just one thing after another, a what and a what and a what', plots are all about the 'How' and the 'Why'. Plots are 'a what *because* of a what *because* of a what'.

In addition, plots will often rearrange the 'natural' sequence of events so that a cause comes after its effects – that is, a 'because' comes after its 'what' – usually in order to give some special emphasis to a 'crisis', while the initial 'situation' and 'complication' are presented to us in flashback. There are a great many reasons why an author might wish to reorder the sequence, but the withholding of causes is clearly crucial to the success of any 'whodunnit', for instance, and by extension will enhance the element of intrigue or mystery in even the most 'literary' of fictions, while the simple device of reversing the order of the first two stages in the five-stage sequence – situation, complication, crisis, climax, resolution – may greatly enhance the impact of shorter fictions especially.

Here is an exercise in reordering the narrative sequence:

---

55. Middle beginning end

Look again at a full-length story you wrote in response to a previous exercise, whether in another chapter or in this one.

Consider this story in terms of the five-stage sequence: situation, complication, crisis, climax, resolution.

Now attempt to reorder the narrative so that the story begins with the 'complication', and offers the 'situation' in the form of a flashback.

Alternatively, or additionally, attempt to reorder the narrative so that the story begins with the 'crisis' and offers both the 'situation' and the 'complication' in the form of a flashback.

The cut and paste facility on a computer may make this seem like a relatively simple operation. Even if you were to adopt Eudora Welty's technique – which I mentioned in Chapter 1 – and make your structural revisions using a pair of scissors and some pins, it might still seem simple enough, little more than a mechanical operation. In fact, a great deal of careful rewriting will be required to achieve smooth and plausible transitions between the parts in the sequence. The following exercise may require a good deal more careful rewriting still:

---

56. End middle beginning

Again, return to a full-length story you wrote in response to a previous exercise, whether in another chapter or in this one. You may choose the same story as last time.

Consider this story in terms of the five-stage sequence: situation, complication, crisis, climax, resolution.

Then attempt to reverse the sequence entirely, so that you retell your story in this order: resolution, climax, crisis, complication, situation.

As these exercises will reveal, the shaping of a plot will often involve some suspension or disruption of ordinary or natural time, and this may liberate the author from the obligation to tell every *next* thing regardless of how humdrum that next thing may be. Instead, the author can skip ahead, or double back, or wander some way off the point, which will allow the incorporation into the narrative of other incidents, other information, and – most importantly – other storylines. A plot, that is to say, will very often involve sub-plots, other 'whats', which may work to underscore the main themes of a narrative, or subtly to counter them, adding layers of complexity and irony. For Grace Paley, one of the masters of the short story form, the coexistence of more than one storyline may even be crucial to the overall meaning:

> a story is made very often of two stories, until you have one story sort of half-contradicting another or corroborating another . . . separately each story would be less interesting, and two stories together really make a third story.

This 'third story' will be implicit rather than spelled out; it will be found in the white space between the lines, unspoken, a matter of suggestion and surmise, and of course it will depend upon the imaginative involvement of the reader. As Paley says, 'every story is completed by the reader', and it is this active engagement in making the story's meaning that will cause it to linger or resonate in the reader's mind long after the reading has ended.

> ### 57. Sub-plotting
>
> This time, select two of the short stories you wrote in response to our earlier exercises. One of these will remain much as it is, and provide your main storyline. The other story will be broken up in order to supply your sub-plot.
>
> Some fairly obvious changes will need to be made to the content – names and locations especially. Technical changes may also be necessary – to point of view and tense, for example.
>
> Your challenge is to attempt to interweave the two stories so that they 'half-contradict' or 'corroborate' each other, and so suggest an unspoken third story.

Each of these last three exercises involves some rearrangement of the narrative sequence, some further disruption of a notional story's strict linearity. A more radical form of disruption might take its lead from one of the most innovative – and largely neglected – of English novelists, B.S. Johnson, whose fourth novel *The Unfortunates* was published in a box containing twenty-seven unbound sections, with only the first and last of these – the beginning and the end – being specified. What Margaret Atwood calls 'the stretch in between' – the middle twenty-five sections – can be read in any sequence the reader chooses.

This departure from literary convention may seem gimmicky to some or formally audacious to others, but it was conceived – like so many literary experiments – as a means of getting closer to the true nature of things. Johnson wasn't just a maverick novelist; he was a jobbing sportswriter, too, and it was while reporting a dreary football match in Nottingham for *The Observer* that he found himself distracted by thoughts of a close friend who had once worked in Nottingham and who had died a few years earlier. The anguished, despairing train of Johnson's thoughts was not linear, and so neither was the novel that developed out of those thoughts. *The Unfortunates* is, then, an attempt to be faithful to the fragmentariness of memory and our awareness of our everyday reality.

---

58. *Shuffling*

Once again, select one of the short stories you wrote in response to an earlier exercise. This may be the story you produced for the previous exercise, 'Sub-plotting'.

Break down your chosen story into its constituent parts. Each of these parts should be a single, significant event, or a passage of description or dialogue, or a stretch of interior monologue. Some parts will be longer than others. Some may be as short as a single sentence.

Spend some time finessing each of these parts so that it is fully self-contained. Then assign each part to a separate sheet of paper.

Decide on your beginning and your end, then shuffle the other sheets.

This is your new story. Read it carefully and consider whether it works in terms of the five-stage sequence: situation, complication, crisis, climax, resolution. If it doesn't, does it nevertheless gain in narrative interest and surprise? And even if it fails in this regard, does it suggest another story, quite different from the original, which you may go on to write next?

If *The Unfortunates* is an attempt to approximate to the randomness of reality and human consciousness, it may be said that most storytelling works in quite the opposite direction by seeking to impose some shape or structure on that reality. The notion that most narratives will conform to a familiar pattern – for instance, a state of equilibrium disturbed by some transforming event, leading to other transforming events, and then to the restoration of a modified state of equilibrium – is itself familiar and has in the past century given rise to numerous attempts to identify the archetypal structures underlying all storytelling. One significant example of this is Vladimir Propp's *Morphology of the Folktale*, published in 1928.

Perhaps the most 'structuralist' of the Russian Formalists, Propp analysed a relatively limited corpus of 115 Russian fairytales in order to identify the recurrent patterns that lay beneath their apparent variety. He then produced an inventory of thirty-one narrative units or key events, which he termed 'functions', such as 'the hero and villain do battle', 'the hero sets out for home', 'the hero is recognised', 'the false hero is exposed', 'the villain is punished'. Not all of the thirty-one functions will appear in every tale – some may be skipped – but they will always occur in the same order, and will be undertaken by seven basic character types, or 'roles': the hero, the villain, the false hero, the dispatcher, the donor, the helper, the princess (and her father).[5]

This is a simplifying account, and if it's already making you uneasy that may be because a sample of just 115 fairytales appears too limited, or because fairytales seem too primitive a literary form compared to the complexity of the contemporary short story and novel, or because character in the psychological sense is again being made secondary to character in the plot sense. It may also be because so schematising a scheme must leave out of the account precisely those non-functional elements that make literary fiction so absorbing (and *literary*): cadence, mood, atmosphere, the very 'thingness' of language, what Flannery O'Connor termed 'the mystery of personality', and so on.

These would be among my own misgivings, certainly. And I find I am no more persuaded by the numerous subsequent attempts to identify the basic plots in world literature, which generally include such archetypal forms as the quest narrative, the narrative of voyage and return, the rags to riches story, the tale of the outsider (a stranger comes to town), and several variations on the theme of man against an adversary, whether that be fate, nature, society, his own inner demons, God, the machine . . .

It isn't that I doubt the rigour or accuracy of such analyses, or the existence of such archetypes, but that I suspect they will be of limited value to the practising writer, for whom specifics are everything: *these* particular characters with just *these* dilemmas in *this* time and *this* place facing *these* unique challenges. As most of the exercises in this chapter are intended to demonstrate, the value of such analytical schemes is more likely to be diagnostic than instructive or prescriptive; their usefulness will come at the revision stage, as a means of determining where a particular story may have gone wrong and where it may be improved.

With this in mind, I would suggest that it's rarely useful for a writer to begin with a definite plan – a timeline, a plot diagram, an itemised synopsis. At least initially, the process should be exploratory, the territory uncharted, since the danger of proceeding from a plan is that you may feel obliged to follow it, to the exclusion of the inspired moment, the possibility of self-surprise, and the discoveries that can only be made when you are fully immersed in the form and the language. Timelines are certainly useful; plot diagrams can be clarifying. But these should emerge from the work rather than determine it.

As an example, the following is the start of the 'map' I produced when I was writing *What I Know*. Pinned over my desk, this allowed me to see at a glance the shape-so-far of my book, which helped me decide where I ought to go

---

[5] Maybe that's eight.

next. By consulting my map, I could gauge whether one or another character was in need of development, or whether some back-story might be required, or whether I needed to quicken the pace or introduce some new turn in the plot.[6]

1. pp1–11. 3533 words   mid-May
My name is Mike Hannah and I am forty years old . . .
Laid out on his back, spying on a student. His dream of Sarah. The Sommers & chopping down their trees. Being a parent. Memory of Sarah drying her hair. *Every marriage is a mystery.* He imagines Sarah as his wife, and regrets his life has no plot. Student stares down at him. He weeps.

2. 12–19. 2484 (6017)   four days later
The blue plastic clock on the chiropractor's wall ticks loudly.
His reflection in the mirror: his body, his anonymity. *Jan however is beautiful.* Sex is rare. He fancies Stella. 'The Holistic Clinic'. He regrets that he's not a 'tactile' person, or a risk-taker.

3. 20–34. 4631 (10,648)   that Sunday
'So,' Jan says, 'are you up to it?'
She leaves for the fun run. Their high social-capital community. St Luke's church & meeting the Sommers. He feels transparent. God does not exist for him. About surveilling insurance claimants, but not adulterers. At the fun run. Anna is drunk; Will and Jan are together.

4. 35–45. 3262 (13,910)   4 years ago
You may or may not have heard of Will.
Rosa's party, where Will talks about himself. Mike pretends to be a decorator. Jan joins them. About becoming a private detective. His hangover the next morning. Jan has Will's address. Mike continues to avoid Will & his books, but collects reviews. He once hoped to be a writer.

5. 46–51. 1656 (15,566)   19 years ago
Write about what you know was the only advice ever given to me as a student.
Sarah sits in his room as he types. About their housemates, and Tony the Tory. Sarah's tears.

---

[6] Each entry gives the chapter number, the pages, the word count, a cumulative word count in brackets, and a note of where the chapter fits chronologically. The italicised line is a reminder of the first sentence; then comes the summary of that chapter's events.

6. 52–64. 4169 (19,735)   **last day in May**

It is evening, the last day in May.
The student's bedroom is empty; Jan is reading Will's book. Mike goes for walk, spying on the neighbours. About 'Rear Window'. About seeing a man masturbating in his garden; his own limited perspective. He creeps into Will & Anna's garden & spies on them. Memory of Anna stroking his hair.

In the writing of longer works especially it can be hard to *see* why a plot is failing. It may be that certain less crucial scenes have been given too much prominence, or that certain less crucial characters have been allowed too much space on the page. The balance of 'now' and 'then' may have gone awry. The narrative may be dwelling too long in the past, leaving certain more promising plot-strands dangling in the present, waiting for development. It could be that the rhythm of narrative unfolding has ceased to keep time, that there are too many short scenes and not enough long ones, or that the longer scenes would benefit by the insertion of interludes, the 'punctuation' of some briefer scenes. Perhaps there is too much 'summary' and not enough 'scene', or exactly the opposite. It could be that there are too many sub-plots, too many tributaries, a profusion of distractions. It could be that a few of the lesser, flatter characters ought to be amalgamated, gathered into composites.

When we are most engaged on a piece of writing, fully absorbed in the task, we can sometimes lose a sense of the bigger picture, the overall structure; we can lose our sense of proportion. And of course we can lose focus. Being too close for too long to a scene can cause us to lose our sense of perspective: the page may start to blur, the simplest of sentences may start to seem uncertain.

There are several strategies for overcoming such difficulties. With shorter fiction especially it can be helpful to read the piece aloud, which may make audible what has ceased to be visible: we will stammer at the missing words, stumble over the clumsy phrasing, become conscious of the drone in our voice when the writing is monotonous. A fresh editorial angle will always be useful, whether that comes from a tutor, a professional editor, or a trusted first reader. The Creative Writing workshop may fulfil this function, too – as I'll explain in Chapter 12 – or the fresh eye may be your own, if you are able to shelve the work for a while, long enough to begin to forget it, which may take weeks rather than days, or months rather than weeks. And then there's the answer my wife Lynne Bryan arrived at when she was writing her first novel, which involves a certain amount of standing on furniture.

Having previously published a collection of short stories, the writing of *Gorgeous* presented Lynne with several formal and structural challenges that she hadn't previously encountered, and after almost two years of drafting and redrafting she found she could no longer hold the novel in her head; she could not see it whole, or see it straight. Her solution – which worked – is the one described in this final exercise:

---

59. Rearranging

Take a pile of scrap paper – A4 torn in half is about the right size – and a black marker pen, thick enough to be read from a distance of a few metres.

Go through your manuscript in order. For each successive scene, number a sheet of scrap paper. Note the main characters in this scene, and how many pages it covers. Give a one or two sentence summary of what happens. Note where and when the action occurs, the time and location.

You are going to lay these sheets in order on the floor, so you will need a room large enough to accommodate them. When you have laid out the entire narrative you may then find there is not enough floor space left for you. You may need to stand on the sofa, the bed, a table.

From this all-encompassing perspective, consider your narrative carefully.

Do your flashbacks occur in the right place? Might some of them be moved? Do you have too many short scenes, too many long? Is the order and balance quite right? Are your sub-plots proliferating, becoming so much clutter? Have you introduced too many characters? Has your main character been eclipsed? Do you have too much 'summary', not enough 'scene'? Are there gaps and dead ends?

As you decide on these issues, move the sheets around. Remove some, add some. Reconsider. Rearrange some more. Eventually you will arrive at a structure that works.

This is clearly suited to a novel-length work, but may be adapted for a short story, which can be printed out in hard-copy, then cut with scissors into paragraphs. These paragraphs can be laid out on a table and manually reordered in similar fashion.

10. Making strange: defamiliarisation

We all have our own little bugbears about language and the way it is used, and the more time we spend in the language the less 'little' these bugbears are likely to seem to us. A couple of commonplace solecisms that irritate me, and which I stumble over repeatedly in my students' writing, are the hyphenation of 'no one' as 'no-one', and the conjoining of 'any more' as 'anymore'. My dictionary supports me on both of these, but they are trivial errors and no doubt in time they will become the accepted convention, in much the same way that 'week-end', for instance, has become 'weekend'. Usage changes, and I notice that 'anymore' is already becoming routine in American English, and increasingly appears in the *Guardian* (despite the advice of the *Guardian*'s own style guide).

Certain more significant errors are those that affect meaning, one example being the widespread misuse of 'disinterested', which actually means 'judiciously impartial, free from bias, objective' and not, as seems to be supposed, the opposite of 'interested' (which would be 'uninterested').[1] Even more widespread, and often more comical, is the use of 'literally' as an intensifier – 'I was literally torn apart by what she said' – when what is meant is the opposite: not 'literally' but 'figuratively' (or 'metaphorically'). If I were literally (actually, truthfully) to be torn apart by what she said, I would be dead. It would be messy.

The irony of 'literally' is that it is usually used in an effort to inject some life into a dead phrase – a cliché – but has in the meantime become a bit of a cliché

---

[1] Interestingly, in the seventeenth century, 'disinterested' was used to mean 'not interested', while 'uninterested' was used to mean 'impartial'. Usage changes. Their meanings have reversed, and may soon merge.

itself. In their newly minted form, figurative or metaphorical expressions such as 'torn apart' can work to revivify the language and reawaken our perceptions; they can allow us to see the world anew. But in their spent form as tired old figures of speech they can become the very thing they were once the answer to: lazy language, dead language. One way in which they might be reanimated, however, is literally to take them literally. What if the expression 'I was literally torn apart by what she said' were to be taken literally? What kind of fiction might result from that?

---

60. Literally

Here are some other figurative expressions:

it was a heart-sinking moment
he was high as a kite
the shit hit the fan
she got her knickers in a twist
he lost his tongue
she gave me the finger
he was running on empty
it cracks me up every time
there was a definite spark between us
butter wouldn't melt in her mouth

    Choose two of these and write a couple of short scenes in which they are taken absolutely literally.

On a similar theme, the following exercise is adapted from Sue Thomas's book *Creative Writing: A Handbook for Workshop Leaders*:

---

61. Figuratively

Here are some similes, all of which have now become clichés:

as pretty as a picture
as ugly as sin
as hard as nails

as easy as pie
as bright as a button
as busy as a bee
as dead as a doorknob
as sick as a dog
as blind as a bat
as sharp as a tack
as cool as a cucumber
as straight as a die
as thick as a brick
as light as a feather
as mad as a hatter
as slow as a snail
as fresh as a daisy
as cheap as chips

Choose six of these, but remove the endings. Think of someone you really don't like. Then write a character sketch in which you use all six similes, with new endings that express your full loathing.

Now think of someone you really like a lot. Using the same similes, write a character sketch in which you change the endings to express your admiration.

It may be helpful to address each of these pieces of writing to the person they're about: 'You are . . .'

The premise of both of these exercises is that certain phrases can become so familiar to us that we lose sight of what they are actually saying, in much the same way that we may become 'blind' to our everyday surroundings, or 'deaf' to certain continuous sounds (as I've become deaf to the hum of the computer on which I'm typing this chapter, for instance).[2]

The promise of both exercises, however, is that everyday language can be made to shed its cloak of invisibility and so reveal the possibilities of a more

---

[2] At least, the hum was inaudible until I drew my own attention to it, since when it has become not only audible but extremely aggravating. In similar fashion, a cliché can very easily come alive for us if we actually pay attention to it. For instance, if you were to concentrate on the idea that somebody's words could be so upsetting as to make you feel as if you were being torn apart – rent in two, ripped down the middle – the effect could be quite startling: visceral and disturbing.

illuminating, literary language – one that 'defamiliarises' the familiar, or 'makes strange' the commonplace. This is a notion I explored in Chapter 4, and touched on again in Chapter 9, where I described it as a cornerstone concept of the school of Russian Formalism. More specifically, it derives from Victor Shklovsky's 1917 essay 'Art as Technique', in which he writes:

> . . . art exists that one may recover the sensation of life; it exists to make one feel things, to make the stone *stony*. The purpose of art is to impart the sensation of things as they are perceived and not as they are known. The technique of art is to make objects 'unfamiliar,' to make forms difficult, to increase the difficulty and length of perception because the process of perception is an aesthetic end in itself and must be prolonged.

For Shklovsky, as for the Formalists more generally, literary language is language that draws attention to itself, that makes us aware of its artfulness. But this is not to insist that literary language must be difficult to the point of impenetrability, or artful for the sake of being artful. Rather, it is to suggest that literary language should resist the already known, the already said, by deviating to some degree from received or conventionalised ways of representing reality. In so doing it will require the reader to engage more actively in 'producing' the meaning of the work, and this element of difficulty or unfamiliarity – which may only be slight – will save the depiction from any 'automatism of perception' and thus bring us closer to a renewed awareness of the 'sensation of life', the sensory truth of our being in the world.

On this account, clearly, defamiliarisation is a defining aspect of all literary works – including those realist novels that allow us, in John Gardner's (much later) words, 'to taste the fictional gazpacho, smell the fictional hyacinths' – and it is significant that Shklovsky illustrates his argument with a series of lengthy quotations from the novels and stories of Leo Tolstoy, one of the giants of literary realism. 'Tolstoy', he says, 'makes the familiar seem strange by not naming the familiar object. He describes an object as if he were seeing it for the first time, an event as if it were happening for the first time.'

Tolstoy, we can be sure, is able 'to make the stone *stony*', just as Chekhov – to return briefly to a theme of Chapter 4 – is able to show us the moon by revealing 'the glint of light on broken glass'. In this sense the injunction 'show don't tell' might be taken as an injunction to defamiliarise in the realist manner described by Shklovsky in 'Art as Technique'.

In a later essay, however, Shklovsky takes one of the most idiosyncratic novels in the literary canon – Laurence Sterne's *Tristram Shandy* – and declares this to be 'the most typical novel in world literature', though certainly not for its ability 'to make the stone *stony*'. The appeal of *The Life and Opinions of Tristram Shandy, Gentleman* is its willingness 'to make forms difficult, to increase the difficulty', since this is a novel that deviates to the maximum degree from received or conventionalised ways of representing reality.

Exhaustively attentive to the trivial, and almost dementedly prone to digression, *Tristram Shandy* gives us considerably more of the *Opinions* than of the *Life*, and is consistently flummoxed by the fact that it takes longer to relate a life than to lead it. The eponymous narrator becomes mired in the minutiae of his conception and birth, and barely manages – even over the course of nine volumes – to get beyond his fifth year, though the problem isn't simply one of material, but of how that material should be organised.

As Shklovsky remarks, 'Everything in the book is displaced; everything is transposed.' And so causes are made to follow consequences; the dedication is delayed until page 15; the preface doesn't appear until page 174; certain chapters are skipped, others presented in the wrong order. The novel makes a comedy of its own chaotic making, and in this way *Tristram Shandy* flaunts its fictionality. It 'accentuates the very structure of the novel', says Shklovsky, and rarely allows the reader to forget that she is reading a novel – even to the extent of excoriating her for reading it wrongly: 'How could you, Madam, be so inattentive in reading the last chapter?'

By these and many other means, Laurence Sterne 'lays bare' his technique, and in the process of 'violating the form', Shklovsky suggests, 'he forces us to attend to it'. In other words, this most challenging and unorthodox of novels is also the most 'typical' because it goes further than almost any other in 'making strange' the conventions for representing reality in the form of a fiction.[3]

Interestingly, in treating *Tristram Shandy* as a metafiction – as a novel about the writing of novels – Victor Shklovsky scrupulously avoids any attempt to explain away or 'naturalise' its eccentricities. He doesn't, for instance, ascribe its disorder to the state of Tristram's chaotic mind or to the peculiarities of his character or upbringing. In focusing on the novel's formal aspects, Shklovsky resists any impulse to reclaim it for realism.

Yet as my account in the previous chapter of B.S. Johnson's *The Unfortunates* should illustrate, a reader's first impulse is often to want to ground a difficult text in reality, to view its formal experimentalism as in some way expressive or mimetic, as an attempt to get closer to the true nature of things – much as the modernist technique of stream of consciousness, for instance,

---

[3] Which is ironical, perhaps, given that *Tristram Shandy* was written 250 years ago, when the emerging form of the novel had yet to become so familiar that it needed rescuing from its own conventionality.

may be understood as a means of representing more accurately the true nature of the everyday mind.

There are however certain experimental writers whose apparent purpose is to evade any possibility of 'naturalisation', largely through the imposition of arbitrary, systematic constraints on their own writing. One example of this might be the loose grouping of mainly French writers and mathematicians known as the Oulipo, an acronym for Ouvroir de Littérature Potentielle, which roughly translates as Workshop of Potential Literature.

Founded in 1960, perhaps the two most famous members of this group are Italo Calvino, who wrote *If On A Winter's Night A Traveller* – a metafiction about a reader attempting to read a book called *If On A Winter's Night A Traveller* – and Georges Perec, who wrote *La Disparition*, a 300-page novel that doesn't contain a single letter *e*. (Both novelists are now dead, which is no constraint, it seems, on continuing membership of the group.)

Perec's novel was translated as *A Void* and is a 'lipogram', a text that excludes a certain letter, but even here – or especially here – the experiment cannot help but signify in human and emotional terms since Perec was orphaned by the Holocaust and in denying himself the possibility of using the letter *e* he is excluding from his novel the presence of words such as *père* ('father'), *mère* ('mother'), *parents* ('parents') and *famille* ('family'). *A Void* is very much a novel about absence, though far from sombre: it is also ironic, parodic, and consistently playful.

The use of such wordgames is typical of the Oulipo, who once defined themselves as 'rats who must build the labyrinth from which they propose to escape'. In essence, their approach is paradoxical, or counter-intuitive. By insisting on the imposition of arbitrary constraints, they seek to generate work that is far more creative – and unfettered – than if the writer were at liberty to write whatever he wished.

The ideal constraint not only requires ingeniousness on the part of the writer, meanwhile; it should also be ingeniously simple in its conception, and will as often be mathematical as alphabetical. This may be illustrated by Raymond Queneau's sequence of ten sonnets, 'Cent Mille Milliards de Poèmes' ('One Hundred Thousand Billion Poems'), which is explained in Warren Motte's *Oulipo: A Primer of Potential Literature*:

> . . . each line of each poem may replace (or be replaced by) its homologue in the nine other poems. Thus, to each of the ten first lines, the reader can add any of ten different second lines; there exist therefore 10^2, or one hundred possible combinations of the first two lines. Given that the sonnet has fourteen lines, the possibilities offered by the collection as a whole are of

the order of 10^{14}, or one hundred trillion sonnets . . . According to his cal-culations, if one read a sonnet per minute, eight hours a day, two hundred days per year, it would take more than a million centuries to finish the text.

It is literary experiments of this kind, perhaps, that David Lodge has in mind when he remarks in *The Art of Fiction*: 'These works are probably more fun to read about than to read.' But as the example of Georges Perec demon-strates, the Oulipian novel can also be affecting – even as it 'makes strange' – and this is nowhere better illustrated than in the work of Richard Beard, one of the most innovative and witty of contemporary British novelists and a writer much influenced by the example of the Oulipo.

Here is the opening to Beard's novel *Damascus*:

> It is the first of November 1993 and somewhere in the Kingdom, in Quarn-don or Northampton or Newry or York, in Kirkaldy or Yeovil or Lincoln or Neath, a baby girl is born. Her name is Hazel. Her father Mr Burns, a salesman, puts the tip of his finger inside her tiny fist. He waves his head from side to side and puts on a childish voice and says:
> 'Who's the most beautiful girl in the whole wide world then?'
> It is the first of November 1993 and somewhere in the Kingdom, in Harlow or Widnes or Swansea or Ayr, in Reading or Glentoran or Nantwich or Hull, a baby boy is born. His name is Spencer. His father Mr Kelly, a warehouseman, circles a tiny upper arm between his thumb and index finger. He frowns and says:
> 'You're not as big as your brother was.'

And here is the start of a later section of the novel, almost a third of the way in:

> It is the first of November 1993 and somewhere in Britain, in Falmouth or Hampton Hill or Llandudno or Oxford, in Devonport or Tranmere or East Stirling or Glenavon, every boy of Spencer's age is having non-stop all-action sex all of the time. They openly admit to it, even though they're only fourteen years old. Spencer doesn't have a girlfriend, but he does have an evolving pattern of facial blemishes. He also has a father who doesn't understand him and a mother who probably takes drugs and an older brother who is about to be married.

And here is the start to a later section still, roughly half-way:

> It is the first of November 1993 and somewhere in Britain, in Lancing or Great Wakering or Gretna or Ascot, in Toller Porcorum or Merthyr or

Richmond or Derby, Hazel Burns is eighteen years old and these are the best days of her life. Her father has given her an allowance and told her so. He has also bought her a car, a small Ford or Vauxhall or Peugeot, so that she can come home whenever she needs a break from her first year, first term, at the University of Warwick or Strathclyde or Oxford or Hull.

An author's note at the end of the book laconically informs us: 'All but twelve of the nouns in *Damascus* can also be found in *The Times* (London) of 1 November 1993.'

Easily overlooked, this reveals the Oulipian constraint that Beard imposed upon himself – to write a novel that contains every noun in a single edition of *The Times*, plus twelve others – which clearly resulted in a surfeit of place names, presumably because that day's paper contained several pages of sports results. His solution was to create the riff that is illustrated by these three examples, and with which numerous other sections of the novel begin. On each occasion the date is the same, but Hazel and Spencer are a year or two older, a little further on in their lives, a little closer to falling in love, and of course the list of locations is always quite different. In this way Beard is able to universalise their love story: the events of the novel could be taking place anywhere in the Kingdom, and Hazel and Spencer could be anyone or everyone. His solution to a simple formal constraint thus becomes something quite touching, and is achieved – as in each of his novels – with a panache that allows him to avoid the fate of so much experimental fiction, which tends often to be more fun in the anticipation than in the actuality (to paraphrase David Lodge).

---

62. Given words

Tear out a page from a broadsheet newspaper.

Circle four nouns from one story or column, four verbs from the next story or column, four adjectives from the next, four adverbs from the next.

Select the names of four people from anywhere on the page.

Now underline one of your names, one noun, one verb, one adjective, one adverb. These have been eliminated.

Underline one of the other names. This is your point of view character.

Using the names, nouns, verbs, adjectives and adverbs that are left, your task is to write a piece of short fiction in which they all appear.

If we take the story that results from this exercise as our given text, we could now subject it to various other constraints. In *Writing Without the Muse*, Beth Joselow suggests writing a short description of a place you know well, then rewriting this description in accordance with a particular mood, which is an excellent exercise both for revealing the way in which a character's personality may influence the depiction of setting, and for allowing us to see the world of our fiction anew, perhaps from quite an unexpected perspective.

---

63. Given moods

Choose two of the following twelve moods and emotions.

anger
love
boredom
anxiety
fear
impatience
shyness
condescension
nostalgia
happiness
desire
weariness

Retaining the same point of view character as in Exercise 62, run your piece of short fiction through the filter of each of your two chosen moods.

The device of subjecting a given text to a series of variations is one exploited to comic, even lunatic excess by Raymond Queneau, in what is possibly his most widely known work, *Exercises in Style*.

This elegant book begins with a short narrative of 130 words entitled 'Notation', which presents – in note form – an account of a young man on a crowded midday bus who accuses a fellow passenger of jostling him, then throws himself into an empty seat. The young man is distinguished – if that is the word – by a felt hat, a long neck, and a snivelling tone. Two hours later the narrator spots him near Saint-Lazare station with a friend, who is advising him to get an extra button put on the lapel of his coat. This fairly unexceptional tale (really little more than an anecdote) is just one of ninety-nine stylistic variations, some of them funny, some baffling, some learned, some silly (my brief précis might stand as a hundredth perhaps, named 'Précis').

To offer a few examples, one sequence of exercises reformulates the story in terms of each of the five senses. Thus in 'Olfactory', Queneau registers 'a certain pungency of anger'; in 'Gustatory' he tastes 'the grapes of wrath and a bunch of bitterness'; in 'Tactile' he remarks on the 'human stupidity, slightly viscous and gummy on account of the heat'; in 'Visual' he writes as if from the point of view of a painter, who applies 'a red triangle to express anger, and just a pissworth of green to portray suppressed bile'; and in 'Auditory' he reports that 'a ludicrous cacophany broke out in which the fury of the double bass was blended with the irritation of the trumpet and the jitters of the bassoon'.

Other thematic variations include 'Botanical', 'Medical', 'Gastronomical'. Among the strictly stylistic variations the tale is retold in the form of a tele-gram, a bureaucratic letter, and the blurb on a book jacket. Among the generic variations it is rewritten as a three-act comedy, a sonnet, an opera, a haiku, an ode. In 'Ignorance' the narrator queries every detail. In 'Awkward' he begins, 'I'm not used to writing. I dunno', and struggles – at some length – to articulate anything. And in 'Exclamations' every astounded, breathless sentence is hyper-excited!

The actual blurb on the jacket of *Exercises in Style* describes the collec-tion as 'a linguistic rust-remover', which is an arresting (or defamiliarising) reformulation of the idea of defamiliarisation. In common with *Tristram Shandy* perhaps, it 'violates the form' and thereby 'forces us to attend to it'. And while the somewhat inconsequential story remains unaltered, the many variations on the style of its telling save it from becoming dulled by familiarity. *Exercises in Style* is above all an exercise in perking up our percep-tions, though less of our world than of the ways in which it is possible to describe it.[4]

I would like to offer an exercise based on *Exercises in Style*, but here first is an anecdote; it is precisely 250 words long and derives from my observational journal:

---

[4] It's also a neat riposte to the claim that we all have a book inside us. We probably do all have a book inside us, but the point is how well, and with what style, what originality, we are able to tell it.

My dog did a dump in the street. I picked up the poo in a scented poo-bag and dropped it in the bin outside the newsagent's, then turned to cross the road.

'Oi!' It was the owner of the newsagent's. 'You wouldn't like that, would you? Someone dropping shit in your bin.'

'Sorry?'

'That stinks when it gets hot – how would you like it?'

'But it's winter,' I said.

He stared at me.

'And there's a picture of a dog on the bin.'

'No there isn't,' he said. 'Look.'

'Ah,' I said. 'Sorry. I misread the sign.'

'You're just inconsiderate.'

'I'm not,' I said, 'I just misread the sign.'

'Well, tell you what,' he said, suddenly angry. 'Here' – he lifted the lid from the bin – 'why don't you take your shit home with you!'

I waited, then shrugged, and as I retrieved my perfumed bag from the bin I said, 'You know, every time I come past here I think it's such a shame because no one ever comes in your shop. And now I know why. I wouldn't want to go in your shop either.'

'Yeah, well, don't, I don't want you!'

'You won't last long,' I told him.

'Oh, fuck off!' he replied. Then, 'Wanker! You fucking wanker!'

I said nothing, and crossed the road. In my imagination I raised my poo-bag in the air, waggled it on the end of my finger. An hour later I was still trembling, still imagining that gesture.

Following Queneau, I could now subject this short short story to a series of re-writings. If I were to adopt the style of 'Exclamations' it might begin, 'My dog did a dump in the street! I picked it up! I had a bag! It was scented!' A version called 'Awkward' might produce – or might not, I'm not sure – something like: 'Shall I tell you about this? What my dog did? Or not really what he did, more the situation I got into because of it. Well, I say situation. It's not worth mentioning really.' While 'Ignorance' might begin: 'Was it my dog? There was a pile of some dog's shit in the street, I think, if I remember rightly. Possibly that street – it could have been a different street.'

Among some other possibilities, I might re-write my story in the vernacular – Queneau's translator comes up with 'Cockney', 'West Indian' and 'For Ze Frrensh'. I might attempt to render every sentence in the grammatical 'passive voice', so that: 'A dump was being done by my dog. The street was receiving his dump. The dump was picked up by me.' Or I might, as in 'Retrograde', tell the story in reverse order, so that it begins: 'I was still trembling an hour later, thinking of myself as I crossed the road from the newsagent's.'

64. *Exercises in style*

Look through your observational journal and identify an incident that could be written up as a piece of very short fiction of precisely 250 words.

Write this story chronologically, in the first person, and in the grammatical past tense.

Choose three of the following fifteen headings from Queneau's *Exercises in Style*:

Notation
Retrograde
Official letter
Blurb
Ignorance
Passive
Exclamations
Cockney (or any other vernacular)
Awkward
Olfactory
Gustatory
Tactile
Visual
Auditory
Telegraphic

Now attempt to rewrite your story in response to your three chosen headings.

Among the most challenging – and least engaging – of Raymond Queneau's variations is a sequence of alphabetical and mathematical permutations whose outcomes are largely unreadable, a series of blocks of text in which sense is sacrificed to surface, the story lost to a seemingly arbitrary arrangement of letters – for example:

Oursl afewh sawhi ateri ninfr magai thega ontof ntlaz resai gross areen conve edina onwit rsati endwh hafri ellin owast ogett ghimt butto hetop sover nofhi aised coatr.

The use of numerical schemes is a standard procedure of the Oulipo, however – and not every scheme need result in this kind of nonsensical outcome. One of the better-known formulas is 'Mathews's Algorithm', the invention of the only American Oulipian, the novelist Harry Mathews. This algorithm may be understood as a kind of machine for producing new literary works from existing works, and is based on a system of permutations similar to those governing Queneau's 'One Hundred Thousand Billion Poems'. Somewhat difficult to describe, the best approach to comprehending it may be to submit to it.

---

65. Mathews's Algorithm (almost)

Take a lengthy short story you have already written, and divide it into nine numbered sections. Each section should be more or less self-contained. Some may be longer than others.

Now take nine index cards and write a number from one to nine on each. Arrange the cards on your desk in this grid:

One   Two   Three
Four   Five   Six
Seven   Eight   Nine

In order to generate your first new text, shift each card in Row One a single place to the left. This will mean card one has to come right round to the other end:

Two   Three   One

Now shift each card in Row Two two places to the left. This will mean card four has to come right round to the other end, and then move along another place, ending up in the middle:

Six   Four   Five

Now shift each element in Row Three a single place to the left:

Eight   Nine   Seven

You will now have the following grid:

Two	Three	One
Six	Four	Five
Eight	Nine	Seven

If you rearrange the sections in your story in accordance with the grid, it will produce this narrative sequence: two, three, one, six, four, five, eight, nine, seven.

You might now want to recombine vertically. Shift Column One a single place down. Shift Column Two two places down. Shift Column Three a single place down. You will now have this grid:

Eight	Four	Seven
Two	Nine	One
Six	Three	Five

If you now rearrange the sections in your story in accordance with this grid, it will produce the following narrative sequence: eight, four, seven, two, nine, one, six, three, five.

Mathews's own algorithm is based on a grid of sixteen, four by four. You can see how this could be combined and recombined to generate a great many different plots. And of course, larger grids might also be employed: six by six, eight by eight, ten by ten . . .

Although Mathews's Algorithm is rule-based, its results will have an air of the arbitrary, mainly because the author of the initial work is denied any authority over the shape of the final work (if ever there can *be* a final work). The author operates the machine, so to speak, but isn't permitted to exercise much in the way of judgement or creativity.

An alternative approach to generating new work by reformulating or 'making strange' an existing work – and one that requires the author to be less like a factory operative – might take its lead from the 'structural linguistics' of another of the Russian Formalists, Roman Jakobson, who proposed (among other things; his was a long and hugely influential career) a model of language arranged along two axes, the horizontal and the vertical.[5]

The horizontal is the axis of 'combination' and is concerned with syntax, or the way in which words are linked together (like the carriages in a train) to

[5] Not to over-complicate matters, Jakobson was following an earlier linguist, Ferdinand de Saussure.

make grammatical sentences. It is concerned with the forward flow of words. And of course there is always more than one way in which the words in a sentence may be combined, or lined up. Consider for instance the first two sentences of my novel, *Pig*:

> It was the pig that woke my grandfather on the morning Gran died. It was squealing outside in the garden.

These words could be ordered or combined quite differently. Some of the words might be eliminated (and others added):

> On the morning Gran died, it was the pig, squealing outside in the garden, that woke my grandfather.

This is recognisably the same story, though the narrative voice is subtly different, the forward flow of the words less regular. It remains grammatical, too, and the sentences are in the same order. Conceivably I could rewrite the whole novel along these lines – taking each sentence in turn – and end up with a novel that is uncannily similar to the original, but also uncannily different. It would be familiar, yet not.

One useful drill for developing your own style is to take a story you have already written and attempt syntactical variations on each of the sentences, experimenting with different word orders, different sentence shapes. The following is a short exercise in such syntactical reordering:

---

66. Horizontal

Take a piece of short fiction that you wrote in response to any earlier exercise. Attempt now to rewrite this story, sentence by sentence, by rearranging the syntax. You should aim to retain as many of the existing words as possible, and to add as few new words as possible. The sentences should remain grammatical. And while the words within each sentence will be reordered, the sequence of the sentences should remain the same.

As any thesaurus will illustrate, for most words there are numerous alternative choices (though in certain contexts the best alternative may not be a straightforward synonym but a metaphor). Jakobson's vertical axis – the axis of 'selection' – takes account of this potential for substituting individual words while retaining the original syntactical structure. With this in mind, I might take my first two sentences and swap each of the nouns for a close cousin:[6]

> It was the sow that woke Pappa on the day that Grams died. It was squeal-ing outside in the yard.

This has the obvious advantage of retaining most of the sense of my original opening. The novel that proceeds from this beginning could go on to tell much the same story, though differently inflected, possessing a somewhat dif-ferent voice. However, should I wish to stretch my source text so that it gener-ates a new novel that bears a less obvious resemblance to the original, I would need to choose my nouns from slightly larger groups of words. For example, instead of synonyms for 'pig' and 'grandparents', I might choose from 'farm animals' and 'family members'. I might also modify the verbs:

> It was the heifer that wakened my sister on the day that Mum died. It was lowing outside in the orchard.

This version has the advantage of still seeming relatively plausible and of occupying a similar vein of realism to *Pig*. Were I now to choose from some-what broader groups of nouns – for instance 'domestic animals', 'people', and 'cultivated spaces' – and vary the verbs more freely, the story would begin to lose such a clear connection to its source, and might begin to shade into the surreal:

> It was the camel that tickled my guru on the morning Millicent graduated. It was bellowing outside in the greenhouse.

Any novel or story that emerged from this beginning would be almost unrecognisable as a sibling or cousin to *Pig*. Yet I have selected from noun groups that are far from illogical, given the original words – 'pig' and 'camel' both belong to 'domestic animals', for instance. I could however broaden my choices yet further, selecting my nouns from the word group 'nouns', and my verbs from the word group 'verbs'. I might also set myself the arbitrary con-straint of making everything alliterate:

---

[6] The metaphor 'close cousin' is a synonym for 'synonym' in this instance. It is also a cliché, of course. I might have said 'near relative', another cliché, or 'farrow mate', an attempt at 'making strange'.

It was the cauliflower that concerned her confederates on the campus the cretins created. It was cogitating close to the clinic.

Bizarre as this has become, it nevertheless remains consistent with the original syntax; for all the changes I've made along the vertical axis, the horizontal axis remains undisturbed. As a final stage of making strange, I might now rearrange these two sentences along the axis of combination:

On the campus the cretins created, her confederates were concerned by the cauliflower. Close to the clinic it cogitated.

This final exercise requires you to experiment with different word choices, and should take you along another axis, the line of increasing strangeness.

---

67. Vertical

Take a piece of short fiction that you wrote in response to any earlier exercise. Making minimal changes along the horizontal axis, attempt the following changes on the vertical axis (that is, retain the syntax but make different word choices).

1. Swap all the nouns for close synonyms. For instance, I swapped 'pig' for 'sow'.
2. Swap all the nouns for other nouns belonging to slightly broader categories. For instance, I swapped 'pig' for another noun within the category 'farm animals', giving 'heifer'.
3. Take your first few sentences only. Swap all the nouns for nouns belonging to much broader categories. For instance, I swapped 'pig' for another noun within the category 'domestic animals', giving 'camel'. Then choose some different verbs. When you have altered all the nouns and verbs in these first few sentences, see if you can generate a brand new story that shares the same surreal logic.
4. Take your first few sentences only. Swap all the nouns for other words belonging to the category 'nouns'. Do the same for 'verbs'. Make each of your alternative words alliterate. If possible, change the next few lines, then the next few. Go as far as you can. But try to retain some semblance of a logical connection between the sentences; however surreal, try to tell a story.

Throughout this chapter I have been concerned with the ways in which a source text – apparently finished – may be subjected to varying degrees of creative destruction in order to generate new and potentially surprising alternatives. These new texts may prove more satisfying to you than the originals, or they may not. If the former, it could be that you are presently writing in a conventional, realist vein that does not suit you; if the latter, it may be that your sensibility, like mine, is fundamentally that of a realist. In either case, the most important consideration is to be aware of the dulling, even deadening effect that the familiar phrase, the clichéd construction or the formulaic solution can have on your writing. For Victor Shklovsky the distinguishing characteristic of the literary is that it should 'make strange', whether at the level of precise observation, as in Tolstoy (my concern in Chapter 4), or at the level of formal construction, as in *Tristram Shandy* (my concern here). But as this chapter should have demonstrated, there are many degrees of defamiliarisation, and many devices for achieving it. The challenge, always, is to find a means of representing reality that not only rings true, but seems new, and is authentically your own.

11. Making clear: revision, grammar and punctuation

In Chapter 3, I introduced the technique of automatic writing with the exercise 'First thoughts'. Here is that exercise again, but this time you should write for thirty minutes instead of fifteen:

---

68. More first thoughts

Think of the person you are closest to in the world, the person whose life you know the most intimately. You are going to write for thirty minutes, describing in detail what you imagine that person to be doing (and thinking and feeling) at this very moment. Write in the present tense, and address it to 'you'.

The rules are these:

- You are free to write illegibly and ungrammatically.
- You are free to be clumsy and clichéd.
- You are free to repeat or contradict yourself.
- You are free to write rubbish.
- You are free to write anything.
- You are free to go completely off the point.
- But you must write without a moment's pause for exactly thirty minutes.

When your thirty minutes are up, put this writing aside. Don't read it. We'll return to it later.

As the word implies, the process of *revision* is a process of looking again. Yet as I suggested in Chapter 9, the intensity of our involvement in a work-in-progress can sometimes cause us to lose our sense of perspective or proportion; we may become blind to its virtues as well as its faults, adding where we need not add, cutting where we needn't cut. The work may also go stale on us, dulled by familiarity, seemingly exhausted of energy.

A fresh eye will then be required, or perhaps a fresh ear: we may need to read the work aloud, or pass it to another reader, or submit it to a workshop, or put it aside for a while – perhaps for a very long while. But whatever strategy we employ, the ultimate aim is the same: to place ourselves in the position of our eventual readers, so that we may gauge the likely effects of our words on them, anticipating their potential misunderstandings or confusions, attempting to guide the nature of their engagement with our fictional world.

For some writers (a very few) that fictional world may appear before their mind's eye as if fully formed, fully illuminated; for others it will be considerably more vague, a matter of glimpses, hints and intimations that will only start to come clear as it begins to emerge on the page.

The issue then will be one of communication; that is, of attempting to convey to the reader at least some of what the writer feels she already knows. And while every story will be slanted differently, depending on the writer's sense (as I put it in Chapter 4) of what to withhold and what to reveal, what to emphasise and what to suggest, there are certain foundational details that a reader will require in order to orientate himself in the fictional world. These will include the basic coordinates of time and place, simple signposts to indicate who speaks and to whom, and issues of 'continuity' such as those that operate in film and TV and ensure that this character will always have a stammer, or that particular window will always look out on the sunrise.

Often, of course, a writer's chief interest or purpose will be to dwell in the realm of the uncertain, exploiting the possibilities of mystery, ambiguity, complexity. And often it's precisely this kind of uncertainty that will draw the reader into the fictional world, and hold him there. But how to depict the mysterious without becoming confusing? How to suggest ambiguity without seeming muddled, or complexity without seeming contradictory?

And how to be perfectly clear when we need to be clear?

In Chapter 3, I paraphrased Dorothea Brande to the effect that every writer is in some way double, a dual personality comprised of adult and child, critic and artist. In her Freudian scheme, the adult-critic is associated with the painstaking discriminations of conscious thought, the child-artist with the more spontaneous, unpredictable processes of the unconscious. The successful writer is able to bridge these two sides of the self, to hold them in balance, and while any work of 'genius' will depend crucially upon the unconscious, it will also rely on the more craftsmanlike processes of the fully conscious mind.

Among the processes that Brande identifies are those of 'weighing, balancing, trimming, expanding', a set of terms that recalls those used by T.S. Eliot in his much-quoted essay 'The Function of Criticism':

> Probably . . . the larger part of the labour of an author in composing his work is critical labour; the labour of sifting, combining, constructing, expunging, correcting, testing: this frightful toil is as much critical as creative.

For Eliot and Brande and numerous others, the writer is always also a critic – which is to say, a self-critic – but the involvement of the critical self need not be deferred until the final stages of the creative process. It has an essential role then, of course. Every work will require later revision, and the more spontaneous it is, the more revision it may require. The final exercise in Chapter 9, 'Rearranging', is an example of the major structural revision that may sometimes be necessary. But there is also a sense in which our critical intelligence is applied incrementally and 'recursively', by which I mean something like 'ongoingly'.

If we assume a first draft written automatically, each subsequent draft will involve the writer more and more in the process of reading and re-reading herself. This will happen both at the level of the sentence – the often enjoyable fuss and fiddle of shaping and reshaping her phrases – and at the level of structure – the often more challenging task of envisioning the shape of the whole narrative and the interrelationship of the many disparate parts that combine to create the overall work, whether they be technical, ethical, thematic or aesthetic.

With this in mind, Dorothea Brande's conception of the writer's dual personality might then be extended to include another doubling: that of reader and writer. In the act of writing we are also, constantly, engaged in the act of reading – that is, reading ourselves – and of adjusting our writing in the light of our reading, and it is this continuous alertness to how we are sounding and what we are saying that allows us to gauge the likely effect of our words on our eventual readers; it's what allows us to depict the mysterious without becoming confusing (or the obvious without becoming *too* obvious).

The middle chapters of this book provide a guide to many of the questions that you might ask of your writing as you read and revise it. Here is a checklist of some of those questions:

69. Checklist

1. Showing and telling
Do you have good balance between showing and telling, dramatising and summarising? Are you merely 'piling up detail'? Is it vivid and particular? Could you be more selective, more economical? Are you appealing to all five senses, and avoiding 'feeble abstraction'? Do your details 'make strange'? Are you telling it slant?

2. Places and people
Do your settings influence or reflect the mood of your characters? Do they resonate with the themes of you   Are your characters revealed through several means: their appearance, possessions, behaviour, dialogue, and the opinions of others? Are they flat when they ought to be round? Do they develop in response to events? Does their development determine the plot?

3. Voices
Does your dialogue sound natural? Do the vernacular voices ring true? Do your characters speak at cross purposes, hide more than they show, communicate more to the reader than they do to each other? Does your dialogue signify on more than one level? Does it help advance the plot or enhance the characterisation? Is it clear who is speaking? Is your punctuation and formatting consistent?

4. Viewpoints
Is your narrator a reliable guide to the world of your fiction? Whether first, second or third person, is the point of view consistent? Do you exploit the difference between 'the time of the told' and 'the time of the telling'? Do you manage the possibilities for narrowing and widening the 'psychic distance'? Is there a difference between 'who speaks?' and 'who sees?' and is it consistent?

5. Structure
Is there a definite beginning, middle and end to your story? Do you have an inciting event? Is your story complete and self-contained? Do the events have a causal connection? Are they in the best order? Do you dwell too long in the past? Do you have too many strands, or not quite enough? Do you have too many short scenes and not enough long ones? Is there a change or reversal or a coming to awareness of some sort? Does the ending resolve things?

Of course there's an element of artificiality in the idea that you might need to consult such a checklist in order to approach the task of revision. Initially, at least, it may prove useful. But over time you should begin to acquire a level of understanding through the continuous practice of writing and reading that will enable you to 'feel' when your fictions are working, without the need for such deliberate or mechanical self-questioning.

A tentative analogy might be drawn with the way in which we come to know and use basic grammar, which will often seem like second nature to us, as much a matter of intuition as conscious intention. And indeed the hope of this guidebook is to offer something like a schooling in the 'grammar' of writing prose fiction. But the analogy must remain tentative, for a couple of reasons: firstly, as the example of Snowy Fulcher in Chapter 7 should illustrate, spoken English frequently tends towards the ungrammatical, even while it continues to communicate; and secondly, as I know from reading hundreds of student works-in-progress, even the most carefully written English can betray a degree of grammatical uncertainty, particularly in the area of punctuation.

I will return to this shortly, but here first is an exercise that should be completed without further recourse to the checklist.

---

70. Next thoughts

Look again at the piece of automatic writing that you wrote in response to the exercise 'More first thoughts'.

You are going to attempt to turn this rough writing into the start of a short story.

As with earlier automatic writing exercises, the phrasing will need some finessing. The order may be wrong. There may be lines you'll want to remove, and lines you'll want to improve. There will be gaps to fill.

But this time you should aim to depict the mysterious. Whatever your character is doing, your description should suggest that something ominous is about to occur. Your character should sense that something is amiss, and your reader should share the uncertainty (without becoming confused).

You may change the point of view to first or third person, but remember to place the emphasis on precise sensory detail.

We will return to this later.

If, as I claimed in Chapter 7, everyday speech verges at times on the incoherent or frankly nonsensical, the problem is never one of punctuation, for there is no punctuation in speech. There is breath, and intonation, and speed of delivery; there's facial expression, hand gesture, and body shape. Each of these is expressive; all of them signify. And dependent on our use of such physical indicators, the same few words can be made to mean a variety of things, sometimes quite contradictory things. Consider, for example, the way in which body language and intonation can alter the meaning of the sentence: 'You're a really funny guy.' This could be sarcastic or enthusiastic, insulting or admiring; in certain contexts it may even convey puzzlement or disappointment.

In addition to being highly flexible, speech is also instantly 'correctable'. So if I sense I'm not getting my message across, or if I know I'm expressing myself poorly, or if my listener looks puzzled – or affronted when I intend her to be amused – I will have an immediate opportunity to amend what I've just said. A shared understanding can be 'negotiated', person to person. Even someone whose speech is loaded with 'ums' and 'arrs' can make himself understood with relative ease in conversation, provided his listener is patient.

None of this can be claimed for writing, however. Compared to speech, writing is really quite inflexible and unexpressive. Or rather, if you wish your writing to be flexible and expressive, you will need to work a lot harder than speech will ever require of you. In order to ensure that your meaning carries to your eventual reader, you will need to be much more exact, much more careful, and one of the ways in which you can achieve this is by engaging with Eliot's 'frightful toil': the testing, correcting and combining that is required at the level of the sentence, and which will depend on an awareness of the rules of grammar and the conventions of punctuation.

This toil needn't always be 'frightful' of course. But it is unavoidable. And if one definition of a writer is 'a person on whom nothing is lost', another might be 'a person for whom commas are crucial'. The critic Louis Menand – a professor of literature and language at Harvard – explains the importance of punctuation in this way:

> Using the relatively small number of symbols on the keyboard, you can record, store, and communicate a virtually infinite range of information, and encode meanings with virtually any degree of complexity. The system works entirely by relationships – the relationship of one symbol to another, of one word to another, of one sentence to another. The function of most punctuation – commas, colons and semicolons, dashes, and so on – is to help organize the relationships among the parts of a sentence. Its role is semantic: to add precision and complexity to meaning. It increases the information potential of strings of words.

Menand wrote this in *The New Yorker*, in a review of Lynne Truss's best-selling book on punctuation, *Eats, Shoots & Leaves*, and both Truss and Menand agree that correct punctuation increases the information potential of words, while being equally alert to the hazards of incorrect punctuation, which can reduce or distort that potential. Elsewhere in his review, Menand refers to punctuation as a 'technology'. Truss herself uses the analogy of a system of traffic signs, which 'tell us when to slow down, notice this, take a detour, and stop'. And of course, should the technology be faulty, or the signs wrongly or poorly positioned, we may get into scrapes, or end up some way from where we were meant to be.

The erroneous comma in the title *Eats, Shoots & Leaves* is a prime example. If we remove it – as we ought to – then 'shoots' and 'leaves' become nouns, the two staples of a panda's diet. But if we leave it in, then 'shoots' and 'leaves' remain as verbs in a bizarre little tale concerning a panda who eats something (perhaps in a restaurant), then shoots (a gun, presumably), and leaves the scene (insouciantly, probably).

In most instances, the context will allow us to retrieve the meaning of an ambiguous sentence almost immediately, but the momentary stumble in our reading will cause the writing to lose a little of its authority. And the more errors there are, the less authority the writing will carry. In the case of fiction, the vivid and continuous dream may be disturbed, possibly terminally. In the case of expository writing, any messiness in the expression will detract from the persuasive power of the argument.

Unfortunately, *Eats, Shoots & Leaves* offers a prime example of this, too. The error in the title is deliberate and illustrative, but throughout her book Lynne Truss persistently misuses semicolons. And once I'd begun to notice this, I started to wonder how much else in her argument was faulty; gradually, I began to lose faith in her authority as a reliable guide to punctuation.

Louis Menand noticed a great deal more that was faulty, and lost faith in her almost before she'd got going. Here is another passage from his review:

> The preface, by Truss, includes a misplaced apostrophe ('printers' marks') and two misused semicolons: one that separates unpunctuated items in a list and one that sets off a dependent clause. About half the semicolons in the rest of the book are either unnecessary or ungrammatical, and the comma is deployed as the mood strikes. Sometimes, phrases such as 'of course' are set off by commas; sometimes, they are not. Doubtful, distracting, and unwarranted commas turn up in front of restrictive phrases ('Naturally we become timid about making our insights known, in such inhospitable conditions'), before correlative conjunctions ('Either this will ring bells for you, or it won't'), and in prepositional phrases ('including

biblical names, and foreign names with an unpronounced final "s"').
Where you most expect punctuation, it may not show up at all . . .

And so he goes on. And if this offers a caution against proposing oneself as
an expert in grammar and punctuation, I ought to declare at once that I am no
expert. I struggle, for a start, to distinguish between restrictive and non-
restrictive phrases. The difference between 'who' and 'whom' gets muddled
in my mind, as does the difference between 'that' and 'which', and 'might' and
'may'. I fear I may sometimes deploy commas as the mood strikes. But I do
believe I have a feel for the fundamentals, even if I have to look up the correct
terminology in order to explain them.[1]

In her essay 'Why I Write', the American writer Joan Didion remarks,
'Grammar is a piano I play by ear, since I seem to have been out of school the
year the rules were mentioned.' And I suspect that a great many of us will feel
that we, too, were out of school when the rules were mentioned, and will also
attempt to play by ear, but that few of us will feel that we play with any great
fluency. On the contrary, we may feel we play woodenly, or clumsily, and could
use some instruction. Didion goes on to say:

> All I know of grammar is its infinite power. To shift the structure of a sen-
> tence alters the meaning of that sentence, as definitely and inflexibly as the
> position of a camera alters the meaning of the object being photographed.
> Many people know about camera angles now, but not so many know about
> sentences.

It is beyond the scope of this book – and certainly beyond my competence
as a linguist – to offer anything like a schooling in the principles and practical-
ities of English grammar and punctuation. But in what remains of this chapter
I will attempt to explain a little about sentences – single-clause, co-ordinate,
complex, and compound-complex – and the ways in which punctuation can
be deployed to shift their structure, alter their meaning, and possibly increase
their power.

Simple

Perhaps the most common understanding of what constitutes an English sentence is that it should contain a subject, a verb and an object, in that order. And

---

[1] The book I most rely on is *Grammar and Writing* by Rebecca Stott and Peter
Chapman. Much of what follows is informed by this book.

there are a great many English sentences of just that type. These are known as single-clause ('simple') sentences, and here's an example:

Andrew wrote a guidebook.

'Andrew' is the subject of this sentence (the active agent), 'wrote' is the verb (it's what he did), and 'a guidebook' is the object (the passive element, the thing that was done or done to). But this would still be a sentence even without an object:

Andrew wrote.

The meaning here is complete and self-contained. We might want to know *what* Andrew wrote, but that wouldn't make this any more of a sentence; it would merely make it longer, and more informative, and marginally more interesting.[2] So, at its simplest, we might propose that even two words can constitute a sentence, provided that one of them is a subject and the other a verb, and provided the meaning is complete and self-contained. But in fact the subject isn't always necessary either. There are four sentence types:

Declarative: to state something – e.g. 'Andrew wrote a book.'
Interrogative: to ask something – e.g. 'What is it about?'
Exclamative: to exclaim – e.g. 'That's exciting!'
Imperative: to command or request something – e.g. 'Let me see.'

With the last of these – the imperative – it is common to have single-word sentences, comprised of just a verb, for instance 'Listen!' The subject here is implicit in the command: imperatives must be addressed to a someone.

But there is something else. The verb here is in a *finite* form, which is to say it is limited to a particular duration ('listen *now*') and attached (even implicitly) to a subject ('*you* listen'). The verb in any sentence must be finite, in fact, otherwise it isn't officially a sentence. And the opposite of a finite verb is a non-finite verb, which doesn't specify a subject or a duration (among other things too tricky to explain).

---

[2] As an aside: verbs that don't require an object are called intransitive, e.g. 'I slept', 'she wept', 'he died'. Verbs that do require an object are called transitive, e.g. 'I threw . . .', 'she caught . . .', 'he took . . .' (the dots represent the missing object). But a great many verbs can be either, depending on the context. 'Andrew wrote' is intransitive. 'Andrew wrote a book' is transitive.

Two of the principal forms that a non-finite verb may take are the infinitive[3] and the present participle. So, for instance, the infinitive of listen is 'to listen', which doesn't limit the verb by duration or to a particular subject, while the present participle of listen is 'listening', which is the *continuous* form of the verb and so, by definition, doesn't impose any limits in terms of duration either.

Bearing this in mind, we might therefore define a sentence at its simplest as comprising a subject, whether implicit or explicit, and a verb in one of its finite forms. But then as a necessary aside I ought to mention the poetic or literary licence that allows constructions such as the following:

Andrew discussed grammar and punctuation. Finally.

'Finally' is an adverb, of course[4] – a word that qualifies or amplifies the meaning of a verb. It isn't an imperative because it isn't an instruction, and it doesn't imply a subject. And like any adverb, its meaning is not complete and self-contained, but entirely dependent on the sentence in which its verb appears. 'Finally' belongs to the verb 'discussed', and strictly speaking it ought to be incorporated into the sentence in which that verb appears:

Andrew discussed grammar and punctuation, finally.

or

Finally, Andrew discussed grammar and punctuation.

or

Andrew finally discussed grammar and punctuation.

Technically, then, 'Finally' is not a sentence. And yet there it sits, capitalised, with its own full stop, for all the world as if it were a sentence. But this

---

[3] The infinitive is the basic form of a verb: 'to be', 'to write', 'to read', 'to daydream', 'to doze'. And one common error is to split the infinitive, which means to place an adverb in the middle of it: 'to carefully write', 'to quickly read'. I call it an error. It makes me wince. It makes many other people wince. But it's probably less of a grammatical error than a stylistic *faux pas*. It doesn't offend a rule so much as a custom, and there are a lot of split infinitives out there, the most famous being 'to boldly go . . .'.

[4] I say 'of course' . . . I really was out of school when the rules of grammar were mentioned, and one memory that continues to make me cringe is having to ask in Malcolm Bradbury's Creative Writing workshop at the age of twenty-two, 'What *are* adjectives and adverbs?' I used them all the time, of course; I just didn't know what they were called.

kind of single-word pseudo-sentence is to be found everywhere in literary English, doing the work that intonation or timing might achieve in speech, adding emphasis, conveying a particular rhetorical charge.

Consider, for instance, the opening to Lynne Bryan's novel *Gorgeous*, which I mentioned in Chapter 9:

> Rita turns into Ashberry Grove. She is still in fourth and her speeding car takes the corner wide. She travels some distance down the wrong side of the street.
> Her passenger, Doreen, clasps her handbag tight, pushing it into her lap. Rita swerves to the left and Doreen inhales. Audibly. Uuhf.

'Audibly' is also an adverb, belonging to the verb 'inhales', while the ono-matopoeic exclamative 'Uuhf' ought really to be contained in speech marks.[5] But the comic and literary effect of this passage depends upon those two words being set apart in this way. Which is perhaps to admit, almost before I've begun, that a strict adherence to correct grammar may actually place a limit on the effectiveness of your prose. It is to admit, perhaps, that you may need to commit some creative damage to the language in order to achieve a style or distinctive 'voice' of your own.

This admission needs to be qualified, however, by a reassertion of the importance of understanding the grammatical rules to which you are commit-ting the damage. And that understanding begins with an appreciation of what constitutes a simple sentence, which thus far I've attempted to define in terms of a minimum number of words. That, too, may need qualification.

Consider this sentence:

> The novelist and Creative Writing tutor put together a guidebook on the writing of prose fiction.

Here the subject (or 'subject element') is six words long: 'The novelist and Creative Writing tutor'. The verb (or 'verb element') is two words: 'put together'. This is known as a phrasal verb, and there are a great many of them in the language: 'calm down', 'clean up', 'write down', 'throw up'. In this case, the phrasal verb 'put together' is transitive and requires an object to complete

---

[5] This may be yet another example of how readily speech is able to accommodate the ungrammatical. A great deal of speech is highly elliptical. For instance, if I were to ask, 'When are you going to start writing your novel?' you might reply, 'Tomorrow, maybe.' This answer lacks a subject, a verb or an object. The conversational context makes it meaningful, however.

its meaning. That object (or 'object element') is another eight words: 'a guide-book on the writing of prose fiction'.

I might lengthen this sentence yet further by the addition of some adverbs and adjectives:

> The *top-notch* novelist and Creative Writing tutor *effortlessly* put together a *superior* guidebook on the writing of prose fiction.

Dubious as the content of this sentence has now become, I could lengthen it yet further by employing what are known as adverbial and adjectival phrases – clusters of words that serve the same purpose as single-word adverbs and adjectives. But still, the underlying structure would remain quite simple: subject, verb, object.

Another name for this kind of minimal grammatical unit is a clause. And a clause whose meaning is complete and self-contained and which contains a finite verb is known as an independent clause – in other words, a sentence in its simplest form.

A single-clause sentence needn't always be expressed in the active voice, however: the subject needn't always come first, followed by the verb, followed by the object (if required). As we saw with my dog's 'dump' in the previous chapter, the order can be reversed, so that the subject comes last, almost as if it's the recipient (or object) of the verb:

> The book was written by Andrew.
> The dump was picked up by me.

This is known as the passive voice and is relatively common in academic writing, especially scientific writing, because the relegation (or even removal) of the active subject creates an appearance of impersonality or objectivity, which is often appropriate to the presentation of fact-based information. In prose fiction, however, the use of the passive voice can seem laboured, long-winded, or simply archaic.

Consider again the opening three sentences of *Gorgeous*, rearranged in the passive voice:

> Ashberry Grove is turned into by her. The corner is taken wide by her speeding car, which is kept in fourth. Some distance down the wrong side of the street is travelled by her.

Arguably, the passive voice has its own distinct – and defamiliarising, and somewhat awkward – style, which could be striking and effective in certain contexts. But clearly the active voice is more direct and concise, and carries more energy, and while I could envisage reading an entire novel written in the active voice, I could not imagine reading one presented entirely in the passive. As a general rule, therefore, I would encourage you to write primarily in the active voice, without entirely eliminating the use of the passive. In effective writing (as with showing and telling) both are required. The key is in the balance (mostly active; occasionally passive).

---

71. Simple

Return to the writing you wrote in response to Exercise 70, 'Next thoughts'.

The aim is to preserve as much as possible of this piece – the same details in the same order – but to rewrite at least the first page entirely in single-clause or 'simple' sentences.

Most of your sentences should comprise a subject, a verb, and an object. Some may dispense with the object. You may include a few single-word 'pseudo-sentences'. But all of your sentences should be written in the active voice.

Compound

If our first type of sentence construction is the single-clause ('simple') sentence, the second is the co-ordinate ('compound') sentence, which is made up of two or more independent clauses. Crucial to the construction of such sentences is the means by which these clauses are connected. Here are two single-clause sentences:

> Lynne Truss wrote a book on punctuation. Louis Menand was far from impressed.[6]

---

[6] Even as I write this, I feel the spectre of Louis Menand hovering over me, distinctly unimpressed. Not to overcomplicate matters, but strictly speaking a clause comprises a subject (whether explicit or implied) and a 'predicate'. A predicate expresses something about the subject. Often, as we have seen, this takes the form of a verb describing an action. But equally it may take the form of a phrase describing a state. The clause 'Louis Menand was far from impressed' tells us not what he did but how he felt. 'Louis Menand' is the subject; 'was' is known as the linking verb; 'far from impressed' (an adjectival phrase) is known as the subject complement. Other examples of this kind of clause are 'I was happy', 'you are sad', 'he is baffled'.

There are two main methods by which these clauses can be joined to make one compound sentence. The first is to use a co-ordinating conjunction, of which there are seven: and, but, or, for, nor, so, yet. In this instance, 'and', 'but' or 'yet' would make a good fit:

Lynne Truss wrote a book on punctuation, and Louis Menand was far from impressed.

Lynne Truss wrote a book on punctuation, but Louis Menand was far from impressed.

Lynne Truss wrote a book on punctuation, yet Louis Menand was far from impressed.

The convention illustrated by these examples is that a comma should be placed before the conjunction, but in shorter sentences it is often acceptable not to:

Lynne laughed and Louis scowled.

The second method for linking independent clauses is to use a semicolon. I think of the semicolon as a 'soft full stop', in that it separates one thematically related clause from another, though not as emphatically as a full stop might. In a sense, it links and separates simultaneously:

Lynne Truss wrote a book on punctuation; Louis Menand was far from impressed.

We can easily extend this, adding a third independent clause, so that we have three single-clause sentences making one large compound sentence. These may be separated by semicolons, or by co-ordinating conjunctions, or by a mixture of both:

Lynne Truss wrote a book on punctuation; Louis Menand was far from impressed; he wrote a stinking review in *The New Yorker*.

or

Lynne Truss wrote a book on punctuation, and Louis Menand was far from impressed, so he wrote a stinking review in *The New Yorker*.

or

Lynne Truss wrote a book on punctuation, but Louis Menand was far from impressed; he wrote a stinking review in *The New Yorker*.

In the last of these examples, the semicolon might be replaced by a colon; indeed, a colon might be a better choice:

> Lynne Truss wrote a book on punctuation, but Louis Menand was far from impressed: he wrote a stinking review in *The New Yorker*.

The effect of a colon is to make a kind of hand gesture towards what comes after it, when what comes after it is an amplification or illustration or explanation of what comes before it. This makes it ideal for introducing quotations or lists, as in the following examples:

> There are three essentials to being a writer: self-discipline, self-belief, and talent.

> There are three essentials to being a writer: an understanding of the need for self-discipline; some degree of self-belief, however undermined by feelings of incompetence; an innate or acquired talent for manipulating language.

In the first of these examples, the items in the list are punctuated by commas, while in the second they are separated by semicolons, and this illustrates the other main use of the semicolon, which is to separate the items in a list when those items are themselves grammatically complex, particularly if they already contain other punctuation, such as commas.

---

72. Compound

Return to the writing you wrote in response to Exercise 71, 'Simple'.

The aim is to preserve as much as possible of this piece – the same clauses in the same order – but to rewrite it entirely in co-ordinate ('compound') sentences. You may use any of the seven co-ordinating conjunctions – and, but, or, for, nor, so, yet – plus semicolons and, where appropriate, colons.

Complex

The one item of punctuation with which you really shouldn't attempt to connect grammatically independent clauses is the comma, and yet this is possibly the error I encounter most often in my students' writing:

> Lynne Truss wrote a book on punctuation, Louis Menand was far from impressed, he wrote a stinking review in *The New Yorker*.

This particular solecism is known as the comma splice, and while it is wrong, and Louis Menand would doubtless disapprove of it – as I very often disapprove of it – there are countless literary examples to support its use. Lynne Truss cites Samuel Beckett, E.M. Forster and Somerset Maugham, and remarks:

> Done knowingly by an established writer, the comma splice is effective, poetic, dashing. Done equally knowingly by people who are not published writers, it can look weak or presumptuous. Done ignorantly by ignorant people, it is awful.

Beware, then, of being ignorant.

Commas do have numerous legitimate uses, however, especially in relation to our third type of sentence construction, the complex sentence. If the clauses in a co-ordinate ('compound') sentence are grammatically equal, the clauses in this third type of sentence are grammatically unequal. In addition to the main clause, there will be one or more subordinate clauses ('sub-clauses'). The role of the comma is to separate them. Here is an example:

> In a complex sentence, the main clause is grammatically independent, whereas the subordinate clauses are not.

The main clause here is in the middle. If we were to capitalise the first letter of this main clause, and place a full stop at the end of it, we would have a complete, self-contained sentence:

> The main clause is grammatically independent.

The same operation could not be performed on the sub-clauses, however, since a sub-clause is entirely dependent on the main clause to complete its meaning. If a sub-clause were to be dressed up as if it were a proper sentence, with a capitalised first letter and a terminal full stop, the result would be what is known as a sentence fragment:

> In a complex sentence.
> Whereas the subordinate clauses are not.

Of course, the main clause in a complex sentence need not always be situated in the middle. In other complex sentences, it may come at the beginning or at the end:

The best way to improve as a writer is to read the work of other writers, no matter how experienced you are.

or

No matter how experienced you are, the best way to improve as a writer is to read the work of other writers.

In this instance, our sub-clause may itself be placed in the middle, which will mean dividing our main clause into two parts:

The best way to improve as a writer, no matter how experienced you are, is to read the work of other writers.

The commas here enclose a parenthetical statement, a sub-clause that might easily be removed without doing damage to the sense of the main clause. The sub-clause is a kind of textual aside; it's a piece of additional, but non-essential information. And it can be punctuated with dashes or brackets instead of commas:

The best way to improve as a writer – no matter how experienced you are – is to read the work of other writers.

or

The best way to improve as a writer (no matter how experienced you are) is to read the work of other writers.

There are quite subtle differences of emphasis here. Dashes are possibly more emphatic than commas, bringing the sub-clause more to the fore. The effect of brackets may be the opposite. But whichever form of punctuation we favour, it's important to remember that the brackets, dashes or commas must come in identical pairs: the parenthesis must be enclosed at both ends. After the comma splice, this is the second most common error I encounter in my students' work, the missing parenthetical comma:

The best way to improve as a writer, no matter how experienced you are is to read the work of other writers.

There are two other useful means by which we might construct complex, multi-claused sentences. The first of these is to use what are known as subordinating conjunctions, of which there are a great many. These are also known as dependent marker words, and here are just a few of them:

> after, although, as, as if, because, before, despite, even if, even though, if, if only, rather than, since, that, though, unless, until, when, where, whereas, whenever, whether, which, while . . .

Unlike co-ordinating conjunctions, which are used to connect two or more independent clauses, the purpose of a subordinating conjunction is to convert what might otherwise stand as an independent clause into a subordinate (dependent) clause. Here are two independent clauses:

> I can't complete my novel. The plot is all in a tangle.

We could yoke these two statements together with a semicolon or with a co-ordinating conjunction – which will give us a compound sentence – or we could attach a subordinating conjunction to one of the two clauses. This will have the effect of subordinating that clause to the other one; its purpose will then be to complete the meaning of the main clause:

> I can't complete my novel *while* the plot is all in a tangle.

or

> *Because* the plot is all in a tangle, I can't complete my novel.

Other subordinate clauses may be added – for instance, the independent clause 'I meant to' could be converted into a subordinate clause by the application of the subordinating conjunction 'even though':

> *Because* the plot is all in a tangle, I can't complete my novel, *even though* I meant to.

The other device by which we might construct complex sentences is through the use of participles, which come in three varieties: the present, which we have seen (verbs ending with -*ing*), the past (verbs ending with -*ed*), and the perfect (*having* plus the past participle form):

> Before *completing* my novel, I first untangled the plot.

or

> With the plot *untangled*, I finally completed my novel.

or

> *Having* untangled the plot, I finally completed my novel.

The positive point to be made about participles is that they offer infinite options for varying the rhythm and shape of your sentences. The problem with them is that they sometimes lead to the third most common error in my students' writing, which is the dangling participle. The participle is said to be dangling because it isn't properly connected – in grammatical terms – to the main clause, and so ends up saying something quite bizarre. Here is an example:

> Finally untangled, I was able to resolve the plot of my novel.

The grammatical rule is that the sub-clause ('finally untangled') should share the same subject as the main clause ('I was able to resolve the plot of my novel'). In this instance, the subject of the main clause is 'I'. And if the sub-clause is to share the same subject (albeit implicitly), this sentence actually ends up saying:

> I was finally untangled. I was therefore able to resolve the plot of my novel.

At its least ambitious, this chapter may be viewed as one large sledgehammer to crack three very small nuts: the comma splice, the missing parenthetical comma, and the dangling participle. If it alerts you to just these three misdemeanours, and stops you offending (or re-offending), that may be enough. More ambitiously, my hope is that it may extend the stylistic possibilities of your prose, not merely increasing the 'information potential' of your 'strings of words', but considerably enhancing their aesthetic effect, as I will emphasise in the final part of this chapter.

---

73. Complex

Return to the writing you wrote in response to Exercise 71, 'Simple'.
   The aim is to preserve as much as possible of this piece, but to rewrite it entirely in complex sentences. Each of your sentences should have one main clause, and one or more sub-clauses. You may need to adjust the order of the clauses. You may need to convert some of the clauses into sub-clauses by employing subordinating conjunctions or participles.

Complex-compound

In Chapter 2, I remarked that the writer's raw material is language, which is to say *words*. But as this chapter should have made clear, punctuation is almost as vital a material.[7] Arguably, the choices you make in constructing your sentences are what will determine your 'voice' – the rhythm, personality or style of your writing – and this is not merely a matter of word choice, but of word order within clauses, and clause order within sentences, both of which will depend upon the accuracy – and sometimes the subtlety – of your punctuation.

This is not necessarily to advocate that you should write in complex sentences, however. Your sensibility or inclination may be to favour simple sentences, in the manner perhaps of the American author, Raymond Carver, one of the most distinctive and influential stylists of the late twentieth century and himself an inheritor of the pared-down, declarative style of Ernest Hemingway.

A former pupil of John Gardner, Carver wrote the foreword to Gardner's posthumous *On Becoming a Novelist*, in which he says of his teacher:

> It was a basic tenet of his that a writer found what he wanted to say in the ongoing process of *seeing* what he'd said. And this seeing, or seeing more clearly, came about through revision. He *believed* in revision, endless revision; it was something very close to his heart and something he felt was vital for writers, at whatever stage of their development.

Carver himself was a scrupulous, painstaking reviser, whose fictions were further revised by his editor, Gordon Lish, to achieve the characteristic Carver tone: taut, deadpan, minimalistic, written largely in simple or compound sentences, and employing a tightly restricted and often rhythmically repetitive vocabulary. Here, by way of illustration, is the beginning of his short story, 'I could see the smallest things':

> I was in bed when I heard the gate. I listened carefully. I didn't hear anything else. But I heard that. I tried to wake Cliff. He was passed out. So I got up and went to the window. A big moon was laid over the mountains that went around the city. It was a white moon and covered with scars. Any damn fool could imagine a face there.

---

[7] I was tempted to write 'just as vital a material' but of course an unpunctuated page of writing will still make some kind of sense whereas a page of punctuation without any words will make no sense whatsoever.

What characterises Carver's fiction is more than just this stark, distilled style, however. There is subject matter, too. In a special issue of the literary magazine *Granta* in 1983, the editor Bill Buford identified in Carver and others a new generation of American writers who were, he claimed, at the forefront of a revival in the American short story. These writers he termed the 'dirty realists' for their shared concern with 'the belly-side of contemporary life', and among them he included Carver's close friend Richard Ford. The stories of the dirty realists, wrote Buford, were:

> unadorned, unfurnished, low-rent tragedies about people who watch day-time television, read cheap romances or listen to country and western music. They are waitresses in roadside cafes, cashiers in supermarkets, construction workers, secretaries and unemployed cowboys. They play bingo, eat cheeseburgers, hunt deer and stay in cheap hotels. They drink a lot and are often in trouble: for stealing a car, breaking a window, pick-pocketing a wallet.

Yet for all that Carver and Ford shared an interest in marginal, disappointed, blue-collar America, Ford was already a more expansive stylist than Carver, and has – since Carver's death in 1988 – developed ever further in the direction of a multi-claused, syntactically complex and thematically capacious prose style, as may be illustrated by this sentence from his 1995 novel, *Independence Day*:

> Last night, sometime after midnight, when I'd already slept for an hour, waked up twice twisting my pillow and fretting about Paul's and my jour-ney, downed a glass of milk, watched the Weather Channel, then settled back to read a chapter of *The Declaration of Independence* – Carl Becker's classic, which, along with *Self-Reliance*, I plan to use as key 'texts' for communicating with my troubled son and thereby transmitting to him important info – Sally called.

The main clause here is very simple indeed: 'Last night Sally called'. Each of the other potentially independent clauses – which include the participles 'waked', 'downed', 'watched' and 'settled' – is subordinated by the dependent marker word 'when'. And this is a typical Ford construction: a main clause trailing an elaborate tail of subordinate clauses. Occasionally, however, he will deploy what is called a compound-complex sentence, which will have two main clauses and two or more sub-clauses. In the following short paragraph, the narrator and his son Paul are taking a road trip to the Basketball Hall of Fame in Springfield, Massachusetts:

In a hasty thirty minutes we slide off 91 into Springfield and go touring round through the old mill town, following the disappearing brown-and-white BB. HALL OF FAME signs until we're all the way north of downtown and pulled to a halt across from a dense brick housing project on a wide and windy trash-strewn boulevard by the on-ramp to the interstate we were just on. Lost.[8]

Here we begin with two independent clauses – essentially 'we slide off' and 'we go touring' – which are connected by the co-ordinating conjunction 'and'. The subordinate clauses are then introduced by the present participle 'following', and furthered by the subordinating conjunction 'until'. This is a very Fordian construction and represents an opposing end of the stylistic spectrum to the Carveresque – a spectrum that has Carver at the pole of simplicity and Ford at the pole of complexity – but while it might be an interesting exercise to rewrite a page of *Independence Day* in the form of Carver's short sentences, or a page of a Carver short story in the form of Ford's more complex sentences, this would be to lose the particular punch and resonance of each author's voice, which has been achieved, as Carver suggests, by 'revision, endless revision'. Which isn't, however, to say that you shouldn't attempt to rewrite a page of your own writing – or indeed that you shouldn't attempt to rewrite, and endlessly revise, your own writing as a matter of course.

---

74. Compound-complex

Return to the writing you wrote in response to Exercise 71, 'Simple'.

The aim this time is to preserve as much as possible of this piece, but to rewrite it entirely as a single, very long, compound-complex sentence, employing independent and subordinate clauses, co-ordinating and subordinating conjunctions, parentheses and all the possibilities of punctuation.

---

[8] Louis Menand criticised Lynne Truss for deploying a semicolon to set off a dependent clause. Now that I come to re-read Richard Ford for his sentence constructions, I realise that his stylistic flexibility extends to breaking this rule more than any other. Awkwardly (for me), there are any number of 'incorrect' semicolons in Ford's writing. I've chosen not to offer an example, but in this paragraph he also concludes with the single-clause pseudo-sentence 'Lost'. There is doubtless a lesson in this.

12. Workshopping

At the start of this book I gave a lengthy list of writers' working routines, since when I've found out that John Steinbeck wrote his novels mainly in pencil, a page a day, and didn't correct or rewrite them until he had a complete draft, and that Mark Twain was another author who did much of his writing in bed, and that Thomas Mann kept to a strict regime of writing every day from nine until one, and that William Trevor will begin work at 7.20 each morning, and take coffee at nine, then attempt one more hour before he stops for the day . . . My list, in other words, might have been a lot lengthier still.

But this isn't the only type of information that interests me. I am equally drawn to what other writers have to say about the craft of writing, and the nature of 'being' a writer, and if I come across something that chimes with my own experience – or even, occasionally, contradicts it – then I will squirrel this away, too; I will copy it to a scrapbook file on my computer which is arranged under such headings as 'inspiration', 'perspiration', 'character', 'dialogue', 'block' and so on. Most of the quotations I've used in this book have come from this store.

Here is a short selection on the theme of 'uncertainty',[1] by way of introduction (a rather roundabout introduction) to some thoughts on the subject of workshopping:

> Paul Auster: 'I sometimes feel that I am wondering in a haze of things that cannot be articulated and the struggle to put things down clearly is

[1] In the main my quotations have come from four sources: newspaper profiles, writers' memoirs, the archive of *The Paris Review*, and the interviews conducted by Chris Bigsby as part of UEA's rolling literary festival and collected in two volumes as *Writers in Conversation*. A fifth source is 'miscellaneous'.

so enormous that I think at times my brain is damaged. I do not think as clearly as other people. The words don't come when I want them. I can spend fifteen or twenty minutes trying to decide between prepositions and then I have no idea which is right any more; absolutely stupid basic stuff, basic grammatical questions. It is just a tremendous puzzle for me all the time.'

E.L. Doctorow: 'You write best when you write to find out what you're writing. It's a writer's dirty little secret that language precedes the intentions . . . I wrote [*Welcome to Hard Times*] crucially because I knew nothing about it. That's how writers write: by trying to find what it is they are writing.'

E.M. Forster: 'How do I know what I think until I see what I say.'

Elizabeth Hardwick: 'As for writing fiction, well, you don't have any primary text, of course. You have to create that, and yet the struggle seems to be to uncover things by language, to find out what you mean and feel by the sheer effort of writing it down. By expression you discover what you wish to express or what can be expressed, by you.'

David Malouf: 'Writers have to be – naive is the wrong word – but in a state of innocence when writing. Everything you think you know you have to let fall out of your head, because the only thing that's going to be interesting in the book is what you don't yet know . . . Although you have to be highly conscious on one level – technique and so on – you also have to be in some 'non-knowing' mode for the book to shape itself.'

William Trevor: 'I believe in not quite knowing. A writer needs to be doubtful, questioning. I write out of curiosity and bewilderment.'

By any measure these are highly accomplished authors who might be supposed to know what they are doing and where they are going, and yet each of them – whether describing their relationship with language, or subject matter, or literary form – appears to be admitting that they do not in fact know, not quite. For some this admission is cheerfully made. For many a degree of uncertainty – or what David Malouf calls 'non-knowing' – is accepted as the necessary precondition for producing surprising or interesting writing. But for others (and Paul Auster is not alone) the puzzlement or bewilderment that accompanies the process of composition is far from benign; the effort to find the right words is often fraught, a struggle, and can be defeating.

In his autobiographical novel *The Wrench*, the chemist and writer Primo Levi offers a particularly wry account of the toll that may be taken on a writer's nerves by dwelling too long, as Keats phrased it, in 'uncertainties, Mysteries, doubts'.

In this novel an unnamed narrator – who happens also to be a chemist and writer – listens attentively to the long-winded anecdotes of another man, a rigger of scaffolds and industrial cranes called Libertino Faussone. The two men are working overseas 'in a very remote factory', and meet regularly in the mess hall, and while there are certain parallels in their respective professions as paint chemist and rigger – not least in their reliance on 'control instruments' to provide them with accurate measurements – the resemblance between rigging and writing is not so apparent until Faussone, after one especially bad day, describes the despair that comes over him when a job goes awry.

The whole of life then seems crooked, he says, and 'you begin to ask yourself questions, maybe even questions that don't make sense, like for example, what are we in this world for?'

But writers have their bad days, too, the writer-chemist informs him; in fact, writers have them more often, because it is so much easier to gauge whether 'a piece of metal structure is "right on the bubble" than a written page'. And so a page, or even a whole book of them, may be written with enthusiasm, only to be revealed in the end as a botch – 'silly, unoriginal, incomplete, excessive, futile':

> and then you turn sad, and you start getting ideas like the ones he had that evening, namely you think of changing jobs, air, skin, and maybe even becoming a rigger. But it can also happen that you write some things that really are botched and futile (and this happens often) but you don't realize it, which is far more possible, because paper is too tolerant a material. You can write any old absurdity on it, and it never complains: it doesn't act like the beams in mine tunnels that creak when they're overburdened and are about to cave in. In the job of writing the instruments, the alarm systems are rudimentary: there isn't even a trustworthy equivalent of the T square or the plumbline. But if a page is wrong the reader notices, and by then it is too late, and the situation is bad, also because that page is your work, only yours: you have no excuses or pretexts; you are totally responsible.

The somewhat tipsy Faussone, whose face is usually 'less expressive than the bottom of a pan', does here become quite animated, and exclaims: 'Just think: for us guys, if they'd never invented control instruments, and we had to do the job just by guesswork . . . it'd be enough to drive you crazy!' Which allows the writer-chemist to claim – or perhaps just to confirm – that many writers do in fact end up 'in the asylum' as a result of their weakened nerves, and 'not only in this century, but also long before', while numerous others 'are melancholy, drink, smoke, can't sleep, and die young'.[2]

Yet much as I recognise in these remarks something of my own relationship to writing, and much as I'm inclined to agree with Primo Levi that paper is far too tolerant a material, and that the writer is pretty much alone in the language – proceeding by guesswork, without dependable instruments to help determine whether a page is 'right on the bubble', and with no one to blame if the writing goes wrong – my main reason for invoking him here is not to insist on this view of writing as a fraught and lonely endeavour, but to make an argument, if only temporarily, against him – and indeed against myself – in favour of an approach to teaching and learning that hasn't so far been broached in this book: the collaborative enterprise that is the Creative Writing workshop.

In his essay 'The Art of Fiction', Henry James says: 'Art lives upon discussion, upon experiment, upon curiosity, upon variety of attempt, upon the exchange of views and the comparison of standpoints.' And one of the many benefits of the workshop is that it provides a forum in which just such an exchange and comparison may take place, while serving also to address the lack of any reliable instrumentation that Primo Levi so laments in *The Wrench*. The workshop operates, so to speak, as a kind of makeshift measuring device comprised of twelve (usually, twelve) additional pairs of squinting eyes, twelve other perspectives on the strength and accuracy of the writer's sentences.

For the workshop to succeed, however, I suspect that the participants should first have achieved a certain level of competence and confidence, not only as practising writers but as thinkers about their own and others' writing. They should have become, to some degree, self-conscious and deliberate in their approach to their craft – as much as they must also be instinctive and 'non-knowing' – and in the process they should have begun to acquire a measure of technical understanding that will allow them to articulate what they feel is 'true' or 'askew' about the works-in-progress that will be laid before them.

The programme of study described in the previous eleven chapters is designed, in other words, to lead up to this point – where the curriculum gives way to conversation, where discussion replaces instruction – on the assumption that the weekly practice of offering constructive criticism on the writing of others will supersede (rather than run alongside) an approach based on timed

---

[2] Of course, this overstates the case in order to make the case, and Faussone is then able, quite rightly, to point to the dangers a rigger is likely to encounter when 'the wind is blowing, and the structure still hasn't been braced, and it's dancing like a boat on the waves, and you see people on the ground like ants . . .'. However hard it might seem to write well, it is never this hazardous.

exercises. For that reason, there are no more exercises in what remains of this book. Instead what follows is a series of suggestions and ruminations on what makes for a successful workshop, based on my own experience of being a participant, both as student and tutor, in good workshops and bad, as well as the experiences of others I've spoken to, some of them colleagues and some of them students of colleagues.

As will become evident, most of the discussion assumes that the workshop is happening in an institutional setting, but of course it could happen anywhere – in someone's living room, for instance.

Distribute the work in advance

The first writers' workshop I attended, aged twenty-one, used to gather in the living room of the poet Robert Hamberger in Kettering (I answered an ad in the local paper); the second took place in Corby's short-lived Community Bookshop (where I worked as a volunteer) and was run by a writer-in-residence, the playwright Rib Davies. Joining both groups was a way of announcing (or admitting) to myself that writing was something that mattered to me, and the gatherings in Robert's front room especially were relaxed and encouraging. The fact that neither workshop was in any way institutional struck me then as important, and it is only now that I can see certain drawbacks, the most significant being that attendance was voluntary, while accessing free (or even affordable) photocopying was almost impossible.[3] As a consequence, we were unable to distribute multiple copies of our work in advance of the meetings, or be confident that anyone besides ourselves would turn up. Instead we had to read our work aloud on the night, sometimes to complete strangers – prospective new members who might never come again – and trust that our words carried, our voices were clear, and the minds of our listeners not too weary or distracted – as my own, I'm afraid, very frequently was.

Inevitably, the responses we received were based not on close scrutiny of our words as they appeared on the page, but on sometimes quite cursory initial impressions, some of them skewed by mishearing or misapprehension, and so, in the main, the best that anyone could offer us was applause – which, over time, is rarely enough, however important it might be at the outset.

---

[3] This was years before email of course, but even though email does make it easier to disseminate work, I discourage my current students from using it. So much can go wrong: the work can be spammed, or misdirected, or prove incompatible with the receiving computer. Some members of the group may not have access to a computer or reliable printer when needed. And besides, as a matter of courtesy, I don't think the recipients should be required to print out the work, in their own time, at their own expense.

I am aware that some highly reputable courses – particularly in Adult Education – are run along similar lines, and I've no doubt that gifted teachers and committed students can make it succeed for them. But one obvious advantage of distributing multiple copies of your work in advance of the workshop is that your sentences can be read, and re-read, and pondered, and written upon. Your readers can see (and correct) your punctuation; they can pause over your phrasing; they can puzzle at length over those passages that don't appear to be working, and appreciate properly those passages where you are right on the bubble. They can attempt to get fully inside your work, and then, in the meeting, they can speak to you thoughtfully as readers and fellow writers, rather than merely as listeners. Collectively they can act as a literary editor might, their reading forensic, engaged and constructive.[4] And they can conclude the discussion by returning your work to you, carefully annotated, so that you can take the copies away to read, and re-read, and ponder, while deciding which of the responses to accept and which, of course, to reject.

Present your work professionally

Assuming the level of engagement I've just described, the least you can do for your readers is ensure that your manuscript is presented to a professional standard: just because it's a rough draft, it needn't look rough (and certainly ought not be handwritten).

White space is important. There needs to be room above and below and to either side of the text for your readers to write their responses. The margins should therefore be generous, and the spacing between the lines should be double, at least. Fancy fonts rarely enliven dull prose; they are irritating, usually, and distracting, and were you ever to submit such work to an agent or editor it would almost certainly be rejected, unread. A sober, unassuming typeface – like the one in which this page is set – allows the reader to concentrate on the writing (not the typesetting). And it should be a decent size, too: 12pt is normal.

It is helpful, if you are submitting an excerpt from a longer work, to offer a brief contextualising note – nothing too detailed; a few sentences will usually suffice, such as I gave in Chapter 2 to introduce an extract from *Common*

---

[4] This may be to overestimate the role of the contemporary literary editor. It's possible, in fact, that the growth of Creative Writing as an academic discipline is due in part to the corporate squeeze on editors, who are allowed less and less time to nurture promising writers, while being placed under more and more pressure to commission the obviously commercial. It may be that academia now provides the close editorial oversight that publishing houses were once able to provide.

Ground. This should come at the head of the work and will usually concern such issues as time and place, as well as any references to characters or events from earlier in the narrative, and the key question of whether the piece is taken from a novel or a short story, which is bound to have some bearing on how your reader engages with the narrative, especially in relation to pacing and structure. It may also be useful to write a brief note at the end of the piece, itemising your own most pressing concerns, those particular features on which you would welcome some feedback. More often than not your reader's remarks[5] will be reassuring, on these aspects at least (the real issues are often to be found lurking elsewhere).

Publishers generally don't like a submission to be fastened or bound, but for the workshop it's essential to staple the pages, given the amount of paper that circulates in the room and the likelihood of it becoming mixed up. Your name and the title of your piece should also appear on each page, and it is vital to number the pages since the discussion in class will so often require your readers to point to particular passages on particular pages: finding page 12 in a twenty-page unnumbered submission can be fiddlesome, time-consuming, and annoying for everyone.

Read and re-read

My remarks on the importance of distributing work in advance give some indication of what I believe are the responsibilities of readers, who should not only read, but re-read a submission, the first time more-or-less innocently, the second editorially.

As far as the writing allows, your initial reading should engage with the work as if it were already published, beyond the realm of revision. It should be read, in John Gardner's terms, as if you were about to embark on a vivid and continuous dream. Of course that dream will be interrupted. Because the work is in draft – by definition in need of rewriting – you will experience any number of jolts and disturbances. Later, once you have a sense of the story, the shape of the whole, you can return to the site of those disturbances, fully awake and equipped with a pen.

The second, editorial reading is the beginning of the conversation you will have with the writer, and here you should be reading meticulously, making

---

[5] I puzzled for some time over whether the reader should be pluralised in this paragraph – i.e. *your readers' likely confusions; a brief note to your readers; how your readers engage; your readers' remarks*. So far as the workshop goes, the reader is plural of course. But when you are writing it is probably best to write for one singular reader, an ideal reader who stands for all readers.

corrections, offering marginal suggestions, highlighting those passages you particularly admire. At this stage it's acceptable to be somewhat pernickety, identifying errors of punctuation, spelling and grammar that it would be too tedious to itemise individually in class. But beyond that, you should be registering your thoughts, succinctly expressed, on how the work might be finessed in order to become a better version of itself. Initially such thoughts should be indicated alongside the text, but it's often additionally helpful to conclude with something like a letter to the author, summarising your main points of concern and encouragement. This end-note should be signed. What isn't acceptable is to use the relative anonymity of the editorial stage to write comments that you wouldn't be prepared to own up to in class.[6]

Lengths

The workshops I teach at undergraduate level are two hours long, at postgraduate level three hours, and in either case I aim to consider three pieces of work in each session. For the purpose of a two-hour class the pieces are between 1,500 and 2,500 words, for a three-hour class between 3,000 and 5,000 words. Each piece is accorded the same amount of discussion time, but first there will be some housekeeping to do – announcements, clarifications, the distribution of work for next time. One essential task in the first session is to agree a workshopping rota for the rest of the term, and most weeks I will distribute or read an exemplary passage from a published work, usually with reference to the discussion in a previous week. The workshop discussions can be intense, and so we will usually have a break of between ten and twenty minutes after we've considered that week's first piece of writing.

Begin by reading aloud

Despite my insistence on the importance of distributing work in advance of the workshop, it can often be useful to begin the session by asking the author to read a couple of pages aloud. Most of us construct our sentences to a particular cadence; whether we are conscious of it or not, our prose will have its own

[6] A colleague once had a student who was virtually silent in the workshop, her posture rigid, her facial expression quite fixed. What was she thinking? If asked, she smirked; sometimes she blushed. But she would not say. Only that week's 'workshopees' would know, though not until after the class: every week, one of the returned copies of their work, unsigned, would be livid with vitriol, scratched all over with damning remarks, some of them quite personal. This didn't make for a particularly relaxed workshop (though it does suggest an interesting short story).

rhythm. In some instances this rhythm will carry – the reader will pick it up from the page – but not always. It can be instructive to hear the work as the author hears it, and this will generally come through in the way that she reads it. Besides which, as I suggested in the previous chapter, reading aloud can also be instructive for the author, revealing to her ear what the eye can no longer see.

And while the rest of us are listening, and the author is concentrating on her reading, those among us who read and annotated the piece several days previously can use the opportunity to glance back through our notes. In those few minutes of being read to, we can settle ourselves, tune in to the work, and surreptitiously remind ourselves of what it was that we wanted to say.

It's not all about the author

If your inclination is to submit the piece of work you have polished the most, and are most proud of, and which you believe will give the best impression of your abilities, then you probably ought not to be bothering with workshops. Either your opinion of the work will be borne out – your writing will prove irreproachable, attracting only admiration – in which case your classmates will have nothing much to discuss, and so nothing to gain, little to learn. Or else you will meet with unanticipated criticism, which will be all the harder to process if your initial assumption is that the work is already as good as it gets: you may then feel compelled to reject the criticism, in which case you will not be able to progress, or you will feel so deflated and defeated you may concede to the criticism but struggle to find the motivation to return to the work.[7]

Conversely, you may be tempted to offer up your least polished work, something approaching writing in the raw, the roughest of rough drafts, containing innumerable errors, inconsistencies, puzzles, which you may only recently have poured onto the page, in the expectation that your classmates will both admire your energy, your ever-brimming inventiveness, and do the bulk of your work for you, correcting the errors, settling the inconsistencies, clarifying the confusions.

Each of these approaches betrays a lack of appreciation of the role of your classmates and the purpose of the workshop.

Of course, the workshop is there to provide your work with an audience, since it is always useful to test the success of your writing on a community of readers. You can gain some idea of what communicates, what carries, and what doesn't. You can think about why certain aspects of your work are

---

[7] As a student, I'm sorry to say, this was usually me.

successful while others are not. You can gain some new perspective on a piece of writing that may have become stale for you.

But there is more to it than this. In submitting your work for discussion you are providing us – the group – with an opportunity to think collectively about some of the key issues in creating successful fictions. These issues may be technical, ethical, perceptual, philosophical; they may be aesthetic or thematic. But regardless of whose writing is currently under discussion, the workshop provides all of its participants with an opportunity to reflect and develop. In analysing one person's work – which should be neither too raw nor too refined – we are each of us pressed into thinking about the issues that this particular work raises, which will almost always widen into a consideration of general principles, which will almost always then produce some new insight into our own practice. For this reason it is important that you participate in every session, whether or not your own work is being discussed, because it is never just about the author; it is never simply one person who benefits.

The role of the tutor

There is an 'ethic of engagement' that all teachers of Creative Writing ought to subscribe to, however 'famous' they are. It isn't enough simply to assume that one's attention – or even attendance – is sufficient, lending legitimacy to the proceedings, conferring some kind of blessing on the students' endeavours. It isn't enough either (though it is certainly better) to offer the occasional remark in the workshop, and the occasional marginal mark on a manuscript, while holding to the view – as I expressed it earlier – that every writer is pretty much alone in the language and needs to find his own way, as you once found yours. I take it as axiomatic that writing is isolating. But equally, I take it as given that the purpose of the workshop is to equip the students with the skills to survive – and perhaps even to thrive – in that isolation.

The tutor will have those skills (in addition to all the uncertainties described by Primo Levi), and chief among them will be the ability to read as a writer, by which I mean the ability to access the inner workings of a sample of writing and to anticipate how those workings might affect a reader's responses. This 'reading of the reader' entails a particularly intense form of imaginative and technical engagement with the way that sentences operate, and in part the tutor's role is to give a practical demonstration of that intensity of engagement in his reading of the student's writing-in-progress.

It ought then to follow that the workshop tutor should be a practising writer, and while I don't necessarily believe that 'practising' must always mean 'published', it should certainly imply an involvement with language and literary form that can only be informed by a regular, hands-on engagement with the challenges of constructing fully-functioning fictions.

Of course it will often be the students' expectation that their tutor has published some books, particularly on the better-known writing courses, and particularly at postgraduate level. Publications lend authority, clearly, and in the writing workshop they can appear to offer more evidence of competence than any amount of teaching experience. But with this authority comes another potential pitfall: not that the tutor will occupy too lofty a position to engage with his students' work, but that he will assume that only one person's opinion matters – his own – and that only one person has the right to the final word – himself. And if such a workshop is to proceed, then the students will have to defer to this view, whether consciously or not, so creating a situation in which everyone becomes, in terms of technique and even imagination, a lesser version of their tutor.

If this is to suggest a somewhat improbable scenario, a more likely version of much the same situation may result from the efforts of an otherwise scrupulous, fully-committed tutor, whose abilities as a teacher, reader and editor are so impressive that they will win the group's unresisting consent, their ready approval, with the result that few of the students will be able to develop fully as writers and self-critics because they are so rarely required to make their own assessments or arrive at their own solutions.

The tutor may well be the most insightful reader in the room. She will almost certainly have spent more years in the language than her students. Possibly she will carry the authority of several publications and prizes. Her role, however, is not to issue instructions, but to point to possibilities. It is not to lay down the law, but to attempt to engage with each student's work on its own terms, and to guide the rest of the group in adopting a similar approach. Ultimately her role is to exemplify a way of reading that is tactful and insightful, meticulous and honest, but which is only ever offered as one reading among numerous others.[8]

---

[8] A problem may arise when all the readings in the room – including the tutor's – are in some way negative. I have several regrets as a teacher – situations I know I got wrong – and one concerns a student whose workshop submission met with nothing but bafflement. To that chorus of complaint I added my own, so leaving the student entirely exposed. The workshop poured down its bad weather, and while I thought I was attempting to summarise the main points of confusion, I was merely adding to the downpour. The student later suggested I should have held an umbrella over her. And she was right. In certain instances – thankfully rare – the most generous thing a tutor can do is unfurl an umbrella.

The role of the students

Where Creative Writing is taught in universities at undergraduate level, it is common for marks or credits to be awarded for class contribution. The following is an extract from some guidance I wrote for my own undergraduates:

> Many students feel their creative writing to be more 'personal' than any other work they do at university, and some may feel nervous about sharing it. The workshop can also seem at odds with the day-to-day reality of writing, which usually involves silence and solitude. And even those of us who *do* feel at ease may struggle to cope with certain kinds of criticism.
>
> It is therefore important that your criticism is *constructive*. You should endeavour always to identify – and praise – what *does* succeed, before you go on to talk about what might not. And in discussing what works less well, you should try always to think about solutions, remedies, the ways in which a difficulty might be resolved.
>
> Needless to say, whatever your feelings about the *writer*, it is the *work* you should be focussed upon. The workshop is not a place to air personal grievances, and the work should never be a pretext for other kinds of criticism. The success of this kind of learning depends on the participants establishing a level of trust and mutual respect. The workshop should therefore be treated as a confidential space, and what is shown or said in class should not be discussed in the form of blogs, journalism, or on social networking sites, etc.
>
> What we're looking for above all is participation. If you don't share your thoughts on your classmates' work then you simply aren't making a contribution. Of course, it may take you a while to get going: allowances will be made. But a whole semester of silence is almost as bad as a whole semester of scene-stealing. The quality of your contribution counts more than the quantity. If you don't have something relevant and useful to say, then wait until you do. And when you do, be concise and be constructive.
>
> Also, be analytical. It isn't enough to say you like this, but don't like that. Try to think about why you like or don't like something: is it because there's a problem in the writing? What is that problem? How might it be mended? And if the writing does work: why do you think it does? There are bound to be reasons, and they will probably relate to technique.
>
> Preparation matters too. Make sure you have actually read the work, and made notes on it, and that you've assembled your thoughts before the class begins. And make sure you are punctual: arriving late disrupts the class and is disrespectful to your classmates, particularly the one who is being workshopped.
>
> Attendance matters even more. There is nothing less respectful than turning up when your own work is under discussion, then absconding when it isn't . . .

Generally older and more mature, the members of a typical Masters workshop may not require quite such explicit instructions. They are also more likely to register impatience with an approach that endeavours 'always to identify – and praise – what *does* succeed' before moving on to 'what works less well', and they may not feel that 'constructive criticism' is necessarily what is required – or possible – in all cases, particularly when they themselves are about to be workshopped.

The success of any workshop will depend on the degree to which the participants are able to achieve a level of trust and mutual understanding that allows them to be honest about each other's works-in-progress without fear of their critique being misconstrued as a personal criticism. All the participants should of course be aware of their responsibility to enter into the discussion with civility, but it should also be recognised that many serious writers will be distrustful of praise; they will want the 'bad news' before the 'good news'; they will want to know what their classmates 'really think'.[9]

A wholly negative, and even vituperative response is unlikely to be anything but undermining and upsetting, of course. And while praise can be uplifting and affirming, it is rarely sustaining. The most useful feedback will often be offered in a spirit of helpfulness – no matter how critical – and will attempt to identify honestly those aspects of the work that are flawed, those passages that are weakest, and then perhaps to suggest some potential solutions. More often than not the criticisms will confirm something the writer already suspects, but hasn't previously been able to articulate. And it's precisely this confirmation or clarification that he may require from his readers. In the midst of so many uncertainties, the writer's most pressing need may be simply to hear that 'Yes, this is askew' or 'No, that's not straight'. Whether the suggested solutions are workable or not is another matter, and can only be tested in the next draft.

Stay schtum

Every tutor will organise things differently, and every workshop will take on its own character. My own procedure, once the 'workshopee' has read a couple of pages from her work, is to invite three of her classmates in succession to offer their thoughts on it. As they speak I will make notes, and attempt to identify

---

[9] This can be taken to an unhelpful extreme. I've heard of two novelists who seek in their workshops (and individual tutorials) to establish a combative, competitive atmosphere, in the belief that this will stir the strongest spirits to produce their best work. Both are male. Neither is a particularly good novelist.

the significant points of agreement or contention, the main issues that this particular work gives rise to. These issues will form the substance of the discussion that follows, which will be relatively unstructured, driven mainly by the passion and urgency of the students, and while I will attempt to draw everyone into the conversation, this will rarely include the writer. She has already had her say: it is represented by the work under discussion.

As the writer you will need to be fully receptive to your classmates' responses, hungry to hear what they have to say. And if that means enduring a series of alarming misreadings, this in itself will be instructive, a sure sign that something has failed to communicate, that your intentions haven't quite carried. Should the conversation concern the implausibility of certain situations, or the unlikelihood of this or that character's behaviour, it is futile to argue that the work is based on actual events, real people. Likewise, should the workshop find your organisation of tenses and time-shifts confusing, it is pointless to plead that this was intentional, a deliberate experiment. Your first responsibility as a writer is to convince your readers that you are in control of your fiction – at the level of character, story and form – and should they fail to be convinced by the words on the page, then the argument has, in a sense, already been lost.

No author of a published work is able to accompany even a single copy of her book home from the bookshop in order to correct that reader's potential misreadings. And however hurtful a scathing review, every writer understands the vanity of attempting to post a reply: no one is listening, and besides, the work should be its own advocate. Similarly in the Creative Writing workshop, you should not feel it is your right or responsibility to defend the work or to explain your intentions, and should the discussion ever become a debate between you and the rest of the group about the worth of the work, then the *writing* has clearly already failed you.

That said, in any such gathering there will be certain readers who 'get' you exactly – your flaws and your virtues – and others who don't, and while it is always interesting to reflect on the responses of your least sympathetic readers, it is the others – the ones best attuned to your sensibility – whose opinions you will want to attend to most closely, and with whom you will probably continue to exchange work long after the workshop. And this, perhaps, is the other main benefit of attending a workshop: it is not just to receive a schooling in becoming your own best critic – your own best 'control instrument' – but to be introduced to your potential first readers, the key individuals who are most on your wavelength and who will most protect you, perhaps, against the future possibility of succumbing to melancholy, and living badly, and not sleeping – or worse.

Nuts and bolts

In the introduction to his book *How Novels Work*, which derives from a long-running series of short articles in the *Guardian*, John Mullan remarks:

> It is striking how much of the talk about fiction that happens on radio or television, or at literary festivals, is talk about content. So often, a novel is discussable for what it is about. One emphasis that I have tried to carry over from academic literary criticism is the emphasis on form and technique. A novel absorbs us, I would say, not because of what it is about, but because of how it is written.

In one obvious sense there is a world of difference between the branch of academic literary criticism that attends to form and technique and the practice of the workshop: the former is concerned with literary works as finished artefacts, the latter with works that are still in progress, or even in embryo; the former attends to 'product', the latter to 'process'. But the emphasis that Mullan describes is one that they share: the writing submitted to the workshop absorbs us not because of what it is about, but because of how it is written – and, beyond that, because of our interest in how it might be *re*written.

This at least is the orthodox view. Within the academic discipline of Creative Writing there are others, and one recurrent theme of certain critiques of the workshop is that it ought to be far more attentive to content; or rather, to content in relation to broader issues of social, political and historical context. The work-in-progress, on these accounts, is to be used as a pretext for other kinds of discussion, which might include the question of what gets published and what doesn't, or whose 'voice' is considered important and whose is marginalised. Which is to say, writing isn't simply about words on the page, but about words as they circulate in society.

Of course, writing is about both, but while my own tendency is to overemphasise the importance of form and technique to the detriment of such interesting questions as what a particular fiction might say about the human heart in conflict with itself, or what it might reveal about contemporary morality, or what it might tell us about the lives of paint chemists and industrial riggers, I would suggest that any extended consideration of these topics should happen in the conversation that continues on from the workshop. In other words, any detailed discussion of the wider contexts of writing probably ought to happen in classes that support or accompany the workshop; indeed, such supplementary classes probably ought to be standard.

The primary concern of the workshop is with the practical problems we encounter in the making of writing, and in this regard one possibly crude analogy might be with car mechanics. It would doubtless benefit the trainee mechanic to have some appreciation of the relationship of car design to fuel efficiency, and of fuel efficiency to the global need to cut carbon emissions, and of the wider issues surrounding car ownership, including the relationship of private car ownership to public transport policy. But the core concern of the mechanic's schooling should be in learning how engines work, how to fix them when they don't, and how to fine-tune them when they do.

All things are imaginable

One immediate challenge to this admittedly mechanical analogy might be the work-in-progress that is misogynist, racist or in some other way offensive or inflammatory, perhaps to religious sensibilities. Addressing content may then be unavoidable, both urgent and necessary, and progressing to a consideration of form and technique may not be possible. Such a scenario returns us to the issues I raised under 'The role of the students', and is offered here somewhat hypothetically: I haven't yet come across quite so contentious a situation; the offensive submission is exceptionally rare.

Respect and courtesy remain the key terms, and while it is possible that a group will arrive at such a level of mutual understanding that almost any work is acceptable, at least initially it may be helpful to abide by a code of conduct, whether formally issued or informally discussed, which might head off the possibility of the objectionable work being submitted in the first place. As a point of interest, however, it is worth being aware that any work that is copied and circulated is, legally speaking, published work, and published work is subject to various laws, including those governing racial hatred, libel, obscenity and blasphemy. So if it is possible to imagine a scenario in which a participant in the workshop submits a piece of work that is utterly offensive to his classmates under one or more of these terms, then it is equally possible to imagine a challenge to that work being made not just in the workshop, but in a court of law. All things are imaginable. That indeed is a fundamental condition for freedom of expression. Whether or not that freedom should be exercised is another question, and one which will depend on the writer's understanding of his responsibilities to his readers.

Afterwards

What makes the workshop particularly exciting and rewarding for me as a teacher is that it's where my teaching and my students' learning come closest to the condition of writing, in that the methods are uncertain, the process exploratory, every solution provisional, the outcomes very often surprising.

The negative aspect of this correspondence between workshop and writing is that a sense of provisionality can linger uncomfortably afterwards, leaving the student unsettled, lacking a definite sense of how to proceed. It might be, for example, that the workshop successfully identifies the weak points in her writing but fails to suggest any workable fixes; it could be that the sole dissenting voice in a clamour of praise is the one that continues to ring loudest in her mind; sometimes the responses can be wholly contradictory, yet all seem equally convincing.

Given the potential for such outcomes, it's important that individual tutorials are offered in support of the workshop, so that the student may reflect on the responses, explain her intentions, ask some straight questions. The tutor may also express certain opinions that might not have seemed sayable in the workshop.[10] Other, more contextual issues might be discussed, including the question of a work's 'publishability'. Some students will require reassurance that they are not deceiving themselves, that they really do have potential. Some may need reminding that *all* they have at this stage is potential, that their writing still requires some work. And occasionally it will be necessary to insist to the student who wants certainty – definite answers about her ability, a promise of future publication for her novel – that the fundamental condition of writing is one of 'non-knowing', and that this is not always such a bad thing.

I began this chapter by quoting at length from Primo Levi's *The Wrench*, and while I have no doubt that the effort to produce something new and worthwhile in writing will require you to proceed from what you already know – about writing, about life, about both – into the realms of what you don't yet know, and that this will require you to climb the equivalent of Faussone's derrick in the wind, before the structure has been braced, when it's dancing about like a boat on the waves, I don't believe – any more than Levi believes – that a lack of reliable instrumentation need always be undermining, the inevitable cause of a structure's collapse.

And so in conclusion to this chapter and this book, I'd like to allow Primo Levi to speak against his own pessimism, for the chapter in *The Wrench* from which I quoted does in fact end with a celebration of the writer's freedom to

---

[10] These are matters of intuition, experience, judgement, but I have sometimes sensed that a workshop was being overly kind, or wrongheadedly critical, and sensed that the writer suspected as much. Sometimes the individual tutorial can be the best place to say so.

be irresponsible, to work against the natural limits of the form, to succeed by taking risks.

Finally, then, here is Primo Levi, being optimistic:

I explained to Faussone that one of the writer's great privileges is the possibility of remaining imprecise and vague, saying and not saying, inventing freely, beyond any rule of caution. After all, on the towers we construct they don't run any high-tension lines; if our structures fall, nobody gets killed, and they don't have to be wind-resistant. In other words, we're irresponsible, and no writer has ever been put on trial or sent to jail because his constructions came apart . . . Working at our tolerance limit, or even beyond the limit, is the joy of our profession. Unlike riggers, when we manage to exceed tolerance, to make an impossible coupling, we are pleased, and they praise us . . .

We agreed then on the good things we have in common. On the advantage of being able to test yourself, not depending on others in the test, reflecting yourself in your work. On the pleasure of seeing your creature grow, beam after beam, bolt after bolt, solid, necessary, symmetrical, suited to its purpose; and when it's finished you look at it and you think that perhaps it will live longer than you, and perhaps it will be of use to someone you don't know, who doesn't know you. Maybe, as an old man, you'll be able to come back and look at it, and it will seem beautiful, and it doesn't really matter so much that it will seem beautiful only to you, and you can say to yourself 'maybe another man wouldn't have brought it off.'[11]

---

[11] Or, of course, another woman . . .

Bibliography

Allott, Miriam, ed., *Novelists on the Novel* (London: Routledge & Kegan Paul, 1965).

Aristotle, *Poetics* (Harmondsworth: Penguin, 1996), trans. Malcolm Heath.

Atwood, Margaret, 'Happy Endings', in *Good Bones and Simple Murders* (New York: Doubleday, 1994).

Atwood, Margaret, *Negotiating with the Dead: A Writer on Writing* (Cambridge: Cambridge University Press, 2002).

Auster, Paul, *The Red Notebook* (London: Faber & Faber, 1995).

Ballard, J.G., *Miracles of Life: Shanghai to Shepperton: An Autobiography* (London: Fourth Estate, 2008).

Barker, Pat, *Regeneration* (London: Viking, 1991).

Beard, Richard, *Damascus* (London: Flamingo, 1999).

Beckett, Samuel, *Worstward Ho* (London: John Calder, 1983).

Bigsby, Christopher, ed., *Writers in Conversation: Volume One* (Norwich: Arthur Miller Centre for American Studies, 2000).

Bigsby, Christopher, ed., *Writers in Conversation: Volume Two* (Norwich: Arthur Miller Centre for American Studies, 2001).

Braine, John, *How to Write a Novel* (London: Methuen, 2000).

Brande, Dorothea, *Becoming a Writer* (Basingstoke: Macmillan, 1996).

Brontë, Charlotte, *Jane Eyre* (Harmondsworth: Penguin, 1996 (1847)).

Brontë, Emily, *Wuthering Heights* (Harmondsworth: Penguin, 1965 (1847)).

Bryan, Lynne, *Gorgeous* (London: Sceptre, 1999).

Buford, Bill, ed., *Granta 8: Dirty Realism: New Writing from America* (Cambridge: Granta, 1983).

Cameron, Julia, *The Artist's Way* (Basingstoke: Pan Macmillan, 1995).

Carver, Raymond, 'I could see the smallest things', in *The Stories of Raymond Carver* (London: Picador, 1985).

Connolly, Cyril, *Enemies of Promise* (Chicago, IL: University of Chicago Press, 2008 (1938)).

Conrad, Joseph, *Heart of Darkness* (Harmondsworth: Penguin, 1983 (1902)).

Conrad, Joseph, *The Collected Letters of Joseph Conrad, Vol. 2, 1898–1902*, ed. Frederick R. Karl and Laurence Davies (Cambridge: Cambridge University Press, 1986).

Cowan, Andrew, *Pig* (London: Sceptre, 2002 (1994)).

Cowan, Andrew, *Common Ground* (London: Penguin, 1997).

Cowan, Andrew, *Crustaceans* (London: Sceptre, 2001).

Cowan, Andrew, *What I Know* (London: Sceptre, 2006).

Cowley, Malcolm, ed., *Writers at Work: The Paris Review Interviews: First Series* (Harmondsworth: Penguin, 1977).

Davey, Mary Agnes, *Hard Up Street: Growing Up in King Street, Norwich, 1919–1947* (Dereham: Larks Press, 1997).

Didion, Joan, 'Why I Write', *The New York Times Magazine*, 5 December 1976.

Doughty, Louise, *A Novel in a Year: A Novelist's Guide to Being a Novelist* (London: Simon & Schuster, 2007).

Duncker, Patricia, *Writing on the Wall* (London: Pandora, 2002).

Eliot, T.S., 'The Function of Criticism' (1923) in selected essays (New York: Harcourt, Brace and World Inc., 1964).

Eugenides, Jeffrey, *The Virgin Suicides* (London: Bloomsbury, 1993).

Faulkner, William, *As I Lay Dying* (Harmondsworth: Penguin, 1988 (1930)).

Fitzgerald, F. Scott, *The Great Gatsby* (Harmondsworth: Penguin, 1950 (1926)).

Foer, Jonathan Safran, *Everything is Illuminated* (Harmondsworth: Penguin, 2003).

Ford, Richard, *Independence Day* (London: Harvill Press, 1996).

Forster, E.M., *Aspects of the Novel* (Harmondsworth: Penguin, 1990 (1927)).

Fowles, John, *The Collector* (London: Vintage, 2004 (1963)).

Frayn, Michael, 'He Said, She Said', in *Speak After the Beep* (London: Methuen, 1995).

Gardner, John, *The Art of Fiction: Notes on Craft for Young Writers* (New York: Vintage, 1991).

Gardner, John, *On Becoming a Novelist* (New York: Norton, 1999).

Genette, Gérard, *Narrative Discourse: An Essay in Method* (Ithaca, NY: Cornell University Press, 1980).

Goldberg, Natalie, *Writing Down the Bones* (Boston, MA: Shambhala, 1986).

Hartley, L.P., *The Go-Between* (London: Penguin, 1958).

Hemingway, Ernest, 'Hills Like White Elephants', in *Men Without Women* (London: Grafton, 1997 (1928)).

Ho Davies, Peter, 'How to Be an Expatriate', in *Equal Love* (London: Granta, 2000).

Hoffman, Eva, 'The Uses of the Past', in *Writing Worlds 1: The Norwich Exchanges*, ed. Vesna Goldsworthy (Norwich: Pen & Inc Press, 2006).

James, Henry, 'The Art of Fiction' (1884), in *The House of Fiction: Essays on the Novel*, ed. Leon Edel (London: Rupert Hart-Davis, 1957).

Johnson, B.S., *The Unfortunates* (London: Picador, 1999 (1969)).

Joselow, Beth, *Writing Without the Muse: 60 Beginning Exercises for the Creative Writer* (Ashland: Story Line Press, 1999).

Joseph, Anjali, *Saraswati Park* (London: Fourth Estate, 2010).

Joyce, James, *A Portrait of the Artist as a Young Man* (London: Jonathan Cape, 1968 (1916)).

Joyce, James, *Ulysses* (London: Bodley Head, 1986 (1922)).

Kelman, James, *How Late It Was, How Late* (London: Secker & Warburg, 1994).

King, Stephen, *On Writing: A Memoir of the Craft* (New York: Pocket Books, 2000).

La Rochefoucauld, *Maxims* (Harmondsworth: Penguin, 1959), trans. L.W. Tancock.

Lee, Nancy, *Dead Girls* (London: Faber and Faber, 2003).

Lemon, Lee T. and Reis, Marion J., eds and trans, *Russian Formalist Criticism: Four Essays* (Lincoln, NE: University of Nebraska Press, 1965).

Levi, Primo, *The Wrench* (London: Abacus, 1988), trans. William Weaver.

Levine, Norman, *Something Happened Here* (Toronto: Penguin, 1991).

Lodge, David, *The Art of Fiction* (London: Penguin, 1992).

McEwan, Ian, *First Love, Last Rites* (London: Jonathan Cape, 1975).

McInerney, Jay, *Bright Lights, Big City* (New York: Vintage, 1984).

McNay, Mark, *Fresh* (Edinburgh: Canongate, 2007).

Maugham, W. Somerset, *A Writer's Notebook* (London: William Heinemann, 1953).

Maxwell, William, *The Chateau* (London: Harvill Press, 2000 (1961)).

Menand, Louis, 'Bad Comma: Lynne Truss's strange grammar', *The New Yorker*, 28 June 2004.

Morley, David, *The Cambridge Introduction to Creative Writing* (Cambridge: Cambridge University Press, 2007).

Motte, Warren, ed. and trans., *Oulipo: A Primer of Potential Literature* (Normal, IL: Dalkey Archive, 1998).

Mullan, John, *How Novels Work* (Oxford: Oxford University Press, 2006).

Novakovich, Josip, *Fiction Writer's Workshop* (Cincinnati: Story Press, 1995).

Oates, Joyce Carol, *The Faith of a Writer: Life, Craft, Art* (New York: Ecco, 2004).

O'Brien, Tim, *The Things They Carried* (London: Flamingo, 1991).

O'Connor, Flannery, *Mystery and Manners* (New York: Farrar, Straus and Giroux, 1970).

O'Connor, Flannery, *A Good Man is Hard to Find* (London: Women's Press, 1980).

Paley, Grace, 'Grace Paley Talking with Cora Kaplan', in *Writing Lives: Conversations Between Women Writers*, ed. Mary Chamberlain (London: Virago, 1988).

Parker, Dorothy, 'But the One on the Right', in *Points of View: An Anthology of Short Stories*, ed. James Moffett and Kenneth R. McElheny (New York: Mentor, 1956).

Perec, Georges, *A Void* (London: Vintage, 2008 (1969)), trans. Gilbert Adair.

Plato, *Theaetetus* (London: Penguin, 1987), trans. Robin Waterfield.

Plimpton, George, ed., *Writers at Work: The Paris Review Interviews: Second Series* (Harmondsworth: Penguin, 1977).

Plimpton, George, ed., *Writers at Work: The Paris Review Interviews: Third Series* (Harmondsworth: Penguin, 1977).

Plimpton, George, ed., *Writers at Work: The Paris Review Interviews: Fourth Series* (Harmondsworth: Penguin, 1977).

Plimpton, George, ed., *Beat Writers at Work: The Paris Review Interviews* (London: Harvill, 1999).

Propp, Vladimir, *Morphology of the Russian Folktale* (Austin, Texas: University of Texas Press, 1968 (1928)).

Queneau, Raymond, *Exercises in Style* (London: Calder, 1981), trans. Barbara Wright.

Queneau, Raymond, *Exercises in Style* (London: Calder, 2009), trans. Barbara Wright.

Read, Herbert, ed., *Writers On Themselves* (London: BBC, 1964).

Roberts, James *et al.*, eds, *Writers On Writing* (Camberwell: Penguin Australia, 2002).

Robinson, Marilynne, *Gilead* (London: Virago, 2005).

Salinger, J.D., *The Catcher in the Rye* (Harmondsworth: Penguin, 1958).

Sellers, Susan, ed., *Taking Reality by Surprise: Writing for Pleasure and Publication* (London: Women's Press, 1991).

Seth, Vikram, *A Suitable Boy* (London: Pheonix, 1994).

Shklovsky, Victor, 'Art as Technique', in Lemon, Lee T and Reis, Marion J, eds & trans, Russian Formalist Criticism: Four Essays (University of Nebraska Press, 1965).

Shklovsky, Victor, 'Sterne's Tristram Shandy: Stylistic Commentary', in Lemon, Lee T and Reis, Marion J, eds & trans, Russian Formalist Criticism: Four Essays (University of Nebraska Press, 1965).

Smith, Ali, *Hotel World* (London: Hamish Hamilton, 2001).

Smith, Ali, *The Accidental* (London: Hamish Hamilton, 2006).

Spender, Stephen, 'The Making of a Poem', in *Creativity*, ed. P.E. Vernon (London: Penguin, 1970).

Sterne, Laurence, *The Life and Opinions of Tristram Shandy, Gentleman* (London: Penguin, 2003 (1759–1767)).

Stott, Rebecca and Chapman, Peter, eds, *Grammar and Writing* (Harlow: Pearson Longman, 2001).

Thomas, Sue, *Creative Writing: A Handbook for Workshop Leaders* (Nottingham: University of Nottingham, 1995).

Tomashevsky, Boris, 'Thematics', in Lemon, Lee T and Reis, Marion J, eds & trans, Russian Formalist Criticism: Four Essays (University of Nebraska Press, 1965).

Truss, Lynne, *Eats, Shoots & Leaves* (London: Profile, 2003).

Woolf, Virginia, *Mrs Dalloway* (Harmondsworth: Penguin, 2000 (1925)).

Index

Page numbers followed by b represent box.

academic writing 189
The Accidental (Smith) 88, 89
Ackroyd, P. 5
active voice 190
Adams, D. 5
adjectival phrases 189
Adult Education 205
adult-critic 42, 179
adverbial phrases 189
adverbs 187, 188, 189
Algonquin Round Table 93
alienation 62
alliteration 119
ambiguity 18, 179
American short story: revival 198
American Southern Gothic
    tradition 56, 112
Amis, M. 6
antithesis 150
apostrophes 184
Archer, J. 6
archetypes 156
Aristotle 144
arrangement of the parts 150
art: purpose of 163; technique
    of 163

The Art of Fiction (James) 21
The Art of Fiction (Lodge) 103, 113
Art as Technique (Shklovsky) 163
articles 49
The Artist's Way (Cameron) 37, 38
Arvon Foundation 1, 2, 13, 20,
    76, 80
As I Lay Dying (Faulkner) 129
Aspects of the Novel (Forster) 84, 98,
    150, 151
assonance 119
Athenian tragedy 144
Atwood, M. 38, 151, 154
Auguries of Innocence (Blake) 67
Auster, P. 6, 62, 68, 200, 201
authenticity 132
authorial summary 103, 117
autobiographical: material 134b;
    work 71; writing 32
autobiographical exercise ('Lost') 71b
automatic writing 34–48, 96b, 97b,
    178, 182b
automatic writing exercise ('More first
    thoughts') 178b
axis of combination exercise
    ('Vertical') 176b

backdrop 26
Ballard, J.G. 13
Barker, P. 80, 110
Barthes, R. 148
Bawden, N. 84
Beard, R. 166, 167
Beat: poets 37; writers 36
Beckett, S. 3, 45
Becoming a Writer (Brande) 8, 39, 46, 47
beginning middle end 143–59, 181b
Beginning middle end (exercise 54) 150b
beginning writers 11
behaviour exercise ('Eye witness') 132b
bereavement exercise ('Lost loves') 71b
Blake, W. 37, 67
body language 183
Bond, E. 6
book recommendations 23
Bowles, J. 6
Bowles, P. 6
brackets 194
Braine, J. 41
Brande, D. 39, 44, 180
Brontë, C. 135
Bryan, L. 158, 188
Buddhism 37
Buford, B. 198
Burroughs, W. 12
But the One on the Right (Parker) 93

Calvino, I. 165
Cambridge Introduction to Creative Writing (Morley) 14
Cameron, J. 37, 38, 42, 44, 46
Captors and captives (exercise 47) 130b, 131b
caricatures 98
Carlyle, T. 41
Carter, A. 80
Cartland, B. 6
Carver, R. 197, 198

The Catcher in the Rye (Salinger) 119, 124, 135
causality 150, 151
character 98, 99, 144; importance of 145; sketch 27b
character exercise ('Envelopes') 91b, 92b
character exercise ('Notes towards a character') 90b, 91b
character exercise ('Q&A gimmick') 89b
characterisation 82, 109
characteristics 98
characters 32, 33, 47, 58, 79, 81, 181b; development 64, 91b; emotions 78; feelings 55, 56b; flat 98, 149; interior world 94; introduction to 122; invention of 84, 85b, 86b, 89, 90b, 91b, 92b; personal possessions 91, 92; physical appearance 92; point of view 51; round 98, 149; secret 91b, 100b; types 156; voice 118
The Chateau (Maxwell) 87, 88
Checklist (exercise 69) 181b
Chekhov, A. 51, 52, 163
child-artist 42, 179
childhood 67, 69b, 74; amnesia 66; experiences 68; memories 76, 97b
childhood attributes exercise ('Lost selves') 70b
childhood friend exercise ('Typical') 74–5b
childhood friend exercise ('Untypical') 75b
childhood places exercise ('Lost lands') 70b
Christ-haunted fanaticism 57
chronology 150
Clark, K. 96
clauses 189, 191, 193, 195, 196, 198, 199
clichés 51, 160, 161b, 162b
climax 145, 146b, 150, 152, 153b, 155b
co-ordinate sentences 190–2

co-ordinating conjunctions 191, 195
The Collector (Fowles) 129
colons 183, 192
comic effect 188
comma splice 193, 196
commas 183, 184, 192, 193, 194, 196
common experiences 32
Common Ground (Cowan) 19, 30, 31,
    121, 122, 125, 127, 139
communication: to the reader 179
Complex (exercise 73) 196b
complex sentences 192–6
complex sentences exercise
    ('Complex') 196b
complex-compound sentences
    197–9
complexity 179
complication 145, 146b, 152,
    153b, 155b
composition: process of 201
Compound (exercise 72) 192b
compound sentences 190–2
compound sentences exercise
    ('Compound') 192b
Compound-complex (exercise 74)
    199b
compound-complex sentences exercise
    ('Compound-complex') 199b
computers 24
concrete detail 75b
Connolly, C. 13
Conrad, J. 45
conscious 42, 46; thought 179
consciousness 122
constructive criticism 211, 212
contextualising notes 205, 206
continuity 179
conventions: exceeding of 88
conversation 27b, 104, 136b
Conversation (exercise 39) 106b
Corso, G. 36, 37
Cowan, A. 30, 31, 74, 102, 103, 126,
    157, 158
creative energy 66

Creative Writing 4, 214; exercises 3;
    growth of 147; teachers 209; teaching
    of 3, 21, 56; workshops 80, 158, 203
*Creative Writing: A Handbook for
    Workshop Leaders* (Thomas) 161
Creative Writing handbooks:
    inspirational guides 35; practical
    guides 35
creativity 88
crisis 145, 146b, 152, 153b, 155b
critical thinking 147
criticism 208; constructive 211, 212
Cross purposes (exercise 42) 113b
crowd scenes 23
Crustaceans (Cowan) 46

Dahl, R. 7
Damascus (Beard) 166, 167
dashes 183, 194
Dead Girls (Lee) 133, 135
declarative sentences 186
deconstructionism 147
defamiliarisation 49, 148, 160, 163,
    169, 177
Departures (exercise 26) 73b
descriptive: intensifiers 109; writing 54
descriptive writing exercise ('Don't
    mention it') 54b
detail 63; selectivity 63; significance 63
Diagnostics (exercise 53) 146b, 147b
dialect speech 114, 116b
dialogue 71b, 75b, 79b, 109, 111b,
    112, 181b; believable 109;
    conventions 111; cross purposes
    113b; formatting 107b, 108b;
    writing 112
dialogue exercise ('Cross purposes')
    113b
dialogue exercise ('Dramatic twist')
    111b
dialogue exercise ('Formatting
    dialogue') 107b, 108b
dialogue exercise ('In summary') 118b
Dickinson, E. 49

diction 115
dictionary 17, 160
Didion, J. 185
dirty realists 198
displacement activities 10
Doctorow, E.L. 201
Don't mention it (exercise 16) 54b
Drabble, M. 6
drafts 206, 208; first 180
Dramatic twist (exercise 41) 111b
dramatised narrator 124
dream state 39
Duncker, P. 38

Eats, Shoots & Leaves (Truss) 184
editing 44
editorial reading 206, 207
Edwards, N. 9
ego 39
Eliot, T.S. 180
emotions 32, 79b, 168b; in concrete
    terms 56b, 57
End middle beginning (exercise 56)
    153b
Enemies of Promise (Connolly) 13
energy 11, 13
English: spoken 182
Envelopes (exercise 35) 91b, 92b
epistolary novel 136
equilibrioception 60
essays 46, 49
ethic of engagement 209
ethnicity 115, 116
events 47, 58, 122, 127
everyday speech 183
exciting force 149, 150
exclamative sentences 186
Exercises in style (exercise 64) 171b
Exercises in Style (Queneau) 168,
    169, 171b
exile 72
experience 21, 23, 32, 76
external narrator 124
Eye witness (exercise 48) 132b

fact and fiction boundary 90
failure 16
fairytales 155, 156
familiarity 68
Faulkner, W. 94
feeble abstraction 56b, 57, 181b
feedback 212
feelings exercise ('How does this feel?')
    55b, 56b
Ferlinghetti, L. 37
fiction 57; nature of 78; successful 77
Fiction Writer's Workshop
    (Novakovich) 71, 105
fictional speech 104
figurative expressions 160, 161
figurative expressions exercise
    ('Literally') 161b
Figuratively (exercise 61) 161b, 162b
film 62, 179
First drafts (exercise 14) 47b, 48b
First Love, Last Rites (McEwan) 58, 59
first person: multiple novel 128, 129;
    narration 132; narrative 127, 136b;
    protagonist narrator 126, 128;
    vernacular 115;
    witness narration 131
first person exercise ('A person') 79b
first person narrative exercise
    ('You, too') 136b
First things (exercise 12) 40b
First thoughts (exercise 11) 36b
First thoughts, second thoughts
    (exercise 13) 43b
First World War 102
Fitzgerald, F.S. 99, 144
flashback 121, 152, 159b
flat characters 98, 149
foes 15
fonts 205
Ford, R. 19, 20, 198
form 214, 215
Formatting dialogue (exercise 40)
    107b, 108b
Forster, E.M. 84, 85, 91, 98, 151, 201

Forster, M. 6
Frankenstein (Shelley) 38
Frayn, M. 106, 107
free indirect style 139; absence of 141
freedom of expression 215
Fresh (McNay) 115
Freud, S. 39
friends 15
Friends and foes (exercise 3) 14b
Fulcher, S. 101, 103, 104
The Function of Criticism (Eliot) 180

Gardner, J. 53, 54, 55, 140, 163
generalising 73; tense 74
Genette, G. 125, 135, 148
genius 41
gesture 55, 56b
Gilead (Robinson) 135, 136
Ginsberg, A. 36
Given moods (exercise 63) 168b
Given words (exercise 62) 167b
The Go-Between (Hartley) 101, 127
Golberg, N. 36, 37
Gorgeous (Bryan) 158, 188, 189
grammar 116b, 182, 185
grammar exercise ('Given words') 167b
grammatical tense 124
Granta 198
The Great Gatsby (Fitzgerald) 131
Greek theatre 144
Greene, G. 27
Guardian 160
guidebooks 133

half-rhyme 119
happening-truth 90
Happy Endings (Atwood) 151
Hard Up Street (Davey) 105
Hardwick, E. 201
harmoniousness 150b
Hartley, L.P. 101
He said, she said (Frayn) 106
Heath, M. 145
Hemingway, E. 6, 48, 109, 110, 141, 197

Hills Like White Elephants
    (Hemingway) 3, 109, 118b, 125, 141
history writing 105
Ho Davies, P. 133
Hoffman, E. 72
Home life (exercise 10) 28b, 29b
homesickness 72
Horizontal (exercise 66) 174b
Hotel World (Smith) 94, 111
How does this feel? (exercise 17)
    55b, 56b
How Late It Was, How Late (Kelman)
    114
How Novels Work (Mullan) 84
How to Be an Expatriate (Ho Davies)
    133, 135
How to Write a Novel (Braine) 41
human interest stories 23
humours 98
Hyacinths (exercise 19) 61b

I could see the smallest things
    (Carver) 197
ideological constructs 147
If On A Winter's Night A Traveller
    (Calvino) 165
images 58
imagination 17, 76, 78, 79b
imagined reader 88; voice of 87
imperative sentences 186
in medias res 121, 149, 150b
In summary (exercise 44) 118b
incidents 26, 27b, 29b, 171b
Independence Day (Ford) 198, 199
indirect speech 117, 118
indirectness 51
inertia 34
inner person 83
inspiration 15, 35, 37, 38, 41, 68
instruction manuals 133
interior monologue 93, 95, 96b, 97b
interrogative sentences 186
interview transcripts 104
interviews 103, 105b

intimacy 133
intonation 183
introspection 23
invention 19, 20, 32, 76
Iowa Writers' Workshop 56

Jakobson, R. 173
Jakobson's horizontal axis 173,
    174b, 176
Jakobson's vertical axis 175, 176b
James, H. 6, 99, 203
Jane Eyre (Brontë) 135
Johnson, B.S. 154
journals: specific 21
Joyce, J. 6, 94, 95, 117, 118, 139

Keats, J. 10
Keeping an observational journal
    (exercise 5) 21b, 22b
Keeping a scrapbook (exercise 6) 23b
Kelman, J. 113, 114
Kerouac, J. 12
King, S. 41, 42, 68
knowability 123

La Rochefoucauld 81, 82
language 17, 18, 58, 67, 81, 160;
    horizontal axis 173, 174b, 176;
    misuse of 160; signals 53; vertical
    axis 175, 176b
Larkin, P. 6, 11
Last Day of Summer (McEwan) 63, 125
Lee, N. 133, 134
letters 136b
Levi, P. 201, 202, 217
Levine, N. 20
lipogram 165
Literally (exercise 60) 161b
literary: canon 2; criticism 214;
    effect 188; language 2, 163;
    realism 147, 163
literary theory 2, 147; history of 3
locations 23
locations exercise ('Departures') 73b

Lodge, D. 78, 103, 113, 114, 141, 166
Losing Battles (Welty) 112
loss 134b
Lost (exercise 25) 71b
Lost lands (exercise 22) 70b
Lost loves (exercise 24) 71b
Lost selves (exercise 23) 70b
Lost things (exercise 21) 69b, 70b

McEwan, I. 59, 63, 64
magazine photographs 22, 23
The Making of a Poem (Spender) 76
Malouf, D. 201
manuscripts 205
materials 17
Mathew's algorithm (almost)
    (exercise 65) 172b, 173b
Mathews, H. 172
Maugham, W.S. 19
Maxims (La Rochefoucauld) 81
Maxwell, W. 87
memories 39, 40, 68, 105
memory 66, 73b, 75b, 79b; and
    imagination 76, 77; as a resource 74
Menand, L. 183, 184, 185
mental space 15
metafiction 151, 164
metaphorical expressions 160, 161
metaphors 53
Middle beginning end (exercise 55)
    152b
migration 71, 72
Mind Writing Slogans 37, 47
monologue 105b, 136b
moods 167, 167b
moods exercise ('Given moods') 168b
moral portraits 81
More first thoughts (exercise 68) 178b
morning pages 37, 38, 39
Morphology of the Folktale (Propp) 155
Motte, W. 165
Mrs Dalloway (Woolf) 94, 140
Mullan, J. 84, 214
multiple storylines 109

Muses 66, 67
mystery 123, 151, 152, 179
mystery exercise ('Next thoughts') 182b

Nabokov, V. 6
narration: temporal gap 127, 128
narrative 26; commentary 54; fiction
    148; focalised 126, 128; poems 67;
    point of view 123b, 124, 125;
    preamble 122; pronouns 126;
    showing 62; unfolding 118
*Narrative Discourse: An Essay in
    Method* (Genette) 125
narrative exercise ('Captors and
    captives') 130b, 131b
narrative exercise ('Something else is
    happening') 128b
narrative exercise ('Something is
    happening out there') 123b
narrative sequence: rearrangement 154
narrative voice 63, 102, 114, 116b, 119,
    120, 124, 139; tone 65
narratives 64, 74
narratology 125, 148
narrator 181b; character of 78;
    confidence in 142; consistency 142;
    voice 118
natural speaking voice 102, 119
natural speech 103, 104, 117
Negotiating with the Dead (Atwood) 38
The New Yorker 87, 93
newspaper clippings 22, 23, 111b
Next thoughts (exercise 70) 182b
non-knowing 201, 203, 216
non-restrictive phrases 185
notebooks 18, 19, 21, 23
Notes towards a character (exercise 34)
    90b, 91b
notetaking 19, 33; benefits 19
Novakovich, J. 71
A Novel in a Year (Doughty) 14
novels 53, 147, 214; English 84; para-
    dox 27; reading 2; Victorian 138
numerical schemes 171, 172

Oates, J.C. 7, 72
oblivion 68, 69
O'Brien, E. 7
O'Brien, T. 89
observational journals 17–33, 78, 97b,
    133, 169, 171b
observational journals exercise
    ('Keeping an observational journal')
    21b, 22b
observations 23, 33; recording 18, 19
observing 19, 33
O'Connor, F. 50, 56, 57, 63, 67,
    73, 156
omniscient: narrator 137; novel 137,
    138, 139; short story 137
On Becoming a Novelist (Gardner)
    53, 55
On Writing: A Memoir of the Craft
    (King) 41
oral history 101
Oral history (exercise 38) 104b, 105b
Orwell, G. 7
Oulipian constraint 165, 166, 167
Oulipo 165, 166, 172
Oulipo: A Primer of Potential Literature
    (Motte) 165
outer person 83

Paley, G. 153
parallel storylines 109
The Paris Review 112
Parker, D. 93, 94
participles 195, 196, 198, 199
particularising 73
particularity 51
passive voice 189
past tense narration 128
pay-off 145
people 181b; remembered 73,
    74–5b
perception 123
Perec, G. 165, 166
perfectionism 35, 38, 44, 45, 46, 47
A person (exercise 30) 79b

persona 94, 131; and personality 97
personal: growth 37; identity 69;
    pronoun 132
phonetic writing 115, 116b
photographs 23; of locations 99b;
    of ordinary people 85b, 99b
photographs exercise ('Twenty
    questions') 85b, 86b
physical detail 56b
physical reaction to setting 55
Pig (Cowan) 12, 101, 174
A place (exercise 29) 76–7b
places 33, 78, 181b; remembered 73,
    76–7b
Plato 67
plays 147
plot 99, 109, 149, 152; definition 144,
    151; diagrams 156, 157, 158;
    five-stage sequence 145, 146b, 152,
    153b, 155b; précis 146b; shaping of
    153; three-act linear structure 145
plot exercise ('Beginning middle end')
    150b
plot exercise ('Diagnostics') 146b, 147b
poems 46, 147
Poetics (Aristotle) 144, 146b, 147, 148
poetry 76, 165, 166
point of view 51, 78, 92b, 123, 125,
    138, 181b; first person 132; shifting
    141; temporal disparity 130
point of view exercise ('Third, and
    finally') 142b
A Portrait of the Artist as a Young Man
    (Joyce) 81, 116, 139
A Portrait of Yourself as You Are Now
    (exercise 31) 83b
post-colonialism 137
poststructuralism 147
Powell, A. 7
procrastination 10, 34
pronouns 4
Propp, V. 155
prose 62; rhythm of 53, 65, 110
pseudo-sentences 190b

psychic distance 139, 140, 181b
publishability 216
published work 215; laws 215
publishers 206
punctuation 109, 182, 185, 193, 194,
    197, 205; correct 184; importance of
    183; misuse of 184; orthodox 110;
    unnecessary 113

Q&A gimmick 88, 89b, 93
Q&A gimmick (exercise 33) 89b
quasi-experience 53
Queneau, R. 165, 168, 169, 171
Queneau's Exercises in Style exercise
    ('Exercises in style') 171b
quotations 23
quoted speech 103, 117

racism 57
raw material 20, 21, 44, 47, 78; for
    fiction 30; language 197
Read, H. 66, 68
reader alienation 62
readers 179; imagination 50
reading 2; act of 180; aloud 158, 179,
    207, 208; continuous practice 182;
    as a writer 2, 53
real: life 67; speech 109
realist fiction 58
rearranging 180
Rearranging (exercise 59) 159b
recipes 133
recollection 67, 68
The Red Notebook (Auster) 62, 68
reflections 23
Regeneration (Barker) 110
regular routines 41
reliability 124
religious faith: decline 137
remembering 77–8, 79, 96b
Remembrance of Things Past
    (Proust) 68
reordering narrative sequence exercise
    ('End middle beginning') 153b

reordering narrative sequence exercise
('Middle beginning end') 152b
resolution 145, 146b, 150, 152,
153b, 155b
restrictive phrases 185
retrieval 68
reverie 38
reviews 49
revision 47, 179, 197, 199
rewriting 46, 152, 153
rhythm 53, 208
Roberts, M. 7
Robinson Crusoe (Defoe) 84
Robinson, M. 136
roles 156
Romantics 38, 41
Roth, P. 7
round characters 98, 149
Ruskin, J. 78
Russian Formalism 148, 155, 163, 173

Salinger, J.D. 119
Sansom, W. 66
Saraswati Park (Joseph) 138, 139
scene-building 73, 74, 109
scene-setting 122
scenes 64, 65b, 71b, 74, 158, 159b
Schachtel, E. 66
scientific writing 189
Scottish writing: contemporary 115
scrapbook exercise ('Keeping
a scrapbook') 23b
second person: narration 133, 137;
pronoun 133
second person exercise ('You') 134b
second thoughts exercise ('First
thoughts, second thoughts') 43b
self-criticism 82, 180
self-discipline 10, 34
self-exploration 81
self-portrait 81, 82, 83b
self-portrait exercise ('A Portrait of
Yourself as You Are Now') 83b
semi-wakefulness 38, 39

semicolons 183, 184, 191,
192, 195
senses 57, 58, 59, 60, 169, 181b
senses exercise ('Hyacinths') 61b
sensory detail 52b, 54b, 58, 59, 60b,
62, 71b
sensory detail exercise ('Sightless')
60b, 61b
sentences: co-ordinate 190–2; complex
192–6; complex-compound 197–9;
compound 190–2; declarative 186;
exclamative 186; imperative 186;
interrogative 186; simple 185–90;
single-clause 185–90
set-up 145
Seth, V. 137
setting 26, 47, 58, 75b, 77, 96b, 109
Shklovsky, V. 163, 164, 177
short stories 46, 133; paradox 27;
poor 64; reading 2; structuring 89
showing 49, 50, 51, 54, 61, 63, 73,
181b
Shuffling (exercise 58) 155b
sight 61b
Sightless (exercise 18) 60b, 61b
similes 161b, 162b
similes exercise ('Figuratively')
161b, 162b
Simple (exercise 71) 190b
simple sentences 185–90
simple sentences exercise ('Simple')
190b
single-clause sentences 185–90
situation 145, 146b, 152, 153b, 155b
Smith, A. 88, 94, 95, 111, 112
social: class 113, 114, 115, 116, 130;
contexts 27b; environments 27b
Socrates 67
Something else is happening (exercise
46) 128b
Something is happening out there
(exercise 45) 123b
Spark, M. 7
speech 55, 56b, 183

speech attributions 109, 111b, 116; avoidance of 110; minimal use of 110
Spender, S. 76, 77
spiritual enlightenment 37
spoken voice 116b
Standard English 115
Steinbeck, J. 119
Still life (exercise 36) 96b, 97b
still life exercise ('Still life') 96b, 97b
stories 53, 65, 147; overly descriptive 64
story 99, 149, 152; definition 144, 151
story vs. plot 143b, 148
Story vs. plot (exercise 52) 143b
story-truth 90
storytelling 65, 67, 76, 109, 155; effective 64; on the stage 144; voice 119
stream of consciousness 94, 95, 114, 140, 141, 142b, 164
Street life (exercise 8) 25b, 26b
A Stroke of Good Fortune (O'Connor) 50, 139
structural linguistics 173
structuralism 147
structure 143–59, 181b
sub-clauses 193, 194, 196, 198
sub-plots 153, 158, 159b
Sub-plotting (exercise 57) 154b
subordinate clauses 195, 199
subordinating conjunctions 195, 199
successful writing: measure of 15
succinctness 50, 51
A Suitable Boy (Seth) 137, 138
summarising 73, 74
summary 64, 65b, 74, 109, 158, 159b
Summary and scene (exercise 20) 65b
suspense 123
synaesthesiac prose 59, 60
synonyms 109
synopsis 64, 156
syntactical reordering exercise ('Horizontal') 174b

syntax 115, 173, 174b, 176
synthesis 150

Taking Reality by Surprise (Sellers) 9, 35
technique 214, 215
telling 49, 50, 51, 54, 61, 64, 73, 181b
Telling it slant (exercise 15) 52b
The Art of Fiction: Notes on Craft for Young Writers (Gardner) 53, 54
theatre: Greek 144
Thematics (Tomashevsky) 148
themes 47, 122
thesaurus 17, 18, 174
thesis 150
The Things They Carried (O'Brien) 3, 90
Third, and finally (exercise 51) 142b
third person: limited narration 139; limited narrator 126, 128b; narration 132, 137; objective narration 141
third story 153, 154b
timed: exercises 36; writing 37
timelines 156
The Times 167
timewasting 11, 12, 13
Timewasting (exercise 2) 9b, 10b
Tolstoy, L. 163
Tomashevsky, B. 148, 149, 150
tools 17
tragedy 144
transparency 58
Tranter, N. 7
Trapido, B. 7
travel writing 71
Trevor, W. 201
Tricks (Levine) 20
Tristram Shandy (Sterne) 163, 164
Trungpa, C. 37
Truss, L. 184, 193
TV 179
Twenty questions (exercise 32) 85b, 86b
Two characters (exercise 37) 99b, 100b

typeface 205
Typical (exercise 27) 74–5b

Ulysses (Joyce) 95
uncommon experiences 33
unconscious 34, 35, 38, 42, 44, 46,
    122, 179
The Unfortunates (Johnson) 154, 164
University of East Anglia 1, 2
Untypical (exercise 28) 75b
Updike, J. 7
The Uses of the Past (Hoffman) 72

verbatim transcription 105b, 106b
verbs 186, 187, 188; finite 186, 187;
    non-finite 186; phrasal 188
vernacular speech exercise ('Vernacular
    voices') 116b
vernacular voice 114, 115
Vernacular voices (exercise 43) 116b
Vertical (exercise 67) 176b
Vietnam War 89, 90
vigil of waiting 41
visual detail 51, 60
visual sense 60, 61b
vivid and continuous fictional dream 53,
    57, 60, 65, 88, 96b, 125, 184
vocabulary 115, 116b
vocation 66
voices 181b
A Void (Perec) 165

Warton, E. 7
Weather report (exercise 7) 24b, 25b
Welty, E. 7, 112
What I Know (Cowan) 74, 156
What where when (exercise 4) 16b
When where what (exercise 1) 8b
whodunnit 152
Wodehouse, P.G. 7
Women's Press 9
Woolf, V. 7, 94, 140

words 17, 67
work-in-progress 214, 215
Workplace (exercise 9) 26b, 27b
workshops 200–17; attendance 211;
    code of conduct 215; distributing
    work 204, 205; length 207; offensive
    submissions 215; participation 211;
    preparation 211; presenting work
    205, 206; purpose 209, 214, 215;
    reading 206, 207; reading aloud 207,
    208; rereading 206, 207; rotas 207;
    students' role 208, 209, 211, 212;
    support 216; tutor's role 209, 210;
    and writing 216
Worstward Ho (Beckett) 3
The Wrench (Levi) 201, 202
writer: characterisation 10; definition of
    183; as a dual personality 42
writer's: block 34, 35, 45; dual
    personality 180; eye 57; voice 80, 81
The Writer's Way (Cameron) 35
writing 2; about what you know 32; act
    of 180; art of 72; continuous practice
    182; courses 80; hindrances to 14;
    practice 16, 36; process 66; and
    remembering 71; routines 5–16,
    9–13, 14, 15, 200; time 12
*The Writing Diet: Write Yourself
    Right-Size* (Cameron) 38
Writing Down the Bones (Goldberg) 35,
    36, 38
writing routines exercise ('Friends and
    foes') 14b
writing routines exercise ('What where
    when') 16b
writing routines exercise ('When where
    what') 8b
Writing Without the Muse (Joselaw) 42,
    69, 168

You (exercise 49) 134b
You, too (exercise 50) 136b